Always an Athlete by Jenne Blackburn is a must read for all athletes and coaches, because Jenne has done a fantastic job of breaking down the anxiety surrounding that transition from active athlete to retirement and how to better equip ourselves for this moment.

Here is the thing . . . as athletes, we know retirement is eventually coming. We worry about a loss of identity, yet, we don't often know how to deal with that loss of identity and community.

Teammates feel like family, and Always an Athlete helps you build a parallel community that also inspires confidence and courage. Most important, Jenne offers fabulous guidance and strategies for athletes and coaches alike, so that BEFORE we hit our "cliff moment" of transitioning out of our sport, the apprehension is replaced by action, knowing sports has given us a platform to soar.

—JULIE FOUDY,
Former captain of USA Women's Soccer Team, 2x Olympic
Gold Medalist, 2x World Cup Champion, and an analyst
and reporter with ESPN and Warner Bros Discovery

For over 50 yrs. I have witnessed firsthand athletes' transition out of their sport. This experience is a massively complicated challenge for many athletes. A whirlwind of change all at once, where mental health, physical health, and athlete identity are disrupted. In Jenne Blackburn's book, the reader will relive the athlete's journey "up the mountain" (youth to professional sports) to the inevitable "cliff" (retirement). Jenne highlights the drivers that impact mental health, physical health, and athletes' loss of identity. More importantly, she provides us with greater awareness AND solutions to better prepare them for the end of their career. This book is an excellent blueprint for athletes, sports parents, coaches, administrators, and communities to align education and events around athlete identity, mental health, and physical health. In completing this read, you will gain insight, the urgency to act, and articulated solutions for your retiring athletes. Always an Athlete® will provide impactful research insight, education curriculum, and community-building activities, better preparing athletes for life after sport. Jenne inspires all of us to do more in preparing athletes for a thriving and celebratory experience in sports and beyond. Her book gives us the roadmap, the tools to traverse the mountain of challenges, and a mindset to leap off that cliff of retirement with a parachute of solutions for a thriving life after sport.

—SUE ENQUIST,
Former UCLA Softball Coach, 11-Time National Champion,
and 6-time Hall of Fame

As a sports medicine physician and former national team rower, I am an advocate for the importance of physical activity and the benefits of being a lifelong athlete. In Always an Athlete, Jenné Blackburn creates an easy-to-follow, but effective roadmap to help former athletes translate their years of athletic hard work and mindset into their next chapter. So many of the skills we develop as athletes are valuable tools for future life happiness and success. She also details important strategies for maintaining a healthy lifestyle and constructing support systems and communities beyond the competition stage. This is a great read for athletes navigating life after they've reached their perceived competitive peak, reminding them that there is life after the climb.

—DR. KATE ACKERMAN,

Former US National Team Lightweight Rower, Medical Director of The Wu Tsai Female Athlete Program, Division of Sports Medicine, Boston Children's Hospital, National Leadership Council—Wu Tsai Human Performance Alliance, Founder and Director of the Female Athlete Conference, Associate Professor of Medicine, Harvard Medical School Chair, and US Rowing Medical Commission and Team Doctor

A former collegiate athlete with an insight into the journey of elite performance takes the reader on the journey that follows. It is a journey which provides guardrails and strategies to make the next phase as enjoyable and successful as the past athletic one. This book should be helpful to the athletes in transition as well as parents and those leaders and organizations who wish to bring the best of the athlete into the best of society. The pillars provide new goals and tools for the next journey where the athlete transitions. The bike serves as an example of a kick start to this next journey – one which might occur on a surfboard or in open water swims or kayaking but in all cases continues with movement and using one's life lessons gained from athletic performance and participation.

—CHRIS VOELZ,

Former Collegiate athlete, coach, and administrator; Executive Director, Collegiate Women Sports Awards; Athletics Director Emerita, University of Minnesota; and Women's Sports Foundation Steward & Ambassador

I have long believed that some of the best employees are those that have had a formative experience with sports—due to the lessons learned of winning, losing and playing well on a team. In this great new book, Jenné Blackburn has created a clear blueprint for athletes of all levels wanting to translate the great skills they learned on the field to be a competitive advantage in life. A must read for any former competitive athlete looking for ways to parlay their experiences into a big fulfilling future!

—SARAH ROBB O'HAGAN,

Corporate Executive; EXOS, Flywheel, Equinox, Gatorade, Nike, Virgin and more; Activist and Entrepreneur; and Founder of Extreme You

Jenne Blackburn perfectly outlines the many positive benefits
that riding a bike can have on all of us,

cycling is a most inclusive activity,

it's good for me, it's good for you, it's good for everyone,
and it's good for our planet,

I love my bike, and the community it creates.

The bike is a wonderful tool for your mental as well as physical health.

It encourages you to get up, get outside and get going—
in the game of life—always forward, and further,

like the song, FIRE ON THE MOUNTAIN,

ride for fun, your bike will take you places that
you can't possibly get to by yourself,

your bike will show you things about yourself, and the
world in general, that you have no idea even exists,

here we go, enjoy the ride, roll on forever,

I thank Jenné Blackburn, and my bike, for my life
—BILL WALTON,
NBA and UCLA Basketball Legend

The bicycle is a wonderful tool for building community. When you plug into
the cycling community, you will find yourself surrounded by like minded
people who—like you—are excited to move their body and make new friends.
A community bike ride is a wonderful event to kickstart this important
conversation around athletes transitioning out of sport into the next phase
of their life. Riding your bike helps you build new relationships and make
lifelong friends. Relationships and community are essential for mental
health, and a bike ride is a great bridge to creating a sense of belonging
. . . similar to what an athlete may have felt when they were competing in
team sport environments. Riding a bike helps your brain and your mental
wellbeing. It takes us outside of our normal schedule, gets us outside and
helps us gain perspective. Cycling helps us get into a routine and create
new rhythms to keep our physical health a priority. The bike provides us
balance and consistency as life changes. Jenné is excited to see people
come together around community bike rides and I am thrilled she is
bringing this idea and message to the larger sports community. No matter
what type of athlete you are, I encourage you to get out and ride!

—KATHRYN BERTINE,
Author, Activist, Filmmaker; CEO, Homestretch Foundation; Former professional
cyclist, former professional figure skater and professional triathlete.

Blackburn weaves in landscape analogies to bring the reader through the athletic journey of multidimensional triumphs, tribulations and transitions, for all sport stakeholders, but especially the athletes, who love or have been impacted by sports. The book ends with a surprising but simple solution for coping with the loss of athletic identity and one I have embraced successfully!

—NICOLE M. LAVOI, PHD,
Director of the Tucker Center for Research on Girls & Women in Sport, former coach, NCAA D-III National Team Champion, and 2x Academic All-American in tennis.

I have been friends with Jenné for over a decade. When she first started talking about this topic to me I was still playing competitively with Team USA Volleyball. Today I am the Assistant Coach. In the years between my two roles, my understanding has grown around the importance of this topic of the athlete transition out of sport, because I now have personally lived it - alongside of my teammates. Now I get it, transitioning out of sport is hard. We don't always get to choose when we step away. Sometimes it is by choice but for others we don't know when the last day will be. What I have noticed is that we can all do a better job of looking ahead past our playing days while still competing. For many, it can be a rude awakening when it is time to step away from the court and the next phase of life hits. The community piece around this topic that Jenné is working to build is huge. It is so important to discuss how people no longer have the structure they once had to connect with others. Finding people going through the same transition season out of sport can really help, especially with mental health struggles. What I hope for all athletes is that they don't hesitate to reach out to others who have gone through or will go through this phase of transition. Thankfully I did some work around my other roles and identities in life before I retired from playing so I feel like I could step away and have some peace of mind. What I was able to tackle head on is that – sport was what I did - and it had been a huge part of life – but it wasn't the only thing. Right now, I am taking the lessons learned as a competitive athlete and transitioning those learnings into this next season of my career as a coach. What we accomplish in life as an athlete does not define us. No matter what level we achieve, we get to be an athlete and move our body for the rest of our lives. There is a community out there waiting to embrace us all when it is time to step away from our competitive days and encourage us to keep pushing on and to keep moving. Let's lean on each other. Some of my teammates are some of my best cheerleaders to this day and sometimes it's the simple things . . . like after a fun bike ride together. I become encouraged that I am not alone in this journey.

—TAMA MIYASHIRO,
USA Volleyball Women's Asst Coach; 2021 Gold Medalist, Coach; 2012 Silver Medalist, Athlete; 2005 NCAA National Champion

One of the things that has brought me a lot of joy over the years is riding my bike. I've always been an outdoors-type person at all points in my life. ... My bike gets me outside, and now as a retired professional and Olympic athlete I'm back into my training athlete mindset where I can just click in and ride for miles. Some of my rides are over 60 miles long. I love the way the breeze gently blows on my face, my arms. It sets me free! What I love about the bike is the community that it creates. I love meeting new friends and building relationships. It is very similar to my years in softball in creating new moments or milestones that I am training for- like triathlons or other long century charity rides. I have been lucky that I have been able to stay so ingrained in the softball culture after my time as a competitive athlete moving into the role of analyst for ESPN. Riding my bike has been a great way for me not only to stay in shape and has definitely helped with my mental health. Rides when my mind just relaxes and the stress of the world disappears as the gentle breezes flow around my body and engulf me as I ride. In this book, Always an Athlete, Jenné makes the call for greater community and resources for athletes as they transition out of competitive sport. She uniquely does not only want to start the conversation—she wants to tie it in with action and support. Community wide bike rides alongside our sport culture at stadiums. How fun?! I'm in and hope you are as well!

—MICHELE SMITH,

Analyst, ESPN; NCAA All-American at Oklahoma State University; Member of three-time U.S. National Team World Championship team; Two-time Olympic Gold Medalist

As an athlete your competing days have an expiration date. When you actually do have to hang up the "cleats" (equipment) it is one of the hardest things to go through. In Jenné Blackburn's book, Always an Athlete, her depiction of an athlete's journey of climbing up "the mountain" in their peak of their careers to describing that there will be an inevitable fall off "the cliff" after they retire is spot on. Her "three pillars of the cliff" offer a roadmap for all athletes in their transition to life away from the playing field. Jenné provides a roadmap that athletes & coaches can have open conversations on what life after playing can look like. Having these open conversations during an athlete's career will better equip them to take on the world after playing.

—NATASHA WATLEY,

2x Softball Olympian, Philanthropist, and Entrepreneur

I knew I wanted to be a professional athlete since I was 13 years old, growing up playing alongside Metta World Peace and Lamar Odom. My mental health issues started when I was 11 or 12 when I went through a lot of emotional challenges as my family situation changed when I was young. Basketball has given me a lot of amazing things. I've seen the world. I've been able to do amazing things for my family and myself. But it did hinder me a lot in my personal growth, things I should have taken care of . . . including a stronger understanding of mental health. Winning those games and winning those championships, it was like the best feeling on earth. I felt like a rockstar, I was on top of the world. I remember when I was at Tennessee, I would regularly talk to Coach Summit . . . even with all the success I was having on the court- still something felt "off balance". In general, I've always known what I wanted, and I would always try to do it by myself. But doing it by myself— didn't work. Now I have learned to pull in my family and my friends into being my support - and this also includes getting the help that I need, including therapy. My self care routines to help deal with my bipolar disorder include:

Weekly Therapy, Staying on Medications, Mediating and Physical Exercise. Like a competitive team has structure, the above is my personal protocol. In order to be a better daughter, partner and friend I need to follow my protocol. I want to use my platform as an athlete and my voice to make a difference. I want to help others, I don't want to see others go through the suffering that I had gone through— suffering in silence. So many people struggle with this illness. Many people have a support system but choose not to use it because we can get stuck in our own heads not wanting to be a burden. If you are feeling sad or lonely, know that there is help. Reach out to experts to talk. It may not be easy, it was not for me, but it is important to take care of yourself. I have spoken to dozens of groups about dealing with mental illness, hoping sharing my story will help others. My mission is to change the conversation. It's ok to say, I need support. If I could impart any advice is that your illness or disorder does not have to define you. You can still live a healthy lifestyle. I appreciate that this book digs into the real Mental Health struggles that athletes deal with as they transition out of sport. Speaking about something that people do not normally talk about—brings the conversation of mental health to the front. Mental Health is just as important as physical well being—and they are deeply connected. As athletes we need to keep moving our bodies when we no longer have the game and structure of a community. Movement of our bodies helps our mental health. I look forward to the resources and stories that Always an Athlete is gathering to help other athletes, at every level, in their personal lifelong athletic journey toward a healthy future.

—CHAMIQUE HOLDSCLAW,
Mental Health Advocate, 3 NCAA Championships, University of Tennessee, 4x All American, Drafted #1 in the WNBA, WNBA Rookie of the Year, 6x WNBA All Star, 2x WNBA Rebounding Champion, and 2x Naismith Award Winner

Jenné felt her own environment and support system change and struggled after retiring—and with a simple bike ride she identified that there was more - not only for her life but for all athletes in sport. We talk about being ready with personal work ethic and hustle when the lights and cameras turn on- but what happens when they turn off? This book outlines the long climb that athletes face at every level of their journey. It identifies that there are real struggles that come after the game ends - no matter what level athletes achieve. More people need to be talking about mental health in sports. During and after. More people need to discuss the real challenges that athletes face when they are no longer in an environment that fosters community and belonging. Let's not only talk about this problem but create solutions and systems to support athletes . . . like a fun bike ride!

—DR. JEN WELTER, PHD,
First Female Coach in NFL, Sport Psychologist, and Author and Motivational Speaker

Always an Athlete resonates with me as a professional athlete but also for humanity as a whole. There is plenty of science, and Jenné shares it, around the positive impacts of getting involved with and staying involved in sports for life. Research shows that athletics are so beneficial and formative in our young years, but what happens when we stop competing and our identity as an athlete seems to fade away? Jenné uses her personal story and at the same time amplifies the experience of millions of athletes who feel a little lost when transitioning from their competitive sport into their next athletic chapter. She reinforces why humans must never retire from sports, but instead shift from competition to exploration and play. This shift in focus comes with all the mental, physical, social benefits of sport and none of the stress and pressure. The best tool to be an athlete for life? A bicycle! She makes a strong case for the bike as a great tool to help in the evolution from competitive lifestyle into wellness lifestyle. As a multi-sport elite athlete I found cycling in my mid 30s and immediately gravitated towards the bike as a way to go places and see things. An unexpected gift from cycling I discovered was the vast community of people to tap into for casual rides, competition, family outings, adventure travel and training. Bottom line, the joy, friendship and benefit we got from the bike as kids is still there for us now as adults, so what are you waiting for? Let's go ride bikes!

—REBECCA RUSCH,
Ultra-endurance professional athlete; Seven-time World Champion; 2x Cycling Hall of Famer; Author, Entrepreneur, Emmy Award Winner, and Motivational Speaker with U.S. Team: 1996, 2000; Elected to NJSIAA Hall of Fame, 1998; First woman analyst for a nationally-televised major league baseball game with TBS, 2012

The power of the bike will always have a place in my heart. I loved biking before, but during COVID I fell in LOVE. My son TJ, myself, and other people in our community bike everyday. We created time together biking, and we were able to have incredible memories and moments.

—NANCY LIEBERMAN,

Naismith Basketball Hall of Famer and Founder Nancy Lieberman Charities

Transitioning out of a sport is a challenging time for competitive athletes. The scaffolds and resources that have been present to assist the competitive athlete during their athletic careers are no longer there. Many struggle with where to start. I believe that people can change their mindset or identity from competitive sport athlete to an athlete who has a healthy lifestyle. Always an Athlete is a great resource for a community of people who have done it. It shares intimate stories and insights from the Always an Athlete community that can help others in their journey into the next chapter of their lives. Always an Athlete can help with the transition by helping people understand that focusing on long-term health is important. In many instances, athletes leave their competitive careers having had injuries or suffer from the wear and tear that comes with the constant repetitive movements that were a part of their sport. Undoing what has been done for years and correcting old injuries can be accomplished by participating in more fitness-based cardiovascular exercises, resistance training, and focusing on sleep and nutrition. Athletes should focus on movement alternatives that are the opposite of the movements that they were constantly exposed to in their athletic careers. Doing so will support long-term joint health. As a coach, when athletes would come back to campus to visit, inevitably, we would end up going on bike rides to reconnect and relax. Sometimes these rides became a race (if they wanted) which would satisfy our craving for competition.

—ANDREA HUDY,

Collegiate Basketball Sports Performance Coach, 9-Time National Championship Teams, National Strength and Conditioning Association (NSCA) Impact Award, 2017, NSCA Coach of the Year, 2012

ALWAYS AN ATHLETE

JENNÉ C. BLACKBURN

ALWAYS AN
ATHLETE

Center for Sport, Peace, and Society
The University of Tennessee

SPORT & PEACE

DEDICATION

To anyone who has ever felt lost after competitive sports
and in their own personal development journey.

I hope that after reading this book you realize you are not alone.

I hope you are encouraged to keep moving your body
and to keep good routines.

I hope you surround yourself with kindness and empathy
in the ups and downs of mental health.

I hope you continue to explore all the multi facets
of your personality and ambitions.

And finally

I hope you find new friends and community where you feel like
you belong and can be your most authentic self.

CONTENTS

THE SPARK THAT IGNITED THE FIRE WITHIN—
A SINGLE BIKE RIDE

PREFACE

Thank you, Athletes!

I want to commend you, the Athlete, for all the effort that you put into your sport. You ran the walls and suicides. You encouraged your teammates. You fought back when the score said it was all over. You sacrificed time with friends to put more hours in at the gym. You competed against your opponent. You competed against yourself. You demanded the best from yourself even if you were not the best on the field or on the court.

You showed up early to warm-ups. You stayed late after practice. You sat on the cold, wooden floor of the gym. You laid in the warm, sunny grass of the field. You stretched to the rhythmic hum of fluorescent lights, thinking and focusing on the task at hand. You lifted weights. You studied game film. You internalized feedback from your coaches, even when you didn't want it or expect it. You implemented it. You rose before the sun came up and went home after the moon came out. You never hit the snooze button, even when your body screamed at you to do it. You ate salads and water while your friends munched on pizza and beer. You avoided "fun" things in the off-season like skateboarding, snowboarding and skydiving if there was any chance it could derail your shot at a championship.

You were highly recruited and started on day one. You walked on and rode the bench without complaint for four years. You changed positions midway through the season because your team needed it, even if you felt out of place in your new role. You cried to your mom and you griped to your dad about problems with coaches and teammates.

You had a "pump up" song in the locker room. You religiously followed superstitions like not walking on the team emblem or growing your playoff beard. You ran out of tunnels, engulfed in smoke, and through countless spirit hands. You and your teammates fed off the crowd's energy. You perfected your celebration dances after scoring, and your towel-biting during close losses.

You paused during lulls in action to soak in the grandeur of the stadium and the arena. You lifted your arms and clapped your hands to get the crowd going. You took a moment to appreciate the roar of the fans. You scanned crowds to make eye contact with your parents, indistinguishable from the crowds in their replica jerseys, face paint and team-colored t-shirts. The whistle snapped you back to attention. Your eyes narrowed on the next play, the next snap, the next pitch, the next serve, the next kick. You battled through the heat, the cold, the wind, the rain, the mud.

You boarded planes at five o'clock in the morning for a single game, only to board a bus to catch a flight back home that afternoon. You collapsed in your bed at one o'clock in the morning after traveling all day for a double-header. You sat on buses for days, traveling to tournaments in order to qualify for other more important tournaments. You never found time to study; you made time to study. You fell asleep on your homework. You failed quizzes, studied harder, and got the B you needed to stay eligible.

You showed up, worked hard and earned your time. The politics of the league, the club and the team never stopped you. The expense of private lessons never stopped you. Some days you battled your opponent. Some days you battled your teammates. But most days you battled yourself. You beat your personal best. You and your teammates were the ultimate underdogs at the beginning of the season. You defied the expectations of the school, the town, the nation. You overcame the odds.

You hit the game-winning shot. You missed the buzzer beater. You supplied momentum that changed the course of the game and the season. You poured water and sprayed champagne over your teammates and coaches after winning the championship game. You cried after losing in the first game of the championship tournament because you knew all that was left was to clean out your locker and go home empty-handed. You forged bonds with your teammates because you trusted them at their strongest, and they encouraged you at your weakest.

Coaches called you. Coaches visited you. They told you that they had the best gym, the best field, the best weight room, the best locker room. They told you they had the best fans and the best traditions. You went to school close to home so your parents and friends could watch you play. You went to school across the country to play for a powerhouse program or a hall-of-fame coach. You didn't know a soul but eventually found yourself calling that school and that town your home. Soon you found yourself playing for that school. Your teammates became your family. They had your back on the field and in the dorm. They helped you move. They borrowed your car. You crashed on their couch. They took you home over the holidays. They visited you during vacations. High school. College. The professional ranks. Your sports family pushed you further than you thought you could go.

Maybe you limped off the field. Maybe you rehabbed after injuries. You fought through pain and tears, trying to get back where you belong: the court, the field, the track. When you came back, maybe things weren't the same. You couldn't move as fast. You couldn't twist like you did before. Maybe your confidence was shot. Or maybe you never made it back at all. Even after months of rehab and workouts you had to look at your coaches, athletic directors and managers when they told you they had to look to the future of the team, even if it meant a future without you.

Maybe you won a gold medal. Maybe you won a national championship. Maybe you never got that varsity letter jacket. Maybe you never made it past junior varsity. But it never mattered because you never tried out for accolades, but to give everything for yourself, your team, and your family. You gave every last ounce of yourself and left everything on the field.

Your sport was not something you did. Your sport, your number, your highlight reel was a part of your DNA. It was a part of who you were. Then one day it ended. You were injured. You graduated. You retired. And even though training camps come and go, and even though you aren't running wind-sprints anymore, and even though you no longer sweat out two-a-days and playbook study sessions, your sport is still an indivisible part of who you are.

No matter how your competitive career ended or will end, you will remain a competitor for the rest of your life. No matter what sport you played, you remain an athlete. You may no longer have the structure of a practice schedule or the muscle-toned body you had at your peak. But you embrace the mindset and the heart of athletes across the land. This is my story, yes. But it is also every athlete's story. All of us, at some point, end our journey up the mountain that we fought so hard to climb. We grapple every day with redefining ourselves and writing the next chapter of our lives. Deep down we always define ourselves as athletes. To you, I say "THANK YOU!" You are my inspiration. You who stepped out of their comfort zones to compete—you are Always an Athlete.

BEHIND THE SCENES HELP AND INSPIRATION

Tyler J Emerson: You listened and helped put structure and outline to this important conversation. Thank you for answering every question that ever bubbled up to mind and for helping me articulate different important parts of this journey. Thank you a million times over for your support and for believing in me that one day it would be complete, printed and in the hands of others. I am not here without you on this book, and I am forever grateful.

Julie and Sue: To be loved and supported by you two has been a dream. I don't know how but I won the lottery on being your friend, but I did and can't thank you enough for being the first two to put your names down to help me get started. From talking to me at the espnW summits and deeply listening, to actively asking how you can help. This entire idea does not exist without your kindness. With you by my side, I thought I had a chance in this crazy sports world . . . that sliver of hope kept me going.

Dr. Sarah: I was certain that I could not do this alone. Why would anyone listen to me? I am not an expert in the world's eyes . . . but you are! A social change expert with the biggest heart – and your Center for Sport Peace and Society and the incredible impact globally was a beacon of hope to me. I wondered if some "impact project" could be started here in the US. You said YES and I was forever changed, inspired and motivated. Hugs and high fives for life!

CSPS Team and University of Tennessee Press: Thank you for your help. Special thanks to Thomas Wells who really let me ask for some nontraditional requests, like longer endorsements. Deeply appreciate you all and your help to get this message to the world.

University of Tennessee Volleyball Team, 2018: Thank you for housing me in Knoxville and getting me to the important meeting with Dr Sarah and the Center. It was through the kindness of friends of friends and the volleyball community that I made it on time, fed and with clothes after a crazy airport snowed in - hitchhiking journey from Chicago to Knoxville. Think "Home Alone" scenes. That was a wild travel story, and it was all worth it.

Laura, Carol, Serita and Rachel: Thank you for making the espnW summits so special and such a powerful place of connection each year. It is amazing to see how much womens sports has grown under your vision and leadership. Thank you for inviting me back year after year and encouraging me to grow into the leader I am today.

John Skipper, Burke Magnus, Rob King, Mark Walker, Kevin Martinez: Individually, thank you for your advice and the time you took to invest in me at the summits. Your quick moments of advice and kindness really made a difference in this journey.

Shelly, Julie and Dianne, Dr. Nicole and Dr. Brooks: Your friendship has meant so much, year after year, summit after summit. Thank you for your open arms and making me feel like I belonged when I showed up as a rookie. You believed in me and my potential. BIG hugs.

Todd Patterson, Brooks Tueting, Chance Siller: thank you for your help and for believing in me when I had nothing but an idea and providing counsel on what I needed to do next. I deeply appreciate all you have done to help me move forward.

Ben Carrol: You were my first call when I wanted to do a bike ride for the Baylor Volleyball team in 2013 after the espnW summit. Thanks for the decades of friendship and willingness to make an impact on the world. Let's go take a bike ride.

Bates and Dudley's: You 4 in all different ways have been such a support. Matt, thanks for bringing helmets and giving me your bike that first day. Ben, thanks for always encouraging me to look upstream when thinking about impact and development. Jamie, thank you for being there through all the Kenya years and Kristen thanks for your incredible friendship when I arrived backrow in the Baylor Volleyball world. Biggest hugs and thanks for teaching me what community looks and feels like so young.

Jenna Fuentes: Thank you for pushing me for more solutions for athletes to be added to the book. Your voice and friendship helped immensely get me to the finish line when I was really tired and stretched thin and I am forever grateful.

Jayme O'Hanlon, Zack Pennachi, Bella Bergfalk, Aries Lopez, and April O: Designers and people who believe in me. Thank you for helping bring visuals of this brand to life. Words pop alongside the visuals you have helped bring to life on social media and the website. You brought color and coding to this world. Thank you for your kindness and amazing patience with me!

Ashima and Karthik: Thank you for believing in the power of mentorship. Proud of how far we come and how the journey will continue to unfold. Entrepreneurship needs community and I am thankful you are in mine.

Former Teammates, Coaches and Trainers: Thank you for kindness and for your ability to laugh when you see the big dream attached to this book. It is outrageously big and I think you will laugh alongside me. One thing I know—you know—is I love FUN and dance parties—basically the bike ride is meant to be a giant fun dance party with tons of high fives and hugs. Kinda like we would have in the locker rooms or gyms. I deeply appreciate your kindness and friendship through the years.

Amanda and David: Thank you for your kindness and deep friendship - all the way from Texas. You both really helped shape my story in different ways, especially helping in moments of mental and physical health crisis. You are the best.

Volleyball Community: I love the game and appreciate all the ways I have been able to give back through coaching and different opportunities. Big thank you to the titan Kathy DeBoer who gave me opportunities to serve each year at the AVCA convention alongside the NCAA tournament. Those years connected to sport while also hustling employed in tech kept me moving forwards finishing this. And thank you Tama and Kathy for writing an endorsement of me and this idea. Forever grateful.

Biking Community: Thank you to everyone who I have met on the road. Special thanks to Eric Garcia and the Moonlight Mash ride in Long Beach who listened to my ideas and continued to cheer me on. What seemed impossible to others did not to you- which was fuel to keep going.

WISE Community: Thank you to everyone who has cheered me on and encouraged me! I love each and every one of you for your incredible kindness. Thank you to my WISE Within Mentors who provided a safe place to keep exploring and pushing the envelope. Special thanks to Nicole Green on this last run as she has given me a belief that a big bike ride is possible. Every nudge, text, open door made me feel like I should not stop because I had kind friends like you who would cheer me on.

Every person who wrote an endorsement or will write one in the future. Thank you for believing in me and the power of this message. I stand on the shoulders of giants and titans of sport and I am so thankful for your support.

THE WHY

1
Why This Book

How can we help them [athletes] understand the realities
of what [the future] looks like? What can we change to give them
a more realistic sense of it? How do we get a handle on that?
How can we provide them with a greater sense
of the realities and what that looks like?

—MARK EMMERT
Former president of the NCAA[1]

Jackie Robinson once famously quipped that every athlete dies twice. The second death is the same that all mortals face. But the first comes sooner and often more surprisingly than the second. The high school track star faces this first death after his last senior meet. The mid-major basketball player faces this first death after his team gets knocked out of the Big Dance in March. The professional baseball player faces this first death after his last at-bat in the majors. The Olympian faces this first death at the podium of her final Games. At some point, every athlete faces this first death. The crowds go home. The lights go out. Lockers are emptied. And the athlete leaves the stadium for the last time. They go to sleep that night on the life they built over years and potentially even decades.

And then the sun rises the next morning.

Few people in the sports industry talk about what happens that next morning, and the next, and the next, and the thousands of mornings after that. Some people do not realize that this silence and the unanswered questions around the transition can be a problem. The questions that can pepper the back of our minds: "what now?" "what is next?" "who will help?" "am I on the right path?" "do I go back to school?" "do I need to see a therapist?" "why do I feel so detached?" "will I be able to do———?" "how do you know where to start?" . . . the questions can be endless . . . and without really even realizing that the athlete is in the thick of the transition, many start to face significant questions and problems—*alone*—without the athletic community that once was so daily present and active in their lives before. The issue is this: athletes lose a significant portion of themselves and their lifestyles after competition ends. The simple fact is that every athlete retires from sports. For most, retirement comes after youth sports or high school. For some, retirement comes after college. And for the few lucky enough to play at the top of the professional ranks or the Olympics, retirement is still on the horizon far sooner than it is for the rest of America. The average retirement age for the American workforce is 63 and rising.[2] The average retirement age for top level athletes in the United States is 33 and dropping.[3] And like most Americans, athletes define themselves, at least in part, by their careers and their ability to compete, whether individually or as a team. For many, competing in sport is a huge part of their story. And the sports ecosystem is where they found themselves growing up, coming of age and finding not only what their body could achieve, but many times their voice in the world.

As the law is for attorneys, medicine is for doctors, and the Gospel is for preachers, sports is not just what athletes do. It is a defining characteristic. Being competitive is inextricably linked to their psyche and their spirit. It is a fundamental piece of who they are, what they enjoy doing, and the path that and journey that they have been climbing. For years and decades, they eat, sleep and drink the ability to play, to compete and to win. It becomes their passion. They hone their skills and their mindset to compete with excellence. But unlike attorneys, doctors and preachers—who may find themselves retiring from their life's work in the twilight of their years—athletes always find themselves retiring from their passion in their teens, 20's, 30's, and maybe 40's if they are ranked among the best of the best. And waking up one morning only to realize that you have to start at the beginning of a new life and a new career just to survive the next twenty, forty, sixty years? Without the support systems in place, this transition is not just daunting- it can seem demoralizing.

For some, it can seem impossible. And too often this major transition is only the beginning of a journey of loss of self, transition and recovery.

Athletes trade in coaches for bosses. Huddles are replaced with water cooler talk. Agents hock real estate—not endorsement deals. Teammates wear ties instead of warm-ups. And achievement is measured in quarterly sales instead of scoreboards. And perhaps to add insult to injury, the last decade of the athlete's life—the late practices, lean meals, hours spent in the weight room, studying playbooks and breaking down game film, injuries and recoveries, sacrifices by family—is summed up by the new people in their lives as quick anecdotes, stories and quick identifiers. "This is my new work buddy. He played in the Final Four," a co-worker tells the barkeeper hoping to grab free drinks off your reputation. "Man, you guys got us really good in that bowl game," the boss says before concluding the job interview. And this is understandable, because sports are a connection point to gain common ground.

You—the athlete—are asked to join the water-cooling and sports-barring masses. The transition from elite athlete to average citizen . . . one of the first times that I really felt this was when I went into my old gym. I was now in the stands, with no access to the back hallways I once roamed freely. Now, I was showing my ticket and seat to the usher to watch the team that I was once a part of.

It's hard to imagine, but this is a reality, in some form, for all athletes after years of focusing on the next play, the next point, the next game to win.

We can all agree, and it has been proven, that the same attributes that made the athlete a great player will translate into making them a great leader in their next career. In this book we will refer to those qualities as the Inner Athlete. Transitioning from being an active competitive athlete to joining in on the discussion *surrounding* sports as a spectator can be isolating and it is at minimum . . . odd.

Few people in the American sports industries acknowledge that most athletes lose a huge part of themselves and their daily routine after they retire. Some influencers have studied and discussed the lifestyles of athletes post-retirement. For instance, much discussion and even regulatory action has been made about the financial difficulties that professional athletes face upon retirement. Sports Illustrated published a 2009 cover feature titled *How (and Why) Athletes Go Broke*. ESPN followed that up with a *30 For 30* documentary on the same subject. Other studies have focused on catastrophic injuries of retired athletes, the most famous being the study of chronic traumatic encephalopathy among former NFL football players. However, few influencers in American sports are investigating and raising questions about the challenges that *all* athletes, specifically younger athletes, uniquely and commonly face after retirement unrelated to the extremes of catastrophic injury, financial meltdown or other tragedy. Even fewer influencers have explored innovative solutions to those problems or provided discussion points.

The greatest obstacle athletes face is mindset: the fallacy that all youth fall victim to, which is that tomorrow never comes. No athlete in any sport begins their career believing their sport will ever be done with them, let alone that it will be done with them before they are done with their sport. They all have high hopes that they will be in that elite group of athletes which includes Tom Brady, Gordie Howe, Nolan Ryan, Kerri Walsh Jennings and Kareem Abdul-Jabbar among the handful of others who have made 20-year careers.[4]

This idea that the athlete's career will take them into their mid-life is perpetuated not just by the athlete him or herself, but by friends and family, coaches and administrators, and the public at large. And this is the real "why" of this book: that we need to change the mindset not just of athletes, but also friends, family, coaches, administrators, the sports media and the sports-going public.

Let's kickstart the conversation and start an ever-building movement that prioritizes our athletes health (mind, body and spirit) and forever connects them to the athletic community in their second life chapter. Let's create energizing events and programming that can unite us in our similarities and highlight resources to our families for those athletes who may be struggling.

We as a society should leave NO ATHLETE BEHIND. (No matter how long they played and competed in their sport). Each of our athletic journeys should not have an expiration date because life is a team sport. In short, we all need to keep our bodies moving and our hearts and minds moving forward. Let's do it together.

So, who is this book for? It's for every person who has ever had sports play a significant role in their lives, either on the field or on the sideline. There is no other language on the planet that brings our global community together like sports. Sports are an integral part of the fabric of the world, so I propose this thesis and book to the world of sports that touches the hearts and minds of all people who partake and enjoy sports.

THE ATHLETES

First and foremost, this book is for the athlete. Athletes come in all shapes and sizes. Each of us are unique: our backgrounds, our hopes for our lives, and even who we root for in sports. If you ever have trained, competed and love being able to move your body— you are an athlete.

I am part of the 99% of this country, my story is much like any athlete who loved playing and then transitioned to the next chapter, and it was a little rougher than I thought it would be . . . so as the author of this book, I hope you know that we are on a journey together. Our stories might be similar and different in some areas, but deep down we know we are stitched together but our love and passion for the game . . . whatever that game is for *you*!

As humans, we can fall into the trap of believing that tomorrow will never come. Many times this could look like being *present* in the moment, taking it "one game at a time" and taking "each season as it comes" or my personal favorite "one point at a time". While this is a healthy mindset to get through a season it does not guard the long term reality of eventual retirement. Being mindful and present in our current situation can lead to great outcomes and memories . . . but it should be balanced with an understanding that competitive sports will end.

When I began playing youth sports, I gave zero thought to a future after athletics. At eleven years old, I had no concept of what I was going to have for breakfast the next morning, let alone visions of a career in volleyball or the eventual end of such a career. Once I hit high school and started playing on club teams, I gave no thought to the *end* of my volleyball career because it was *just beginning*! Who wants to think about retirement when you are sorting a to-do list for collegiate recruitment and for the lucky "blue chip" athletes, sorting through a handful of collegiate offers? It was not until my freshman year playing at Baylor University that my future started coming into focus; but *only* because I tore my ACL. But I was convinced it was just a scare and nothing more. I was confident that I would spend a few weeks on crutches, spend a year in rehab and the gym to get back to fighting form and be back in time to help my Bears win a Big 12 championship and get to the NCAA tournament.

But then my sophomore year came. I was working out. I was ready to play and saw the court a couple of key times for my team. And then I received a rude awakening, my knee was not getting stronger as I played and trained, it was slowly deteriorating in the form of yet another injury.

This one would be the cause of my first death, as Robinson called it: a career-ending tear. I had to confront the truth: at 20 years old, I was nowhere close to being done with volleyball. But volleyball was done with me because my body could not keep up with the physical grind at that Division 1 level. And, frankly, I had other competing interests that allowed me to shine in other ways on campus that were heavy on my heart. In short, because of my ACL tear in High School, I never was able to bounce back and compete at the level that I trained so diligently in my youth sports career.

When I was younger, I never considered retirement before then because I did not want to think it could happen. I never made it to a professional roster. I never joined the national team. It wasn't my time yet! I had so much more to accomplish! But it did not matter. Does it ever?

Over time, I watched my friends pass me by as they went on to play at those levels. And as we have gotten older, I have watched nearly all of them die this first death. I have watched them go through the same struggles that I confronted only a few years earlier. A decade later, I watched a new generation in every sport go through the same moment when their sports career ends. The sports family and belonging that they once felt slowly but surely dissipates.

The loud buzzer goes off—the final whistle blows—the clock runs out.

And it is heartbreaking to watch athletes struggle with "what's next?"

I believe that most athletes go through a similar progression. No child thinks about the "early" retirement that accompanies a career in sports. "Transition" is not a word we hear from coaches or choose to think about when we can be thinking about upcoming games and weight room goals instead. As athletes move through their careers, none like to admit that their sports will be done with them before they are really ready. And thoughts of life post-retirement—even if it is conceptually understood that it will come someday—is put off because, as we all know, someday never comes. Right? For the athletes like me out there, this book serves as a wake-up call and gentle reminder that your "what's next" will come someday and that while you are an athlete, *you are also so much more! Start exploring all the sides of your personality and passion—now! Your new life has just begun!* If we athletes can alter our mindset, we can prepare ourselves mentally, emotionally and physically for when we put two-a-days and training tables behind us.

The hope is that this book and subsequent materials can help make the inevitable transition much smoother for all athletes, at any level, anywhere that sports are being played and enjoyed.

THE COACHES AND EXECUTIVES

This book is also for coaches, administrators, athletic directors, general managers and other executives at every level—from high school on up through the professional ranks. Chances are high that if you are in one of these positions of authority, you also played sports at some point in your youth. YOU LOVE THE GAME, THE COMPETITION AND EVERYTHING GOOD THAT SPORTS REPRESENT! No matter which season of life in which you participated, sports has likely helped give you a sense of competitiveness and leadership qualities that have translated to corporate life and the boardroom. There is a likelihood that you have gone through the transition yourself, whether it was a life after playing or a life after coaching. You know the struggles your athletes go through during the transition on a daily basis, whether it is people coming back to school after graduation to spend time with teammates in classes behind them, or whether it is former players showing up at anniversaries and fan events.

You hear firsthand the uncertainty and the confusion in the questions that your athletes are facing as they transition. You are essential to this conversation on how to help athletes. You have the opportunity to be on the leading edge of the conversation about how and why we need to help athletes begin the transition *before* the locker room is exited for the last time.

If you fall into one of these categories, then you know that you play a unique role in your players' athletic careers. What you may not consider so often, though, is that you have an opportunity to play a unique role in your players' lives beyond sports. I have met a lot of players like me, and many of us agree that while we may not be able to remember every one of our teachers, we remember every coach we've ever played for—from youth sports all the way up through the pro ranks. You may internalize the role you play in the lives of your athletes beyond sports: you have been to your players' weddings, they have brought their kids by your office, and maybe you even grab a beer when they come back for reunion weekends. Regardless of the level you play at, though, you are *the coach*, in a role that necessarily focuses on winning. This book is not to denigrate the fact that you have a job to do. This book is designed to remind you that you also have the opportunity to influence more than just your players' performance on the court or field. You play a pivotal role in the trajectory of your athletes' lives, even long after they exit your locker room.

You have the opportunity to build and maintain a growing sense of belonging and community for your current players, alumni and overall program.

For many athletes, sports are a calling. As athletes, when we find our sport, we fall in love easy. For some of us, something just clicks and it feels like you were meant to play! Maybe in the beginning it didn't matter what sport but just the opportunity to *play*. To be active and competitive and to use your body. The same is true for coaches and administrators. The competitive imperative means that not just anybody can do your job. And, frankly, you would not want somebody doing your job who is only a "paycheck player." This makes the relationship between player and coach or player and executive less employer-employee and more mentor-mentee. Furthermore, the career of nearly every athlete occurs and ends in their twenties. During this period when you are expecting them to perform at the highest physical level possible, you are also in a position of tremendous influence over what neurologists call "emerging adults."

Recent research into how the human brain develops "suggests that people are better equipped to make major life decisions in their late 20s than earlier in the decade. The brain, once thought to be fully grown after puberty, is still evolving into its adult shape well into a person's third decade, pruning away unused connections and strengthening those that remain."[5,6] Related research suggests that all twentysomethings—including athletes—are still developing neural bridges that connect the emotional and motor centers of the brain and develop an "executive" region responsible for, among other things, inhibiting impulses and tempering bubbling emotions.[7] During this period when the human brain is still developing, you have the opportunity to lay long-term foundations and emphasize the need for future planning for the transition. You are on the front lines, and the things you emphasize as a coach or administrator will be internalized by your athletes. You have perhaps the greatest influence on their decision to begin planning for a healthy transition in their futures before their futures catch up with them.

Success is measured in many ways. Bottom lines are important. But as Dallas Mavericks owner Mark Cuban says, "we in the sports business don't sell the game. We sell unique, emotional experiences."[8] For your average fan, those unique, emotional experiences will begin and end with the tradition and history of your team or program, which begins and ends with your former players. This means that your bottom line lives and breathes with the fans who day by day become more and more savvy about the sports business. At the end of the day, the guys who remember an old Yankees Stadium with plaques dedicated to Murderer's Row are the ones the Steinbrenner family has to rely on to pass on those pin-stripe traditions to their kids who may not even know who Derek Jeter is. In an age of constant conference realignment, schools like the University of Kansas rely on the fans who remember watching Danny and the Miracles in 1988 to pass on those traditions to their kids. At the end of the day, your fans still thrive on tradition and care about the "old guys" that have long since found other paths in life. You are the front-line influencers to move the discussion toward how we, as a society, can better prepare our athletes beyond their financial health, and into how we care for our players' mental health, emotional health and physical health as a further retirement benefit. To care about your retired players is to care about your fans who care about your retired players. So this book is for you. The ones with the platform to influence and the power to make change. I challenge you to not only read it but to respond to the call put forth.

THE PARENTS

This book is for the parents of our athletes at every level. You want the absolute best for your children. You want them to grow into the amazing men and women that you know they can become. You are going to create memories and lasting traditions within your family around shared activities. Maybe sports will be one of those activities.

Your family's support of your athlete is invaluable. From the earliest age, parental involvement in an athlete's career can either make or break the sporting experience. Parents support their athletes because they know that sports improve social interactions with other people, it increases self-confidence, sports improve communication skills and, of course, sports can improve overall physical health. The NCAA recognizes that parent involvement is integral during the transition to college athletics. Even at the most elite levels, for better and for worse, we see the impact that parents have on their children playing in the professional leagues and the Olympics.

What you may not realize, though, as your child climbs their personal sport's Mountain (I'll get to that later!) is just how important you will be when their competitive sporting days are over. If you have a parent who has retired, or if you have colleagues who have retired, you have seen how important family and a strong support system is in those first days after a career ends. When your child's coaches and teammates are focusing on the next season, you and the family will be the foundation ensuring that your athlete has a healthy transition. Family should be the first preventative measure by taking proactive measures prior to your child's retirement from competitive athletics. At the end of the day, you will be the one they lean on to get them through those days when they begin to miss the practices, doubleheaders and even grouchy coaches. This book is meant to help you understand what your child has gone through, is going through, or will go through, in the hopes of giving you the opportunity to help them before the day inevitably comes that they enter the next chapter of their lives.

THE FANS AND THE MEDIA

The public. The fans. The media. You fun, crazy people are ready to buy t-shirts for every championship, wear the same jersey every game and engage in postseason rituals involving underwear and socks. You tear down goal posts and burn couches when your team wins key games and championships. You are the people who buy the tickets and religiously watch the game. Some of you may even taunt the opponents with home-made signs and go into the chat rooms online to learn the stories of the athletes on the field. You make sport more than just the game. Because of your fandom, you have made sports its own ecosystem. This book is for you because, at the end of the day, you have the greatest influence on how we—as a society—treat, support and encourage our players. You are the economic driver behind the sports industry.

It is the policy in this country to support our returning soldiers, sailors, airmen and Marines. They have sacrificed their bodies, their time and their energy for us. And when they leave the service, their mental, emotional and physical health can become negatively symptomatic as their bodies and minds react to letting go of constant high-stakes, the constant need to push their bodies to the max, and the stress of giving up control to rely and trust on the person next to them to achieve a common goal. And, while not intending to compare athletic achievement to what President Lincoln called "the last full measure of devotion," our athletes also sacrifice their bodies, time and energy for us in many ways.

The Tar Heel basketball player and the Tar Heel fan share that Tar Heel identity. The Cleveland Brown and the Brownie in the Dawg Pound share that Cleveland identity. If you are from Seattle, the Seahawks, the Mariners or the Seattle Storm represent you and your city. If you are a New Yorker, the Yankees, the Giants and the Knicks represent you (or mix it up with being a Mets fan or Jets fan)! If you are from Chicago, it was a point of pride even during the Curse of the Billy Goat to say "I'm a Cubs fan!" How many fathers and sons have developed their relationships over a team? How many friendships have developed between season ticket holders sitting side-by-side? It is through the traditions, history and memory that would not have happened without the players who went before that we weave sentiments of community and belonging, at least a little bit. As the players have given it to you, I now ask you to pay it back to the players.

In the same way that the public has taken an interest in athlete concussions and finances, I call on the fans and media to now drive the conversation about helping our athletes who have sacrificed so much to provide everything from simple entertainment to being a proxy for home-town pride and honor. So, I call on you to be a part of the conversation to help those that have represented our cities, our alma maters, and us (the fans) at the end of the day. This book is for you to understand and, hopefully, to influence our athletes, administrators and coaches to help our athletes move through the transition period, into their next chapter as a human and as an athlete, efficiently and in a healthy way. I'm going to call on you to participate in events and conversations that will help them bridge the gap. We hope for you to bring the same passion to this movement that you bring to the sports atmosphere!

SO . . .

This book is for many people. It is for every person who has played sports. It is for every person who has coached sports. It is for every person who has managed sports. At the end of the day, this book is for every person who has ever loved sports in some form or who has been impacted by sports. Each of you has a unique and necessary role to play in moving the discussion forward and to ensure that each of our athletes remains in an athletic posture— mind, body and spirit.

Together, as an athletic community, we should encourage all athletes to stay in an athletic state of mind, even after we have hung up their pads, cleats and jerseys.

So, let's get this party started.

THE MOUNTAIN

2

Introduction
The Mountain and The Cliff

I had climbed my Mount Everest and the
view was beautiful from the top.

—ANNIKA SORENSTAM
Professional Golfer[1]

As a kid, I grew up in Southern California. And SoCal takes its sports seriously. Los Angeles hosted the 1984 Summer Olympics, which still holds the record for the most profitable Olympic Games of all time. The LA84 Foundation continues to support youth and amateur athletics in the region. As of this writing, Los Angeles prepares to host the 2028 Summer Olympic Games. I grew up with the Angels and the Dodgers, the Lakers and the Clippers, the LA Galaxy and the Los Angeles Raiders. Just ten minutes down the road from where I grew up, Anaheim plays home to the United States Olympic Volleyball Team and an NHL franchise, the Ducks. No matter what season it is, SoCal is surrounded by sports.

In the fall, I could follow Trojan football. In the winter, I could watch Bruin basketball. Not to mention the numerous other universities and colleges fielding nationally recognized athletic programs in a variety of other sports. If you are ever feeling social, it always felt like someone, or some team, was competing and there was a game to go to.

But all of that starts in one geographical location. What you may not know is that southern California—and Orange County in particular, where I grew up—is one of the most important recruiting hotbeds in the nation. Perennial powerhouse high school programs like Mater Dei High School in Santa Ana and up-and-coming programs such as my alma mater, Tesoro High School in Rancho Santa Margarita, feed into nationally recognized college programs. College basketball recruiters regularly stake out tournaments hosted by the Amateur Athletic Union (better known as the AAU) because SoCal features some of the most dominant and dynamic youth basketball in the nation. College volleyball recruiters travel to the national mecca of club volleyball to scout high school and club programs located up and down the coast. In turn, these high school and club programs are fed by countless numbers of Pop Warner youth football programs, AYSO soccer leagues, and YMCA baseball, softball and Biddy Basketball programs for athletes as young as four years old.

Youth sports is big business, and it seems like it is even further amplified by our countless days of sunshine.

Youth sports feed into high school and club sports. High school and club sports feed into college sports. And college sports feed into professional and Olympic sports. This is a brief look at what I like to call "The Athletic Mountain"—the path that every athlete climbs. Many end their ascent before high school. A select few reach the highest peaks. But if you are playing sports today, then you are climbing the Mountain. If you are a parent with kids in youth sports today, your kids are right now climbing the Mountain. If you are playing at that "next level" on traveling teams or on your high school varsity team, you are climbing the Mountain. If you are on a collegiate roster, you are climbing the Mountain. If you are training for a Super Bowl or the Olympic Games, you are climbing the Mountain. Regardless of how high you have climbed or how high you will climb, taking one step at a time, putting one foot in front of the other. You are climbing your Athletic Mountain today.

Someday, after you have climbed the Mountain as far as you can, you will reach and you will fall off the Cliff at the top of your Mountain. Every athlete falls off the Cliff. How hard that fall is will be impacted by how high you climb. It is over the course of that journey that we develop our identities as athletes, we develop physical and dietary habits, and we face unique mental stressors. And so to better understand the Cliff, it's important to reflect on the journey up the Mountain.

3
Youth Sports
The Foothills

Somewhere behind the athlete you've become and hours
of practice and the coaches who have pushed you, is a little girl
who fell in love with the game and never looked back.

—MIA HAMM
Captain, 1999 FIFA Women's World Cup Champion[1]

The bottom of the Mountain is plentiful with youth participants, though nobody knows just how plentiful it is yet. Youth sports are traditionally defined as organized sporting activities for children and adolescents not yet in high school, capping out at age 14. In 2013, ESPN reported that youth sports in the United States (which I define as sports for kids prior to high school) is so massively popular that, up to that point, there had been no organized effort to accurately measure the level of nationwide youth sports participation.[2] Responding to the lack of quantitative analysis, the Aspen Institute, a bi-partisan think tank and research organization, launched its Sports & Society Program. The purpose of this program is to study under-researched aspects of sports and athletics in the United States.[3] In support of this mission, the Sports & Society Program in 2014 launched what it calls its "Project Play" initiative. Described by the Aspen Institute as "a multi-year, multi-stage effort to provide the thought leadership . . . to build 'Sport for All, Play for Life' Communities, the first phase of which focused exclusively on youth sports.[4]

In 2014, estimates suggested that between 40 and 45 million American children played organized youth sports.[5] That represents roughly three out of every four American families with school-aged children.[6] The next year, in 2015, Project Play reported that more than HALF of all American children between the ages of six and twelve participated in team sports alone. Additionally, more than forty percent participated as "core participants," meaning children who participated on a regular basis.[7] Based on numbers like this, nobody can argue with Olympian and International Olympic Committeewoman Anita DeFrantz who stated that "sports are a birthright."[8] This is how big the base of the Mountain likely is.

When I think about youth sports, the image that most immediately comes to mind for me is a large group of five-year-olds in luminescent jerseys chasing a soccer ball around the field. They chase the ball instead of passing it, ignoring their coaches' pleas to "spread out." In some parts of the country, they call it "bunch ball." On the west coast, where I'm from, we call it "swarm ball." But regardless what you call it, where you are from, or even ultimately whether you end your journey up the Soccer Mountain, the Basketball Mountain, the Softball Mountain, or even the Swimming or Track & Field or Gymnastics Mountain, this image defines where almost all of us began our concepts of sports: playing (many times with a with a ball) having fun with your friends and burning off some energy.

The ball is ubiquitous in childhood. Even before we can walk, somebody is tossing a ball to us. As infants and toddlers, parents give their children balls to entertain their growing curiosity about the world. At two or three years old, physical movement is "the epicenter of children's lives and is crucial to all aspects of a child's development."[9] At this age, kids get their first taste of play, sports, athletics—throwing, catching and kicking balls for the first time. This early-stage ball play stimulates brain development and function, and is key to building the foundation, organization and capabilities of the brain.[10] And the ball is the element common to every athlete, even if they leave the ball at the bottom of their Mountain as they get older. Parents roll and toss balls at their youngsters. They set up small backboards and encourage their kids to push the ball through the hoop. They might set up a small net and encourage their kids to kick the ball into the net, working those motor skills at an early age. Kids play with bounce balls or throw tennis balls at the wall. Across cultures, across borders, across generations, the ball is perhaps one of the most important elements of early childhood development. It is so important that in 2016, a documentary titled *Bounce: How The Ball Taught The World To Play* premiered at the prestigious South By Southwest Film Festival about what else? The impact the ball has on each of us! Kids play with balls, of all different sorts, by the boatload.

During those early years, we engage in free play with the ball. There are no rules, there is no score. It is simply a universal object with which we explore our world. And then, once old enough (typically once attaining school age), the child's world meshes the ball with something brand new to each of us: organized sports. Suddenly, the ball is not simply a tool to explore the world, but an object teaching us systems. Almost immediately the ball has a bigger meaning with rules, scores, strategies and—ultimately—a sense of competition. Before we ever imagined the finer techniques of the give-and-go, the pick-and-pop and top spin, we found our competitive edge learning to play kickball, tetherball and foursquare. When I was a younger girl, tetherball was my favorite. Even after breaking my arm, I would still play with my cast on because it was so fun! And according to sports satisfaction surveys, "having fun" is the main reason that most children want to participate in youth sports.[11]

Not surprisingly, the most-cited reason that parents enroll their kids into youth sports is for the physical benefits to their children. In a 2015 Harvard University survey, 88 percent of parents with kids enrolled in youth sports reported it having a positive impact on their children's physical well-being.[12] Since 1990, societal evolutions including proliferation of technology, the national financial crisis, cloistered suburbanization, two-income households (which lead to more "meals on the go") and fast food have combined to facilitate a more sedentary lifestyle with a greater consumption of high-calorie, bad-for-health foods.[13] This has led to an epidemic of childhood obesity rates in the United States that directly correlates to physical health problems in later life, including increased risk of heart disease and diabetes, not to mention the psychological tolls that such children face including diminished quality of life, learning difficulties, decreased self-confidence and social discrimination.[14] Meanwhile, a child's motor skills acquisition and movement improves the likelihood they will participate in physical activity into adulthood.

But parents enroll their kids into youth sports for other reasons, too. According to that same 2015 survey, parents also identified youth sports' positive impact on "giving a child something to do" (83%).[15] While I don't have kids yet, I sympathize with my friends when their kids go crazy from time to time. And I certainly remember my mom dropping me off at practice when I had energy to burn, her hand waving with a "dad will pick you up!" With kids that age, it's no wonder this is the top response. But other reasons for parents to enroll their kids in youth sports include teaching discipline and dedication (81%), teaching children how to get along with others (78%), children's mental health (73%), children's social life (65%), children's skills to help in future schooling (56%) and children's skills to help in future careers (55%). Other benefits include physical development, weight control in an era of a childhood obesity epidemic, improved endurance, greater self-esteem, perseverance, promotion of healthy competition, and providing guidance to young people face to face coaches and other mentors.[16] No matter how short an individual athlete's journey up the Mountain is, athletics are a great way to teach life lessons. It's no wonder that a vast majority of industrial titans and world leaders participated in sports in their youth.[17]

It makes sense, sports teach so many important life lessons that no matter what age you play, those characteristics and social norms help an athlete adapt to society at large. To quote a fabulous 501c3 organization, Positive Coach Alliance, "When done right, sports teach."[18]

A quick anecdote to illustrate the values that parents place on participation in youth sports. Amy Roegler and her husband, Octavio Herrera, live with their kids, Jake and Alyssa, in Los Angeles. They are die-hard Dodgers fans, and "Jake loved balls even as a baby," according to his father.[19] According to Octavio, "[w]e have a picture of him as a 3-month-old with a little Dodger jersey and a glove, so he was definitely going to be introduced to sports early, and he took to it right away."[20] And for Amy, the benefits of youth sports go beyond physical exercise. At this age, kids are introduced to non-family social structures for the first time as they head off to school. They are introduced to informal "team" building and are learning that there are rules for general behavior. Kids are taught to share, sacrificing instant gratification. And while we may not call it as such, this is the age when we all first internalize the idea of "winning" and "losing." We get judged by our peers. We get scored on tests. For better or worse, we slowly begin to evolve out of our "play" phase of life and begin to enter the "performance" phase that will dominate our worldview for decades to come. These lessons are internalized in the most acute way in youth sports. As Amy says, "when you do sports as a kid, you learn how to win and how to lose. You learn what it's like to put in lots of work and have things not turn out terrifically. And you learn what it feels like to put in a lot of work—and then win."[21]

With this evolution from play to performance, which begins often between ages 5 and 8, many children begin to move into organized sports for the first time. There, this evolution is more pronounced. The offerings are aplenty, with nationally recognized youth sports organizations present in most states including American Youth Soccer Organization (AYSO) soccer leagues, Pop Warner football leagues, YMCA and Little League tee-ball, baseball and softball leagues, USAV volleyball leagues and T-Ball, YMCA and Boys and Girls Club basketball leagues.

But in addition to these community and rec leagues, other local and regional leagues have popped up that advertise more "elite level" competition for childhood athletes. The primary commonality between these elite leagues—regardless of sport—is often their reference as "club" or "traveling" team leagues. During this period, while young athletes are still developing mentally, emotionally and especially physically, they may encounter a sports culture that simultaneously begins their indoctrination into the "athlete identity" while also having potential for emotional and physical scarring down the line. A recent development and current trend has conquered youth sports: specialization. For better or for worse, specialization is the first step that most athletes take in order to climb beyond the base of the Mountain.

The late Kobe Bryant was a huge advocate to create a better, less specialized and more equitable youth sports system. "You try to overload these kids and get them to be the best in one year. It is absolutely ridiculous."[22]

Specialization is defined as a shift that adolescent athletes undergo in which their focus moves away from broad "physical literacy" to a focus on one sport, usually year-round, typically in an effort to maximize a child's "athletic potential." The Aspen Institute defines "physical literacy" as a combination of physical ability ("competency in basic movement skills and an overall fitness that allows individuals to engage in a variety of games and activities"), confidence ("knowing that you have the ability to play sports or enjoy other physical activities") and desire ("intrinsic enthusiasm for physical activity").[23] Specialization, on the other hand, promotes a focus on competency in advanced-but-narrow skillsets applicable to a single sport. Often confidence and especially desire are the greatest cost of specialization. It is characterized by a child's shift away from sport "grazing," in which they play multiple sports, typically only in-season, and participate in casual playground or so-called "pick-up" games, and begin focusing on a single sport year-round. A sport becomes a child's life lens. It is the way that they experience the world and the way they identify themselves to others. In other words, specialization is when a child athlete's entire life can be summed up in one word: "insert chosen sport here."

For most athletes climbing the Mountain, specialization occurs as they get older and move out of youth sports onto varsity school teams and elite club teams in their late teens. However, it is beginning to occur in younger and younger youth sport athletes in America, as illustrated by ESPN's 2013 story about a grade school soccer player Tyler Ward. At just two years old, Ward's mother enrolled him in one of the best toddler soccer classes in New York City. By the time he was five years old, Ward's coaches had identified him as one of the best players on the six-and-under team and was groomed to join his club's pre-travel program. By the time he was 11 years old, he was one of the standouts on his club's eleven-and-under team and advanced all the way to the final tryout for the U.S. Youth Soccer Olympic Development Program before getting cut. His team practices on Tuesdays, Thursdays and Saturdays and most Fridays. He plays in games and tournaments every Sunday during the season.

In addition to his regular club team, he also made his league's "select squad," effectively an all-star lineup of fourth graders from every team in the area. This required Ward to make a three-hour round trip drive from his home in New York City to New Jersey every other Monday, in addition to his club team's practice schedule. During the off-season, Ward's father enrolled him in futsal—a modified version of indoor soccer—one day a week, in addition to a recreational league which Ward's father coaches. In the summers, Ward's father took him to Europe where he was enrolled in soccer camps in Italy, France and the Netherlands. For Ward, there effectively is no off-season. *Soccer for this eleven-year-old was a full-time job.*[24]

The young athlete is forced to rise to the level of competition with whom they are competing. And the most ambitious desire to rise to the challenge because they will be around teammates who match their intensity and commitment to the game. As Ward said, "it's frustrating when you're trying your hardest and the other kids on your team are making bad passes and not taking it seriously. In travel soccer, it's more intense—everybody wants to win."[25] This young soccer stud is ready to become the next Pelé, Cobi Jones or Ronaldo and it is clear he won't let anyone else's slack drag him down (Tyler, I wish you all the best as you climb your Mountain! Go get 'em!).

But clearly this early emphasis on specialization can be laid squarely at the feet of parents and coaches. Working with the National Collegiate Athletic Association (NCAA), Project Play added questions to the NCAA's annual survey of its athletes. This survey captured, for the first time, NCAA athletes' opinions on their youth sports experiences. Across four sports, including revenue sports men's basketball and football, nearly half of all male athletes said that they believed they played in too many games as kids. More than half of all college athletes across multiple sports indicated that their families *"expected* them to become college athletes 'since [they were] young.'"[26]

For most families, youth sports are a great experience for kids. New friends. Ice cream after wins. Sunshine and the outdoors. Physical activity. Spirit tunnels and a taste of the pageantry of the "big kid" sports they watch with their parents at home. Not to mention how cute is it to dress the littlest kids up in tiny team jerseys? I have to admit that as an "auntie" to several of my old teammates' kids, we love game days when the girls throw on cheerleading uniforms for the team we're all watching that day. On the kids' game days, their moms and I will put them in their pink jerseys that are so big they look more like dresses than shirts. I am not immune to enjoying this with my old friends. But quickly, "the adults" can take over.

At the espnW conference in 2014, the Aspen Institute presented survey data demonstrating that among parents of children at this age, two out of every three parents agree that there is too much emphasis placed on winning and not enough emphasis on having fun.[27] However, while a majority of parents may say that fun is more important than winning, it is hard to say how many of those parents put those words into action. After all, if more than 65% of all parents of school-age kids believe "fun" is more important than "winning," then why are elite youth sports now a $15 billion per year industry,[28] of which $7 billion is annually accounted for from travel team and tournament youth sports alone?[29] And these numbers have only continue to increase. The parents are paying to advance and develop their kids skills as well as their social emotional skills. It certainly isn't the third-grade soccer player emptying his piggy bank to pay those expenses.

I believe that the reason for this is clear. Parents in today's sports climate are encouraged directly and indirectly to sign their kids up for competitive teams earlier and earlier in their children's development. With scholarships available, and professional sports contracts in the hundreds of millions of dollars, parents are pushing their kids more and more to become "elite" at a younger and younger age. And, unfortunately, many parents have subscribed to the so-called "10,000 Hour Rule" perpetuated across parenting websites around the world.

The 10,000 Hour Rule goes all the way back to 1973. That year, researchers Herbert Simon and William Chase published their findings from research they conducted at Carnegie-Mellon University on the skill level presented by chess players. Buried in that study lay the foundations for the 10,000 Hour Rule:

> [T]here are no instant experts in chess—certainly no instant masters or grandmasters. There appears not to be on record any case (including Bobby Fischer) where a person has reached grandmaster level with less than about a decade's intense preoccupation with the game [of chess]. We would estimate, very roughly, that a master has spent perhaps 10,000 to 50,000 hours staring at chess positions, and a Class A player 1,000 to 5,000 hours. For the master, these times are comparable to the times that highly literate people have spent in reading by the time they reach adulthood.[30]

Despite the fact that Simon and Chase were using the phrase "master" in the highly-contextualized setting of competitive chess, the phrase took on a life of its own. Later researchers suggested that *mastery* of *any* skill required a minimum of ten years or 10,000 hours. The most significant of these was John Hayes in the 1989 re-printing of his book *The Complete Problem Solver*, in which he declared that with few exceptions it took the greatest masters of classical music "ten years of silence" toiling at their craft before they produced their masterworks.[31] Then, in 2008, Malcolm Gladwell's book *Outliers* popularized the idea that it takes 10,000 hours of practice to become an expert at *anything*—including sports.[32] In the middle of his book, Gladwell wrote the statement that doomed today's young athletes to specialization:

> It's all but impossible to reach that number all by yourself by the time you're a young adult. You have to have parents who encourage and support you. You can't be poor, because if you have to hold down a part-time job on the side to help make ends meet, there won't be time left in the day to practice enough. In fact, most people can reach that number only

if they get into some kind of special program—like a hockey all-star squad—or if they get some kind of extraordinary opportunity that gives them a chance to put in those hours.[33]

And so, it began.

Today, parents are encouraged both directly and indirectly to sign their kids up for competitive teams earlier and earlier in their child's development. Many parents believe that they need to expose their children to highly competitive sports at a young age so that their kids can survive the competition in their own age bracket. Books have even been written by "sports parents," wherein such parents dispense advice about the need to get kids involved in "deliberate practice" and the 10,000-hour rule despite the fact that they provide the outright caveat that such practice "requires effort, and is not inherently enjoyable" for the young athlete.[34]

The researchers whose work formed the basis for Gladwell's 10,000 Hour Rule have since rebuked it. While noting that the rule "captures this fundamental truth—that in many areas of human endeavor it takes many, many years of practice to become one of the best in the world," the rule itself is too easy: "The final problem with the ten-thousand-hour rule is that, although Gladwell himself didn't say this, many people have interpreted it as a promise that almost anyone can become an expert in a given field by putting in ten thousand hours of practice" when it just isn't so.[35] There has been some reprimand from all-star players about the state of youth sports having been co-opted by this 10,000 rule.

Before his tragic death in January of 2020, Kobe Bryant was a leader in this space. He talked about the state of AAU basketball, calling it "horrible, terrible."[36] Bryant advocated, instead, a focus on fundamentals and having fun: "Right now, I think we're putting too much pressure on these kids too early. . . . It winds up eating away at their confidence. As teachers, we need to have patience to teach things piece by piece by piece. Over time, they'll develop as basketball players, but you can't just rush it all at once."[37]

Despite the opinions of all-stars legends like Kobe, elite traveling teams, out-of-season camps, personal trainers and other forms of specialization have taken over. While other athletes have failed to call specialization healthy, they have certainly noted the necessity of specializing if the young athlete wants to move up instead of out of his sport. 2015 NBA lottery-pick D'Angelo Russell calls playing AAU basketball "a big milestone." As he put it, "[i]f you're not playing AAU, you'll be lucky to get out of your own city."[38] It even permeates the non-sports playing public's consciousness. Who can forget after Tiger Woods' first Masters victory when he was only 21 years old? And who can forget the marketing blitz that immediately followed featuring video clips of a two-year-old Tiger smacking golf balls in front of television legend Bob Hope?[39] And what parent praying for a scholarship for their child would *not* put their child on that path after seeing highly-publicized instances of eighth-graders fielding scholarship offers from college football powerhouses like Alabama and USC?[40] Even so-called "non-revenue" sports are not immune, with college power houses recruiting middle school-aged volleyball players, soccer players and even field hockey and lacrosse players.[41] An entire cottage industry has sprung up to rank third-grade basketball players, and parents have bought into the idea that a nine-year-old's ranking in any way shapes a college coach's belief about his future collegiate ability.[42]

Experts like the NBA and USA Basketball are calling for guidelines to "trigger *less* one-sport specialization" and more importantly to "foster peer relationships, self-esteem and better health."[43] (Thank you Adam Silver and team for your leadership in taking a first step!) But how can parents ignore the "warnings" from the people on the frontlines: youth coaches and other parents? After all, Kevin Ward, the pre-pubescent soccer star's father, says that "[n]owadays, if you want to play a sport at the highest level, you're expected to play it year-round."[44] And coaches invariably promote this dynamic. Gary Pinkney was the director of Maryland's Finest, an AAU basketball program. In his words "[a]t 13 or 14, it's too late" to begin specializing. "Seven or eight years old is where it starts," he says." "If you don't start putting in the work, then you're not doing what you need to do to succeed in sports these days."[45] And what parent is going to argue with the man whose second-graders won the AAU eight-and-under national championship (yes, apparently there is such a thing . . .). Then there are the actual experts that *do* push specialization and elitism at an early age. U.S. Youth Soccer (a subsidiary of USA Soccer) begins weeding kids out as early as 11-years-old. Sam Snow, director of coaching for U.S.Y.S. states that "it's intended to be part of the ladder of getting to the highest level."[46] *So who is to say what is right for kids from ages 8 to 14?*

What can be said as those kids get older, though, is that specialization impacts their identities early on. It goes without saying that at the youth sports age, young kids begin the process of developing an athletic identity. During the years between ages 6 and 14, children become competent, independent, self-aware and involved in the world. Biological and cognitive changes begin to transform their minds and bodies, and their relationships and social roles change as they enter school, join activities and socialize.[47] During this period, kids begin to develop their identity based on their experiences, relationships and emerging senses of social roles.[48] These are often impacted by introduction to activities that can include music, Boy Scouts and Girl Scouts and, yes, sports. It is around age nine that children who have participated in youth sports begin to self-identify as an athlete or not.[49]

As early as 1993, researchers defined "athletic identity" as "the degree to which an individual identifies with the athlete role" that they play.[50] That role is often developed by a person's passion for particular activity. But there is more to the process by which one develops this identity from mere activity as laid out by Eric Martin, professor at Boise State University:

> For an activity to become a passion, it must be significant in individuals' lives, be liked by them, and be something that they engage in frequently. More specifically, the activity that an individual may feel passionate about may not be merely an activity in which she or he participates. Rather, that activity actually becomes a central portion of that person's identity. . . . People who are highly passionate about activities such as football, writing, or teaching, do not merely play football, write or teach. Rather they are, or they have become, football players, writers and teachers.[51]

Even in the less-competitive leagues, kids are likely engaging in their sports frequently with one or two practices per week and at least one game on the weekends. If they are engaging in more than one sport at a time, play unorganized or "rec" games during their free time, and even watch sports regularly with friends and family, it is fair to say that sports—as a general proposition—is becoming a significant activity in addition to engaging them frequently. In those instances, it would not be difficult to see a kid beginning to develop a sense-of-self centered on sports and athletics. If those kids become specialized and begin participating in the highly-competitive leagues with elite squads, traveling to camps and getting one-on-one training outside of practice, it likely goes without saying that those kids are certainly engaged frequently *and* that their *singular* sport has a significant place in their life. In those instances, it is not hard to see those kids going one step beyond developing a more generalized "athlete" identity, but developing a "player" identity: "I am a 'fill-in-the-blank' player."

A whole nother chapter could be written around this formation of athletic identity by the young athletes family taking pictures and capturing the moments of their young athlete. Us 90's kids did not have the same pressure as this young generation added a layer of social media. Pictures of kids playing sports and the streaming comments that can come in from all the family's social connections.

As this identity takes hold, and the youth athlete becomes aware, it is not surprising when the athletic identity takes hold at the next level.

Without discussing the merit of specialization at such an early age, what is apparent is that of the 45 million kids, give or take, who participate in youth sports each year, as many as 75 to 80 percent will quit sports completely by the time they reach 15 years of age—sometime before the end of their freshman year in high school.[52]

This can be because children find other interests outside of sports. For many, they may feel burnout. Whatever the reason, it is clear that as a function of pure numbers, this is as high up the Mountain as most kids will go. If a child's sports journey ends before high school, we need to explore opportunities to engage them again in sports or recreational athletic activities, because, like Nike's mission statement says, "if you have a body, you are an athlete."[53]

"Don't Retire Kid" was a campaign that launched in the summer of 2019 by ESPN's department of Corporate Social Responsibility.[54] If you have not seen the powerful images and messages of young athletes announcing their retirement from sports, I encourage you to look it up or Youtube the video campaigns. You will see the message that encourages young athletes to *have fun* and for them to stay in the game!

I personally hope that we can reverse this statistic and keep as many of those kids playing sports as long as possible, because it is unclear how many of these kids will pick up sports again later in life,[55] and we need to keep this country active and healthy.

4
High School Sports
The Base of the Athletic Mountain

These six individuals have made a choice to work,
a choice to sacrifice, to put themselves on the line
twenty-three nights in the next four months to represent you,
this high school. That kind of commitment and effort deserves
and demands your respect. This is your team.

—GENE HACKMAN,
Coach Norman Dale, "Hoosiers"[1]

Perhaps you or your athlete is one of the 20 to 30 percent of youth sports kids who moved up to the next level by joining high school teams and ever-more elite traveling teams.[2] Interestingly, while there is a 70 to 80 percent attrition rate by the time high school starts, a National Public Radio and Harvard University survey conducted in 2013 revealed that 72% of children in middle school and high school play at least one sport. In 2016, the National Federation of State High School Associations reported that high school participation in sports increased for the 27th year in a row, reaching an all-time high of 7,868,900 students participating in high school athletics.[3]

As we go from youth sports and middle school teams—after all of the hours spent at games and practices—something CLICKS! The athlete finds his or her rhythm. Games and tournaments become more entertaining. Passion starts to unfold as we worry less and less about the rules and fundamentals of the game, and more and more about advanced skills and strategy of the game. The shift to taking sports "seriously" occurs as the athlete begins to form adolescent relationships with teammates that can become lifelong friendships and carry weight in social circles. Not to mention that as our bodies change during puberty, sports and a player's identity give us something to aspire to in terms of physical form when we may lack confidence or struggle with self-esteem as we deal with braces, acne, and changing voices (at least for the boys).

This is also a period when sports truly become a family activity. How many of you remember a time when your mom or dad sat you down and asked you if you wanted to keep playing? Did you enjoy it? Do you like your coaches and teammates? For many families, playing sports at the high school level—whether it's varsity sports at school or club sports—becomes a commitment of both time and money. Expenses for registrations, new uniforms and new equipment—sometimes for multiple teams per year—add up. Costs of travel, private lessons and personal training add up. In fact, the cost to continue playing at this age is estimated to be the greatest barrier-to-entry, per Project Play:

> While only 20% of U.S. households report an annual income of at least $100,000, 33% of households participating in sports enjoy that income level. Travel-team parents spend an average of $2,266 annually on their child's sports participation, and at the elite levels some families spend more than $20,000 per year. In 2015, less than one in three parents (32%) from households making less than $50,000/year told researchers that sports cost too much and make it difficult for their child to continue participating.[4]

I know that from my playing days, my parents paid for private lessons and plyometrics with the legendary Marv Marinovich to make sure I had the greatest competitive edge available (I loved my time with Marv! He had other clients, but always pushed me to make sure *I*—Jenné Blackburn—excelled, training right next to future Chicago Bear and fellow Capo Unified School District alumnus, Mark Sanchez). My lessons and training sessions could range from anywhere from twenty to seventy-five dollars per hour. I had high school registration and uniform fees. I went to every club camp to increase my ranking and increase my visibility within the elite Laguna Beach Volleyball Club. And this was just to be able to *play* in high school and club, in hopes of getting noticed by colleges.

When you are a developing athlete, you don't realize all the outside financial struggles of families just to be given the opportunity to train and compete.

For the collegiate athlete, there are other expenses simply because the market to receive a full or partial college scholarship is so competitive. As I played through high school, I remember my dad sitting up at night cutting videos for recruiters and college coaches with a video camera and VCR/TV combo when he wasn't at my games with a camera in hand. My dad is a unique man with many interests. While other parents would have the inexpensive Walmart tripod out, my dad insisted on using an old Army tripod from the 1950's that went three times as high as everyone else's just to get the right shot. I remember him getting to the court early so that he could stake out territory and crank his tripod ten feet higher than everyone else's. He called me "One Take Blackburn" before pushing the record button as he recorded my intros. As committed to volleyball as I was, sometimes I think maybe my dad's commitment to getting the perfect shot for volleyball recruiters may have been even greater. (I have such gratitude to have all my greatest sports memories to both my father and mother for believing in my volleyball dreams, and even now with this dream for athletes to be fully supported in their second chapter)

Today, video cameras and editing systems are available on smart phones, but with coaches' email addresses available on websites, the field is deeper and wider. As Matt Tyner, a recruiter and baseball coach at Richmond University said, "the good news is, I have access to worldwide talent. Guess what the bad news is? I have access to worldwide talent," increasing the number of recruits from the hundreds he had to look at in the 1990s to thousands today.[4] But how does the high school athlete stand out today? Parents can shell out anywhere from $500 to $700 for their kids to attend showcases for their talent, and many are paying fees upwards of $3,000 for recruitment consulting firms to put their kids in front of as many college coaches and recruiters as possible.[5] Recruiting today is big business. Looking back, I finally realize how much my dad sacrificed to make sure I had an opportunity to play at the next level. He worked overtime just for an extra couple hundred dollars anytime I played at away tournaments. Growing up in Orange County, where I realize I grew up surrounded by a lot of privilege (safety—security—education) from an early age, I knew other players whose families really had to work and sacrifice for the money because all of the extra practice, tournaments, personal training, and recruitment activities were not really "extras." These expenses were necessities and non-negotiable in order to get us to that next level. Even for the athlete who only plays varsity sports at school, those costs can skyrocket.

With the commitment of both time and money, it is no wonder that the athletic identifier becomes much more important to the individual athlete as we feel the need for that time and money to "pay off." As athletes transition from elementary school playgrounds and youth sports through middle school, institutional pride is amplified as athletes play for fans that—for the first time perhaps—don't include their family. For the first time, they may run into a coach quoting Arsenal F.C. defenseman Tony Adams: "Play for the name on the front of the shirt, and they'll remember the name on the back,"[6] or Olympic Hockey coach Herb Brooks, of Miracle on Ice fame, when he said the "name on the front of the sweater is more important than the one the back."[7] At this point on the path up the Athletic Mountain, athletes are often associated in the public with larger community groups like teams, schools, and even entire hometowns. If it hasn't already, sports begins to be about performance and not simply participation anymore. Kids want to win titles—not just participation trophies. Even in the 21st Century, varsity letter jackets are still a point of pride for the high school athlete; an obvious billboard advertising their athletic achievement. Local media begins to cover their games and print their scores, times and stats. Booster clubs and fundraisers all add into the equation.

I believe that there are two types of high school athletes: the "varsity athlete" and the "collegiate athlete." I believe that *both* are athletes, though they differ in one main respect: where the varsity athlete participates on his or her high school's team simply because he or she wants to play on the team, the collegiate athlete actively hopes for and pursues opportunities to play in college. There are many reasons that an athlete may choose a varsity role over a collegiate role. And athletes may also *change* that role throughout high school. In 2010, researcher Katie Helms published a study about athletic identity and transitional loss in former high school athletes at the University of Arkansas, Fayetteville. In her study, Helms found that 75 percent of high school freshman athletes expect to play college sports, while only 54 percent of high school senior athletes have the same expectations,[8] indicating that many high school athletes accept that they likely will not play competitive sports beyond high school. Then, of course, there is the rare varsity athlete who becomes a collegiate athlete during high school; the varsity athlete who did not necessarily set out to get noticed by colleges, but gets noticed anyway. NFL legend Jerry Rice perhaps fits this model, forced to choose between playing football or expulsion for playing hooky.[9] But what makes a high school athlete a varsity athlete or a collegiate athlete? A quick story.

One of my friends is the quintessential college athlete. Tall. Broad shoulders. Zero body fat. Veritable Greek god. A few years ago, he married another amazing athlete. Then these two athletes had kids. I was invited to their house over the holidays a few years ago and remarked that their oldest son seemed very tall for his age. His dad told me that in addition to being tall, their son scored remarkably above the normal range for his age group in motor skills. Then something unexpected. His dad then grinned and sang a jingle.

"Deck the halls with future scholarships."

I laughed, of course. But my friend's joke has always stuck with me because I knew he was only half kidding. His grin underscores a difficult issue that many parents face today: the cost of higher education. Since roughly 1970, the cost of attendance at universities has outpaced the rate of inflation nearly tenfold.[10] Today, the average nationwide cost of *tuition alone* at a four-year public university for in-state students is over $9,410 per year. This figure does not include room, board and other living expenses.[11] There is certainly a lot of debate about how valuable a college degree really is these days, but nobody disputes the idea that getting a college degree *at all* is a good idea.[12,13] And for the athlete who has his or her eye on the peak of the Mountain (*i.e.* professional sports or the Olympic Games), with few exceptions intercollegiate athletics is the *sole and exclusive* path to reach the Mountaintop. So, whether you or your athlete is looking for a way to go to college inexpensively or a way to reach the professional or Olympic level, chances are that a college scholarship, or at least making a roster, is your goal while in high school.

Much has been researched and written about the actual chances that high school students have of playing at the collegiate level, so I'll keep this part brief. The NCAA keeps the most regular statistics, the latest demonstrating that of the nearly eight million students presently participating in high school athletics, only 5.8 percent can ever expect to make an NCAA roster—at any division.[14] And only 2 percent of all high school participants in NCAA sports can expect to play on a Division I team[15]—the highest, most prestigious division among National Collegiate Athletic Association institutions. For the family that is looking at sports as a vehicle to help put their athletes through college, though, those numbers may not be as awful as they first appear because they do not take into account the full scope of college sports opportunities.

NCAA alternatives include the small, private schools in the National Association of Intercollegiate Athletics, better known as NAIA; as well as the numerous junior colleges (sometimes called "community colleges") in the National Junior College Athletic Association (the NJCAA) that offer both scholarships and opportunities to play after high school. NAIA and NJCAA schools sponsor and field nearly all of the same sports as the NCAA. The NAIA Eligibility Center reports that there are over 65,000 student-athletes across its institutions every year who receive over $500 million in financial aid each year.[16] Roughly 45,300 students compete in the NJCAA each year as well, also with scholarship opportunities.[17] Accounting for programs at institutions under these three major collegiate athletic governing bodies, high school students have a 7.3 percent chance of making *any* college roster.

I advise high school athletes not to discount these non-NCAA opportunities. First, it is still an opportunity to play sports at the next level. Second, it is still an opportunity to help pay for a quality education. And as anyone who has watched the hit Netflix series, *Last Chance U*, knows, the NJCAA and NAIA offer platforms for athletes to move up to NCAA Division I programs to audition for professional leagues. NJCAA Executive Director, Dr. Chris Parker, touts the advantages of the NJCAA for the high school athlete looking to move up to the next level:

> On many occasions, kids haven't quite hit their stride and realized their full potential by the time they need to make a college decision. Or, maybe they do get an offer from a 4-year school, but they don't figure into the mix of playing time until their junior or senior year. Those are both scenarios in which a student-athlete should strongly consider going the junior college route. A junior college gives you the advantage of honing your physical skills because you can get on the field and get those reps you're needing to develop.
>
> Junior colleges also present an amazing cost-saving opportunity for student-athletes . . . If you haven't decided on a major or you're just not in love with any of your college options, think about a junior college. The cost of attending a junior college is far less than most 4-year schools.[18]

After all, Cam Newton, Bryce Harper and Jimmy Butler all came out of the NJCAA ranks.[19] And NAIA even regularly reports on the numerous people its programs have sent to the professional ranks,[20,21] including NBA All-Star legends Dennis Rodman and Scottie Pippen[22] who famously joined Michael Jordan during the Chicago Bulls' dynasty in the 1990s. However, the message is clear—it is extremely difficult to make that college roster, and harder still to get that scholarship.

My friend's joke highlights this phenomena during the high school years. National Public Radio, the Robert Wood Johnson Foundation and Harvard University announced in a recent study that 26 percent—more than a quarter—of parents of high school athletes harbor desires that their lettermen and women will go on to play professional sports.[23] In families with incomes below $50,000, that number jumps to 39 percent.[24] Those numbers may be betraying, though. In a recent survey of athletes across all three divisions and numerous sports, the NCAA found—on average—more than 25 percent of all respondents—men, women, Division I, Division II, Division III and across 25 different sports—reported that their family not only *hoped* they would become professional and Olympic athletes, but *expected* that they would become college athletes.[25,26] Despite the well-publicized odds, families place more and more pressure on their kids each year to get that scholarship. In some cases, to get that pro contract even while they are still going through puberty. But one thing is clear—parents and family pressure play a very large part in what type of high school experience the athlete gets: varsity sports and the letter jacket, or college prep, prep, prep.

Chances are, if you played sports in high school sometime between 2005 and now, with an eye on playing in college, you specialized as soon as you hit your freshman or sophomore year. As always, the question is who is the expert when it comes to specialization in sports. While far from a consensus, certainly the majority of researchers believe prior to high school is too early. But what about in high school?

Take the case of 19-year-old prep school senior Chase Bly. After playing baseball and soccer through elementary school, he picked up lacrosse in middle school.[27] After attending a lacrosse camp the summer before his freshman year of high school, he arranged a tryout for an elite club team in Baltimore—a five hour drive from his hometown of Pittsburgh—without discussing the matter with his parents. After explaining his passion to his parents, Bly's mother drove him the nine-hour round trip twice a week for three years.[28] But even through it all, he did not dedicate himself solely to lacrosse:

> Chase made a concerted effort to sample as many offerings as he could from the sports menu. Freshman year, he made his high school's varsity basketball team. Sophomore year, it was cross country. Junior year, he played squash. None of them held a candle to lacrosse. . . . For Chase Bly, who played anything and everything before ultimately settling on

a sport of his own choosing at a developmentally appropriate age, the answer is yes. As for other, less well-rounded youth athletes, the answer is probably not.[29]

Certainly, a strong case can be made for specialization where the athlete makes the choice for him or herself, like Chase did (incidentally, Chase ended up signing with the University of Richmond to play lacrosse.[30]) But Chase's world seems so different than it did only a few years ago when he would not have been considered odd at all for trying those other athletic opportunities during high school. Prior to 2005, America still celebrated "athletes" as distinct from great "players." Names that popped up in the "greatest athletes" categories belonged to the nearly-forgotten Jim Thorpe and the legendary Vincent Edward "Bo" Jackson, who some consider legendary *only* because he was a Major League Baseball All-Star *and* an NFL Pro Bowler. (I'd suggest that he's an All-Star and a Pro Bowler because he was simply such a remarkable athlete!)

Other names that have come along in recent years include one of my fellow Baylor alums, Robert Griffin III, who famously won the Heisman Trophy *after* breaking Big 12 Conference and NCAA records in the 400 meter hurdles and reached the semifinals at the U.S. Olympic trials.[31] And yet another name that people put into the "elite" category simply because he participated in multiple sports in college is most recently Jameis Winston, who quarterbacked the Florida State Seminoles to the final BCS National Championship in 2014, before heading to the mound for the Seminoles throwing an impressive E.R.A. of 1.08 on 24 starts and seven saves that same year.[32] Interestingly, both Griffin and Jameis made their decisions on where to go to college based on representations by their respective universities that they would be allowed to pursue athletic opportunities beyond gridiron football.[33,34] Fascinatingly, these people were celebrated *because* they were the exceptions to the rule. They were the exceptions to specialization. And it bears mentioning at this plateau on the Mountain that they made their collegiate choices based on which universities would let them continue their high school multisport careers.

Some of the biggest names in college coaching have jumped on this same bandwagon—getting high school athletes off the specialization train. Some coaches have done this expressly and intentionally, while some have put the principles into practice without calling it what it is.

Two powerful coaches have placed great value on the multi-sport athlete coming out of high school: Urban Meyer, the former head coach of Ohio State University and Dabo Swinney at Clemson University.[35] As the New York Times reported:

> With their embrace of multisport participation, Meyer and Swinney are swimming against a tide of specialization in youth and high school sports . . . that dragged Meyer, as a parent, into its undertow. Against his wishes, his daughter Gigi, the middle child of three, gave up basketball in high school to participate in year-round volleyball at the club level. Meyer said he had been overruled by his wife, Shelley, who was adamant that a full-time commitment to volleyball was necessary if their daughter wanted to play the sport in college.
>
> His daughter did become a four-year starter at Florida Gulf Coast University, following the path of her older sister, Nicki, who played volleyball at Georgia Tech. But Gigi also competed in wakeboarding while in college and became a national champion, validating her father's model, too.[36]

Coach Swinney, a three-sport athlete at Pelham High School in Alabama in his youth, puts it more succinctly: "I want the multisport guy. I just love that."[37] As to specialization in high school, Swinney believes it is a disservice because it limits an athlete's room for growth at the collegiate level:

> I think sometimes you see some of these kids that specialize so early, and they're much closer to their ceiling. I see it all the time—one sport since the fifth grade, and that's all they've done. They've been to every clinic, every camp, every teaching session, and everything's been squeezed out of them. There's just not that much room for them to get any better.[38]

Swinney, of course, went on to beat Alabama for the national championship. But it is not just in football where coaches see the benefits of cross-training.

Recent Naismith Basketball Hall of Fame inductee and basketball coach at the University of Kansas, Bill Self, has become notorious the last several years for finding "big men "—centers and power forwards—with multi-sport backgrounds. "There was a time I gave up basketball and started playing volleyball," says Jeff Withey, who was one of the most prolific shot-blockers in NCAA, Big 12 and KU basketball since the beginning of the millennium.[39] He credits volleyball and strength and conditioning coach, Andrea Hudy (no longer at KU), for helping him go from lanky sophomore transfer to Big 12 record holder for blocked shots and National Defensive Player of the Year.[40] Then Coach Self took Joel Embiid—a Cameroonian native on his third sport, after soccer and volleyball, and turned him into the third pick in the 2014 NBA Draft.[41] Embiid did not dribble a basketball until he was 12 years old.[42] Most recently, Coach Self had the chance to work with phenom Udoka Azubuike, who hails from Nigeria where he grew up playing soccer.[43] As Doke—as he is affectionately called by the Jayhawk fan base—says, soccer "helped me with footwork and being able to keep my balance. You see an NBA player like Steve Nash . . . he played soccer." Coach Self puts it simply: "I see parallels of kids that play soccer having better footwork."

I tend to join the bandwagon of Coaches Meyer, Swinney and Self. Growing up, I was simply athletic. Or, more appropriately, just plain energetic and active. I was a terror. Too much pent-up energy and not enough outlets for it. My mother likes to tell a story about how when I was little she would make me run laps around the outside of our block to get me out of her hair and to try to get me to burn off some of that energy. It worked . . . sometimes. So, it wasn't too long before my parents enrolled me in sports. They enrolled me and never looked back. I grew up playing soccer when I was younger. Through middle school, I played softball, basketball and even tried my hand at cheerleading (Yes, cheerleaders are athletes, too! I see you Navaro Cheer!).

If I'm honest with myself, I really joined cheerleading because all the "cool girls" were cheerleaders. And I liked the uniforms. But really, I enjoyed cheerleading in theory more than I did in practice. I wanted to be a "flyer," but my body destined me for nothing more than the base of the pyramid and supporting basket catches. That's what happens when you are a five foot, nine-inch, broad shouldered, strong girl. The little girl that my mother made run around the block was simply not satisfied with holding up other girls. And so, in middle school, I tried my hand at basketball. My dad was very successful playing high school basketball in California. In the early 1970's, he was name to the "George Ingalls" tournament all-state high school team which had recognized Bill Walton the year before. Anyway, my dad figured that basketball was a good sport for me to try.

The point I make here is that SO MUCH CAN HAPPEN BETWEEN THE TIME THAT WE MOVE OUT OF YOUTH SPORTS AND INTO HIGH SCHOOL SPORTS! No person can argue that there is a *huge* difference in skill level between the eleven-year-old athlete and the same athlete at eighteen. Moving from middle school to high school brings as many challenges for the average freshman as does moving from middle school sports to high school sports. But there is little doubt that this is the point in time for many athletes that my coaches' advice became real: "When you get good, things get to be *really* fun!" It is fun to hit a home run! To dunk the basketball! Or to sink a tournament winning putt!

As sports begin to get fun, though, they also can take over even more of your life. Recent research has found that athletic identity takes over much more once a person becomes focused on sports in high school. In 2011 at the University of Houston, researchers found that "the 'role engulfment' presumed to be associated with sports participation may occur earlier than expected. . . . [I]t is possible that the physical and psychological variables previously linked to college athletics, including pressure from coaches and teammates, the belief that a narrow focus on sport is necessary to excel, and restrictiveness of the athletic environment, may be trickling down to high school athletics."[44] Unfortunately, the stress of trying to make a team, stay on a team, keep a starting position, and any other number of stressors at that age—in addition to maintaining *academic* eligibility—can take hold in the high school athlete. As Dr. Stankovich has found:

> The greater their athletic identity, the greater their risk for problems as well. These are the athletes willing to do whatever it takes to be on the team, to maintain their starting position and/or to be a top player—even if it involves unhealthy, unethical and even illegal means—like performance enhancing drugs. The use of such drugs to gain speed, strength and endurance is on the rise among teens, with 11% of high school sophomores, juniors and seniors reporting having used synthetic human growth hormone without a prescription (up from just 5% the previous year). Athletes have also reported using recreational drugs in a poor attempt to relieve stress from the pressure they feel to perform—which may also be associated with athletics identity.[45]

Unfortunately, too little has been studied about the development of athlete identity in high schoolers specifically. And while this area of research continues to grow, it will not be unexpected if we find that with greater specialization and with a higher intensity focus on sports at the high school level compared to youth sports, high school kids are setting themselves up for falls off the Cliff that may be greater than they were in the past.

5

College Sports
The Air's Getting Thin

Let me tell it to you as clean as I can. We have 95 players here
so accomplished as athletes in high school, we gave them full
scholarships to the best football program in the country. NCAA
regulations allow us to dress just 60 for home games, which
means at least 35 scholarship players are gonna be watching the
game from the stands. So, if any of you have any fantasies about
running out of that stadium tunnel with your gold helmet shining
in the sun, you best leave them right here.

—JOHN BEASLEY,
"Coach Warren" in *Rudy*[1]

I've been ready for this my whole life!

—SEAN ASTIN,
"Rudy" in *Rudy*[2]

Congratulations! Hoping beyond hope, you've somehow managed to be
in the seven and a half percent of all high school players who made it
onto a college roster. The spectacle and the spotlight are now brighter
than they have ever been in your sports journey thus far. All the hours of
practice, travel, private training and competing paid off and you made it
to the next plateau up the Mountain. *You are an intercollegiate athlete!*
Once you make it to this level, you are a "baller," as one of my former
coaches once described it. You may have been a highly recruited scholarship player starting on your school's team in a high-profile revenue
sport like basketball or basketball. Or you may have received a partial
scholarship in an Olympic sport like rowing or track. Or you may not
have received a scholarship at all, showing up as a walk-on. But none of
this matters. You are an athlete at that next level! You are now cemented

as an influencer and in some cases a celebrity on campus. Whether your name was already touted in the online blogs before you even arrived on your university campus or if you are relatively unknown, your world is about to completely change.

There should be a big, flashing neon sign as athletes begin their climb up this particular part of the Mountain that reads: "Welcome to Big Money Athletics." As early as 1986, then-athletic director at Florida State University Cecil "Hootie" Ingram put it succinctly: "I'm not afraid to say it: it's a business."[3] To be clear, this is not a criticism. It is simply stating facts.

In the 1980's, the New York Times reported that "scores of football and basketball coaches command annual incomes of $300,000, with some said to get upward of $500,000."[4] The NCAA basketball tournament generated revenues of "nearly $40 million."[5] And CBS Sports paid $60 million for 175 hours of college sports in 1985.[6] And no matter what edition this is or what year you are reading this—*the value of "live sports" and specifically "college sports" keeps climbing.*

Today, head coach salaries continue to soar. Google the top 25 highest paid college football coaches, and you will consistently find Jim Harbaugh, Nick Saban, Kirby Smart and Dabo Swinney battling it out on who will set a new record.

This past summer Nick Saban signed an eight year contract extension worth 93.6 million dollars, that made him once again the highest paid coach in the country after renegotiating his newest contract extension. Georgia Bulldogs, Kirby Smart agree to new 10-year, $ 112.5 million contract, making him the second highest-paid coach in college football.[7]

Seven post-season football games alone generated media rights contracts worth over $608 million per year.[8] And the NCAA will distribute to its member institutions (i.e. colleges) roughly 96 percent of the more than $890 million per year it will earn through 2032 through the media rights licensing of the March Madness tournament.[9]

In 2011, sports economist Andrew Zimbalist estimated that athletics were worth $8 billion per year to the universities.[10] And in 2012, the NCAA estimated college athletics to be worth $10.6 billion.[11] In 2019 the NCAA estimated that the market is now work $18 billion.[12]

Understandably, the US collegiate sports body suffered heavy losses during the Covid-19 pandemic, with the cancellation of the men's March Madness basketball tournament alone costing the NCAA $800 million in missed multimedia and ticket revenue.[13]

Thankfully sports are rebounding. The National Collegiate Athletic Association (NCAA) generated record revenues of US$1.16 billion for the 2021 fiscal year ending 31st August, marking an increase from US$519 million in 2020.[14] Honestly, it is a great thing for sports in general to see this type of bounce back from the pandemic. Resiliency is a word I resonate with a lot. These numbers bounce back in revenue reaffirms that the sports industry continues to hold its value.

Presumably, those numbers have increased and continue to increase. These numbers also do not include the economic impact of Division II, Division III, NAIA and NCJAA which can still generate more than $1 million for one weekend of post-season play in any given sport.[15] So it is fair to say that what Mr. Ingram forgot to mention is that college sports are *big* business. And as athletes begin to climb this face of the Mountain, the expectations they face tend to increase exponentially. Expectations from fans, from Athletic administrators, from coaches and, yes, from themselves.

In college athletics, athletes enter a very public performance space, often for the first time. In high school and club sports, winning was always important. At the end of the day, it was always the most important benchmark for the athlete. In some spaces, high school sports could easily look like college or even professional sports. Especially with the hype and never sleeping eyes of social media coverage and behind the scenes videos. Buzz Bissinger's book *Friday Night Lights* accurately portrays the extreme to which high school sports can go, in which high schools have legitimate booster clubs and fans having no relation to the players on the field. But for many athletes, their high school and club teams are vehicles to show off the individual athlete, to create that recruitment tape, to #getthatbag, or secure the scholarship. For many, college is the first time in their careers that they have expectations thrust upon them by total strangers. And not unreasonably, either.

Without commenting on how healthy it is for the athlete, it bears stating as fact that American culture has created a particular college sports ecosystem in which the athlete plays a fundamental role. And understanding the impact of that environment on the athlete is fundamental to understanding the way in which this phase of the Athletic Mountain impacts the athlete's stark transition and fall off the Cliff. But best to start at the beginning. And the college sports ecosystem starts with the alumni, the fans and the donors. They want great universities which start with great presidents and chancellors. The savvy college president today joins in with the many administrators who recognize athletics as the "front porch" of their universities.[16,17,18] For instance, Calvin Brown is the former director of alumni relations for the University of Alabama. In his words, "many times, athletics provide the window through which people first see the university."[19] As he says in reference to the Crimson Tide's living legend, football coach Nick Saban, Brown explains that "the way he's run that program, people that may not have had any familiarity with the University of Alabama got their first glimpse into the university through that program."[20]

College administrators are very aware of a phenomena called the "Flutie Effect." In 1984, Boston College played the University of Miami in a nationally televised game that served as the *de facto* national championship game that year (in the era before the Bowl Championship Series). In the waning seconds of the game, quarterback Doug Flutie fired a Hail Mary touchdown pass to Gerard Phelan in the end-zone to win the game for Boston College. Flutie would go on to win the Heisman Trophy later that year. But perhaps the bigger winner was Boston College. During the two years following Flutie's miracle play, Boston College experienced an incredible 30 percent surge in applications from prospective students.[21] Since then, researchers like Dr. Doug Chung at Harvard Business School have noted that this phenomena—"an increase in exposure and prominence of an *academic* institution due to the success of its *athletic* program" is not peculiar to Boston. Between 1982 and 1985, basketball coach John Thompson and future NBA All-Star Patrick Ewing took the Georgetown Hoyas to the Final Four three times with a national championship. During that same period, Georgetown University saw a 45 percent increase in the number of applications it received from prospective students.[22] Northwestern University enjoyed a 21 percent increase in applications in 1994 following their Big Ten football championship.[23]

Even small-conference and small-market schools reap the benefits of athletic success on the field. Boise State University saw increased applications after its football team earned a perfect record capped by a Fiesta Bowl Championship over perennial power Oklahoma in 2007.[24] Wichita State University saw increased applications after beating top-seeded Gonzaga to go to the Final Four for the first time since the 1960's.[25] The Class of 2022 at Loyola-Chicago is the largest in school history, attributable by the dean of admissions (at least in part) to the Ramblers' improbable Final Four run in 2018.[26] And then there is the story of George Mason University which set the bar. After George Mason made an incredible run to the Final Four in 2006, the capital fundraising campaign came and went without a hitch, merchandise sales at the campus bookstore skyrocketed to over $800,000 in sales in one month (more than the rest of the year combined), the number of active alumni jumped 25 percent, freshman applications increased by 22 percent and out-of-state applications increased by a whopping 54 percent![27]

Beyond this, though, is the ultimate impact of athletic success for universities. Rodney Fort, a sports economist and professor of sports management at the University of Michigan, has stated that the Flutie Effect has a consequence beyond just raising the number of applications: "the quality of applications also increases."[28] As applicants become greater in number and better in quality, the academic side of universities sees greater improvement. There has been some correlation between success in big-time college sports and academics at universities. Norvin Richards, a professor *emeritus* at Alabama, states:

> It's a hard sell to go out and convince people in other parts of the country that [the University of Alabama] is where you should go, that this is a good place academically. So, one side of the coin is to ride the 'football horse' to get the money, to help you attract academic talent, as you have nothing else that will generate that kind of money.[29]

In addition to *more* students and *better* students, athletic success also correlates with another important issue for the institution riding the Flutie wave. The Knight Commission on Intercollegiate Athletics was founded in 1989 to research and promote reforms that strengthen the educational mission of college sports. In 2009, the Knight Commission on Intercollegiate Athletics published a study tending to corroborate Richards' statement. While the Knight Commission found no correlation between spending and winning, there is a correlation between winning and receiving. Gifts, that is:

> As for donations, while winning records do not necessarily increase gifts, football bowl game appearances do, [Cornell University economist Robert H.] Frank wrote, to the tune of $6.50 per alumnus at public universities and $40 per year per alumnus at private schools.[30]

These results have been corroborated by other researchers as well, such as Jonathan Meer in 2008[31] and Michael Anderson in 2012,[32] both published by the National Bureau for Economic Research.[33,34]

Even when direct gifts are not the issue, the Flutie effect and college athletics in general generate millions of dollars in unpaid advertising and publicity for the institution. For instance, the Washington Post estimates that Robert Griffin III's Heisman was worth $250 million in publicity for Baylor University alone.[35] Even at the junior college level, the publicity associated with athletics often results in greater interest and earlier enrollment. Former Independence Community College president Dan Barwick noted in 2018 that summer enrollment at the Coffeyville, Kansas junior college increased by 45 percent immediately following the premiere of Netflix's *Last Chance U.*[36] Even when universities' athletic programs are embroiled in scandal, the enrollment generated by athletic success does not cease.[37,38]

Universities fight over every potential student. Those students turn into alumni who turn into donors. In the fall of 2022, University of Texas spent over $600,000 to land highlight touted Arch Manning (nephew of Peyton and Eli Manning) and other top recruits. And Texas's investment paid off with 16 of the 23 recruits that they had on campus committing.[39]

The financial stakes are simply *huge* at this level. Understanding how much there is to gain, then, it is not surprising that university and college administrators put pressure on athletic directors and coaches to win.

College coaches and athletic administrators regularly get caught up in questions about the "product" that they put on the field. With so much at stake—students, alumni, donors, money, ultimately their jobs, reputations and prestige all entwined together—it is no wonder the pressure coaches are under to win. And win they must, since *their* livelihoods are dependent upon their record. No administrator is safe. Only three games into the 2017 football season, the University of Nebraska fired athletic director Shawn Eichorst after a loss to Northern Illinois. The reason? According to University President Hank Bounds, "Our fans and our student-athletes deserve leadership that drives the highest levels of competitiveness on the field, as well as across all facets across Husker athletics. The fact of the matter is that we need to raise our on-field competitiveness. Competing at a high level is required for the long-term success of Nebraska athletics."[40]

That same year, a plane flew a banner over Lawrence, Kansas before the Jayhawks' game with cross-state rival Kansas State that simply read "Fire Zenger," in reference to former KU athletic director Sheahon Zenger, who oversaw the hiring of three separate football coaches who amassed a dismal 10-62 record under his leadership.[41]

Interesting fact: Bleacher Report found that the turnover rate for NCAA football coaches at the FBS level increased from 18 percent between 1991 and 2005, to 22 percent between 2006 and 2010, to 24 percent in 2013.[42] Even high-profile coaches in high-profile sports get the ax, *despite* objective success. The University of Texas pushed its second-winningest coach of all time out when Mack Brown failed to reach double-digit wins his last four years in Austin. Larry Coker was fired by the University of Miami after six seasons that included a national title and three conference titles.[43] In 2016, Louisiana State University fired Les Miles after only four games and a .500 record.[44]

But it is not just high-profile sports and coaches that get this pressure. At Independence Community College, *Last Chance U* personality and former head football coach Jason Brown made $65,000. His defensive coordinator and assistant coach, Jason Martin, made less than a public school teacher in Kansas, with a salary of $36,000.[45] To help stretch that dollar and to be available for his wife and two small children, Martin also moved his family into the dormitories on campus instead of buying or renting a home in town.[46] Then there are the assistants who have to get the teenagers in their units to perform, while making less than $10,000 per year from coaching in Division II, Division III, NAIA and junior college programs like Bill Vasko.[47]

In 2017, Clemson University was paying then-volleyball coach Hugh Hernesman only $90,000 per year (a drop in the bucket compared to revenue sports coaches), but let him go after only two seasons due to a 6-26 overall record.[48] Mid-major schools are not immune, as three weeks later, Indiana State of the Missouri Valley Conference let softball coach Shane Bouman go in the middle of his season after recording a 118-172 record over six years.[49] Back in 2015, the University of Kansas fired women's basketball coach Bonnie Henrickson after 11 seasons, and two Sweet 16 appearances. After two losing seasons in a row, however, athletic director Sheahon Zenger put it more honestly than most athletic directors when he said "there's not one thing about Bonnie Henrickson that we in this department, and this campus, don't love working with. Great ambassador. Great teammate. We just expect to win on the court."[50] For better or for worse, the message that universities are sending to their athletics administrators and coaches is clear: you have one job—win.

I don't want to get into whether these expectations are fair or not. Merely I wish to say that they are what they are. And these expectations, in turn, trickle down to the athlete because coaches have to get teams of teenagers and early twenty-somethings ready to compete. The best coaches are the ones who not only find ways to get the most out of their athletes, but also demonstrate a first-level care for them as humans. The epitome of this is Clemson University football coach Dabo Swinney. As a headline about Dabo Swinney on the Clemson World website states, "[i]t's *how* you win that matters:"[51]

> In Swinney's relationship driven model, he says, 'We want our players to graduate, to leave here equipped with tools for life. Because of our program, they are equipped, they know what discipline means, they know how to show up on time, they know how to handle adversity, respect others, be a good teammate.
>
> They understand what it means to be a part of something bigger than yourself. No sense of entitlement, and they know how to win and lose. Those are the tools for life. If we do a great job with that, whether they make All-American, or never get above third team, they will still have a great experience.[52]

Of course, it's hard to argue with a man who is getting the winning part done. Swinney has three ACC conference championships and a national championship to his name since taking over as head coach in 2008. But it's clear that he is getting the "taking care of your players" part done, too. Unfortunately, some people will argue with that. While attending the espnW conference in 2014, I pitched an idea called "Ball2Bike" to help athletes transition (more on this later at the end of the book). The gist is that I re-discovered cycling as a means of regaining some of what I lost when I was forced to retire from volleyball. For me, the bicycle is a great vehicle (no pun intended) to help athletes, after they retire, from falling too hard off the Cliff (also something you will read about later). Many of my friends and other athletes I meet refer to themselves as "ex"-athletes, as though they have given that part of themselves up, and who struggle through the next phase of their lives. For me, it was always about the *total* welfare of our retired athletes. And so, I was excited to talk to people about it. I expected that at a conference featuring *numerous* retired athletes, this concern would be shared. For the most part, it was. Unfortunately, I did run into some pushback on the idea that *anybody* cares about athletes. I vividly remember one attendee telling me the following: "It will never change. People don't care about the players. They only care about the wins. Good luck finding anyone to take your idea of athletes' well-being seriously, though." I only wish that I was making that up or paraphrasing. It was so nonchalant, but also so in-your-face that I wrote it down when I got home. But, no, that was—verbatim—what I was told by a supposed thought leader in sports and athletics in America. I thought, what a bummer attitude! And especially in an environment that was supposed to be inspiring and empowering. But, you know what? Challenge accepted! Because there *are* people who care, like Coach Swinney. As I said, who knows whether he would be given the latitude to tout the fact that his is the only program in America ranked in the top 10 academically *and* the top 15 athletically four years in a row.[53] But for now, it doesn't matter, because Coach Swinney demonstrates that you *can* win, and you *can* care about your athletes at the same time. But, I digress . . . For most college athletes, they do take that pressure on themselves, and they do feel the pressure that big-money sports is putting on them for the first time.

This pressure can manifest before the athlete even steps onto campus for freshman orientation, creating divisions and different college sports experiences even between people on the same team. While the joys of camaraderie and athletic prowess may be similar between you and your teammates, there are many ways in which college athletes—even those on the same team—can differ from each other. First of all, you and your teammates may have had completely different recruiting experiences. You may or may not have been recruited as a scholarship player. The NCAA shares that more than $2.7 billion in financial aid annually being distributed among 150,000 athletes. But less than 2 percent of high school athletes will ever be awarded an athletic scholarship of *any* kind.[54]

Of those who receive scholarships, very few will get the coveted "full-ride" and the dream of a free college education. On its website, the NCAA explains that "full scholarships" cover tuition, fees, room, board and course-related textbooks and materials. But "most student-athletes who receive athletics scholarships receive an amount covering a portion of these costs."[55] Still today in 2022, only six of the NCAA's 24 sports, across three divisions, were deemed "head count" sports.

Head count sports include only football, men's basketball, women's basketball, women's tennis, women's gymnastics and women's volley-ball. These are referred to as "head count" sports because pursuant to NCAA rules, schools may only offer a limited number of scholarships per athlete. In other words, a $500 scholarship and a full-ride scholarship are counted the same, and so economically it makes the most sense to make *every* scholarship for such sports full scholarships. All other sports, on the other hand, are deemed "equivalency sports." In these sports, a coach is limited not in the number of *scholarships*, but in the amount of scholarship *dollars*. In other words, a coach may divide up the amount of money that would go toward one *full* scholarship for one athlete into several *partial* scholarships for *multiple* athletes. This results in the more numerous *per capita* partial scholarships that may not cover tuition or books, let alone the cost of attendance. In 2012, the average scholarship—nationwide, for both out-of-state and in-state student-athletes, and across both public and private universities—was only $11,000.[56] Put into perspective, the National Center for Education Statistics reports that in school year 2011–2013, the average cost of tuition, fees, room and board (not including books and living expenses) was $19,741. In 2012–2013, that cost climbed to over $20,000 for the first time ever.[57] So, athletes feel the pressure immediately in order to *keep* their scholarships to avoid becoming part of the ever-growing student loan bubble in America.

Also affecting the college athlete are the myriad of social hierarchies to navigate not just on the campus at large, but within the athletic department and even on the team. If you are an athlete in any sport, you already may receive various benefits the rest of the student body does not: first shot at registering for classes, dining hall privileges, a floor in dormitories dedicated to the team, tutoring and specialized academic counseling, access to weight rooms and athletic training light years beyond anything available to Joe College at the student rec center (though that is open to you, too!). But then there are others: travel across the country and even the globe, free athletic gear and clothes, and not to mention the sweet swag given out at conference tournaments. But even the distinctions between athletes at the same school, and even on the same *team*, make that neon sign on this Mountain path brighter screaming "Big Money Sports!"

The first way that the college sports experience can differ for athletes is in the simple hierarchy that exists between the so-called "revenue sports," traditionally football, basketball, and baseball or hockey depending on whether the school is located in a state long the Canadian border or not, and the so-called "non-revenue sports" *i.e.* everything else. The revenue sports are called such because, as a general proposition, they generate the greatest share of sports revenues for universities and athletic departments. For proof, all we need to look at are sell-outs in 80,000 seat football stadiums and billion-dollar deals networks are willing to pay to air March Madness. However, there is a symbiosis between the revenue sports and the non-revenue sports.

Revenue sports overwhelmingly generate the money that finances the operations of the non-revenue sports,[58] while non-revenue sports ultimately fulfill the mission of college sports which is to support the "collegiate model of athletics in which students participate *as an avocation*, balancing their academic, social and athletics experiences."[59] This is not to speak harshly against any football or basketball player. For many of them, the college experience provides exactly what it has always been intended to provide: training ground for a professional career. And what football or basketball player in college has never expressed a desire to play professionally? Even Time Magazine has made a cogent argument that perhaps in those sports where there are major professional leagues, it would not be out of line to allow football players to major in "Football Performance" and basketball players to major in "Basketball Performance," any more than it would be out of line to permit fine arts students to major in studio art and viola performance.[60]

For athletes in the non-revenue sports, Olympian and former NCAA rower Megan Kalmoe puts it succinctly on her blog:

> [W]hether you like it or not, all athletes who are participating in NCAA athletics are there first and foremost to: win an NCAA championship? . . . make money for the University? . . . impress alumni and supporters who don't know what they're talking about? Sadly, no. NCAA athletes are all at their respective universities to earn college degrees. They're there to study, to work hard, and give themselves the best possible chance to be successful adults when they leave their University.[61]

Furthermore, Kalmoe explains the long-term symbiotic relationship between non-revenue athletes and the university:

> [T]he 'little guys' are the ones who are quiet, successful leaders who work thanklessly to represent ourselves and our school, even if 'no one cares' but us. We will go on to be successful professionals, and to make up the majority of your Olympic Team every four years. And we are the ones who organize extensive alumni networks in order to create financial legacies for generations.[62]

The revenue and non-revenue athlete put in as much effort, and sacrifice often as much time and experiences as the revenue athlete to make it to this level. But, there is a difference there that can later impact not only professional sports prospects (based simply on the fact that there are more professional opportunities later on in some sports as opposed to others), but approaches to collegiate sports which have bearing on the Cliff later on.

Another major distinction is the difference between those participating in head count sports versus equivalency sports. For the head count sport athlete, because the university invests so much into them—a full scholarship—they often are at the top of the pile and in the biggest spotlight. If they win or lose, their classmates know about it. This is all accentuated and elevated by the use of social media. #MeanTweets takes on a new meaning when you are 18 and 19 years old when scrolling through your feed after a tough game. If an athlete gets in trouble with the police or has a fight with their girlfriend or boyfriend, and the police are called, everybody in town hears about it. This is further tied into the distinction between revenue and non-revenue sports, as there is a lot of overlap. Because even in perennial powerhouse programs in equivalency sports, a star athlete may or may not be receiving a grant-in-aid that accurately reflects their commitment. In 2012 for instance, Paul Mainieri—head baseball coach at Louisiana State University—said of his equivalency sport athletes, "I don't know that I've ever had a player receive a scholarship in the amount which was commensurate to his value,"[63] despite the fact that since 1991 LSU had won six national championships in baseball to the football team's two. In these cases, especially when the sport is not only an equivalency sport but also a non-revenue sport, the passion for the sport may be the driving force for the athlete at this level and may also temper any expectations of making it to the next level up the Mountain.

The last major distinction between collegiate athletic experiences is whether you are a scholarship player (partial or full-ride) or whether you are a walk-on. "*Rudy*" is one of my favorite movies of all time. I curl up on the couch every fall to watch it. He's the most famous walk-on in the world, and I think that is what I like about him. I'm reminded of myself every time I watch the movie because I was a walk-on. But what is the "walk-on?" In 1984, Sports Illustrated articulated it clearly:

A rare breed of tough-minded, stubborn and dedicated college athlete . . . He arrives on campus with no scholarship, no reputation and, quite often, no chance. He just shows up and says, 'I want to play.' He's the ultimate odds-beater. He pays his own freight, carries his own weight and, in some quarters, sparks a lot of debate.[64]

A walk-on is the purest athlete at this level—the one who shows up simply because he loves the game or the team.

However, the hierarchy between the walk-on and scholarship player can be acute. While problems like these have long since been abated (for the most part), there was a time when locker rooms simply weren't large enough, and walk-ons could be pushed into hallways and closets to change. "You might be on the eighth team, but if you're on scholarship you're in the varsity locker room" said Chuck Nelson, a walk-on at the University of Washington football team before becoming a Los Angeles Ram in the 1980s.[65] But there are other distinctions. For a time, walk-ons were permitted to eat with their scholarship colleagues, but had to pay for their own meal in order to conform to NCAA regulations. But there are other minor differences.

Perhaps the second-most famous walk-on after Notre Dame defensive end Rudy Ruettiger is Mark Titus, former walk-on shooting guard for Ohio State basketball and founder of Club Tril. In his 2012 book, *Don't Put Me In, Coach*, Titus illustrates the difference perfectly between walk-ons like him and scholarship players, like his teammate, friend and number one NBA Draft pick in 2007:

> After a few steps, though, he [Buckeye head coach Thad Matta] turned around and said, 'I forgot to mention. Now that you're on the team, I'm going to have to ask you to shave your beard. It's nothing personal. Just a team rule.'
>
> As I told him that it wasn't a big deal because I actually planned on shaving it anyway and just hadn't gotten around to it yet, Greg walked by sporting a ferocious beard that made my beard look like Sidney Crosby's wispy excuse for facial hair. When I pointed to Greg with a confused look on my face, Coach Matta laughed and said, 'Well, he's Greg Oden. You understand, right?'[66]

Such is often the life of the walk-on, even in the non-revenue and Olympic sports.

Interestingly, even among *walk-ons* there is a hierarchy. Preferred walk-ons may have received promises of future scholarships, when recruited walk-ons are merely expected to try out. And then there is the rarest of all—the "true" walk-on who makes his or her way to the open tryout. I was a preferred walk-on at Baylor. When I took my recruiting trip there, it was expected that I would be on the team my freshman year and that scholarships would likely follow the year after that. I overstate the difference in terms of an actual hierarchy between walk-ons and scholarship players, of course. But as to how those experiences shape their identities, each role on a college sports roster may create a greater probability of a harder fall off the Cliff someday.

Whether the athlete is a scholarship player or walk-on, full-ride or partial scholarship player, football player or badminton player, they all have performance expectations to meet. Most college athletes burn the candle at both ends during their season at school. In the NCAA, athletes' in-season practices are limited to twenty hours per week. However, in recent litigation against the University of North Carolina at Chapel Hill, it has been alleged that this rule is inadequate as it is undercut by numerous loopholes and cutouts:

> The 20-hour rule itself is also rife with loopholes. Administrative meetings, weight-lifting, conditioning, film study, and activities incidental to participation, such as taping, visits to the trainer, and rehabilitation, do not count towards the 20-hour limit. Nor do 'voluntary' activities where no coach is present. Game days count as three total hours, even though they often require travel and hours of pre- and post-game meetings and activities.[67]

That same suit also cited a 2006 NCAA survey that found—on average—college "athletes dedicate an average of 45 hours per week to their athletic endeavors."[68] A similar study by the NCAA in 2010 revealed roughly the same results.[69]

Interestingly, though, Inside Higher Ed reported that college athletes are not so bothered by a lot of the time commitments:

> Getting rid of late evening games? The athletes said they like playing during prime time. Realigning conferences so that athletes don't have to travel so far? The athletes said they enjoy traveling across the country.[70]

I believe most athletes enjoy these parts of the college sports experience. After all, if you don't like playing on the big stage, why are you playing on the big stage? However, this is not to say that we don't suffer from pressure we also put on ourselves.

Self-created pressure to perform often exacerbates such pressure from outside sources. For some, this comes from an inner place and a pure desire to compete—walk-ons especially. But for many others, like scholarship players and revenue sport athletes, this plateau up the Mountain is simply the last stepping stone before moving up to the peak of the Mountain: professional sports or Olympic teams. Much has been written about the statistical chances college athletes in the United States have of making major professional league rosters, but a significant number of college athletes believe they will beat the odds. According to the NCAA, over half of NCAA Division I football players believe they will be playing on Sundays when they leave school despite the fact that 98 percent will never go pro.[71] According to NCAA surveys, in 2015, more than 60 percent of Division I ice hockey players believed they would play professionally, even though less than one percent would ever reach the NHL. 45 percent of Division I women's basketball players believed they would play professionally, even though less than one percent are drafted by WNBA teams. And despite the fact that only 1.2 percent of college basketball players will ever be drafted by NBA teams, more than 75 percent of Division I men's basketball players believed they would play professionally, more than half of Division II men's basketball players believed they would play professionally, and more than 20 percent of Division III players believed they would play professionally.[72]

Now, to be fair to the basketball players, there are also many overseas options available to play professional basketball. Tennis players and golfers can go on their respective professional circuits if they choose. Baseball in the United States and Canada includes the minor leagues and semi-professional leagues, not to mention other leagues across Latin America and Japan. And soccer and volleyball players can find opportunities in organized professional leagues overseas. Of course, the flip side of this equation is how many athletes from NJCAA and NAIA ranks come out of the college system each year, which pushes the chances of going pro after college even higher if all we care about is "after *college*" and not just "after *NCAA* colleges." Accounting for all of that, the odds are slight that an American student-athlete will go pro in their sport. It's no wonder, then, that since 2007 the NCAA has regularly publicized its service announcement to "go pro in something other than sports."[73,74]

During this period, the stress of remaining academically eligible while managing what amounts to a full-time sports career manifests itself more often and in greater magnitude than it does for the general student population. The Atlantic Journal reported in 2014 that:

> College athletes are at greater risk of developing particular mental health maladies than the rest of the student body. In sports that reward leanness, like running and gymnastics, eating disorders are common, particularly among women. Those playing contact sports like football are more apt to abuse alcohol than those who don't, said Chris Carr, a counseling sports psychologist and coordinator of Sport and Performance Psychology Services at St. Vincent Sports Performance in Indiana. Depression cuts across all teams, genders, and divisions.[75]

Other mental health problems that college athletes suffer from include gambling addictions, sleep disturbances, mood disorders and suicidal thoughts and tendencies.[76]

At this level, if you never identified yourself as an athlete before, you certainly will now. Here, the athlete often moves out of the development of the athletic identity and into what many researchers refer to as "identity foreclosure." In other words, the college athlete develops the athlete identity as their *sole* identity, to the exclusion of all others. This is likely not surprising, as nearly all activity at this level is dedicated to athletic performance. Practices and training sessions are the obvious activities devoted to athletic pursuits. But so are the less obvious activities. Tutoring time, academic counseling and homework time is devoted to remaining academically eligible in order to compete. Eating at training table can be highly regimented, with rules and guidelines established by team nutritionists. Even the act of grabbing a meal on campus is in furtherance of athletic performance. With every activity every waking hour of every day devoted to remaining at peak performance, it is no wonder that college athletes have no time to discover other roles they may inhabit. Even students at the community and junior college level show increased levels of athletic identity:

> Community college student athletes, for example, generally compete well outside the national athletic spotlight. However, the degree to which they identify with the athletic role may remain as strong as their more athletically gifted peers who received athletic scholarships [at NCAA institutions]. In the case of community colleges, it may sometimes be easy to overlook student athlete issues. This is because community col-

leges rely less on athletics for institutional identity and as a means of assimilating students into the [social] mores of the institution.[77]

Regardless of your situation, once you make it to the collegiate level you ought to be proud of your athletic accomplishment. And if you are lucky enough to reach the peak of the Mountain, then particular high fives and fist bumps to you! When the opportunity extends to you by your university to connect with the next generation of athletes, I personally hope you take it! Your teammates are your brothers and sisters in sweat for life.

6

Professional and Olympic Sports

The Peak of the Mountain

Champions keep playing until they get it right.[1]

—BILLIE JEAN KING,
Sports Icon and Equality Champion

You graduated! Or you managed to play well enough to get drafted! You went into free agency. You fulfilled your draft obligations out of school (if you played baseball). You made your national team! You are headed to the Olympic trials! However it happened, you are at the peak of the Mountain!

I believe that there are really two different peaks for the modern day athlete. One is in a traditional professional league, whether it is in the highest major league such as the National Football League, the National Basketball Association, Major League Baseball, or any number of professional sports leagues in a myriad of other sports overseas. The other is for athletes whose interests lie in Olympic sports; those athletes who may have no interest in professional sports or, alternatively, for whom there are no professional opportunities to make a living at their sport. For some, both professional and Olympic opportunities are available in their sports. While these two roads to the peak of the Mountain have different characteristics that make for different experiences, the athlete at each level is fundamentally the same: an athlete who has pushed his or her body to peak performance. The other characteristic for all athletes at this level is that aside from a Super Bowl championship, a World Series ring, or an Olympic gold medal, there is no further step up the Mountain.

PROFESSIONAL SPORTS

It seems today that there are professional opportunities for more and more athletes in more and more sports. For clarification, I define "professional sports" by whether an athlete is paid specifically to play their sport by either a team organization or a national body of some sort. For purposes of this book, while an athlete may be a professional based on sponsorship and endorsement income, I attach those sources of revenue more closely to the idea that the athlete is getting paid to represent or endorse a particular brand—not necessarily to win (though such bonuses may be included in sponsorship and endorsement deals). An Olympic sprinter may be a professional sprinter, but the "professional" part comes from paid sponsorships and endorsements—not necessarily for being a part of a team. I discuss this more in the Olympic Sports section below.

In the United States alone, there is a major professional league for football, baseball, basketball, hockey and soccer. There are major American professional opportunities for tennis and golf, whereby athletes at the top of those circuits can actually pay the rent by playing. If American athletes are willing to look overseas, their options open up. For basketball, athletes who do not go to the NBA can join teams in the elite Euro-League, the Spanish Liga ACB, Turkey's BSL, Russia's VTB United League, Italy's LBA, France's LNB Pro A, and Australia's NBL. Football players can go to the Canadian Football League or even stay home in the Arena Football League.

Women basketball players often find professional opportunities overseas more financially satisfying than the WNBA. This is why we see WNBA stars like Britney Griner play in Europe and Asia to maximize the time that they are in peak condition to get paid more. #GetTheBag is real for these athletes who have to split their time between the US and other countries. According to Barbara Barker at Newsday, in 2016 WNBA MVP Nneka Ogwumike made the league maximum base salary of $109,000 while players in her talent range can make 15 times that on overseas teams during the WNBA off-season.[2] According to Barker,

UMMC Ekaterinburg pays women's basketball superstar Diana Taurasi $1.5 million per year.[3]

A big update to the economics of the country's longest-running women's professional sports league, the WNBA, came at the beginning 2020. The collective bargaining agreement increased salaries from $117,000 to $215,000. (An NBA player will make no less than $898,000 this year.) Much smaller improvements were given to the rookie minimum (from $41,965 to $57,000) and veteran minimum (from $56,375 to $68,000).

Nnekas Ogwumike's case, we have seen her contract values increase since the first versions of this book. In 2022, she signed a 2 year / $386,817 contract with the Los Angeles Sparks, which creates an annual average salary of $193,409.[4] While there is much to unpack in this equality discussion of womens and men's sports, it is a huge step in the right direction.[5]

Even in sports that Americans may not think of as professionally aspirational there are not only opportunities to make money playing the game we love, but *lucrative* opportunities. Tim Kelly owns Bring It Promotions, a sports agency, where he represents more than 200 athletes around the world including both men's and women's professional volleyball players. In the lead-up to the 2016 Olympic Games in Rio de Janiero, he said that "the average sports fan would be blown away if they found out that anyone was making a million dollars net play volleyball. That continues to shock people."[6] Even in places with social unrest like Turkey[7] and Iraq[8], American athletes are finding opportunities to extend their careers just a little bit longer and find ways to hold on to that big piece of self they call "athlete."

Of course, it's not all glitz and glamor at this level—despite what your friends, family, and certainly the general public might think. Whether an athlete plays in the minor leagues or developmental leagues, at the highest level, or overseas, many things remain the same across the spectrum. At this level, sports is no longer just an avocation—it becomes your vocation. This game is now what pays the rent or mortgage, puts food on the table, gas in the car and birthday presents for parents and kids. Olympic volleyball player Courtney Thompson puts it best:

> The first year, I remember that every time they [her team] would give me a check—which wasn't much every month—I would say, 'Thank you, thank you so much, thank you.' And finally, my boss was like: 'Courtney, you can stop thanking me. This is your job.'[9]

At the end of the day, you are still one of the lucky ones because some-body is paying you to play your level best in a sport that you love.

Everyone hears the stories about the biggest names in the biggest sports in America. Who hasn't heard of Tiger Woods, LeBron James, Tom Brady and Serena Williams? And that's just in America. How about Lionel Messi, Roger Federer, and Usain Bolt? Everyone sees them on the cover of Sports Illustrated and watches them give interviews on Sports Center. But there is a whole wide world outside of North America for professional athletes out there who are "judged, valued, and promoted based on how well you use your body," says minor-league soccer player Clint Irwin.[10] But for all professional players—perhaps *especially* those in the minor leagues—this level is about playing because you love it. The sacrifices for so many are just so big that it *must* be for love of the game. Irwin kept a journal of his journey through minor league professional soccer in North America and shared some outtakes from 2011 which demonstrate this "love of the game:"

> I signed a deal with Capital City FC for $500 a month and they are paying for my living expenses. Bonuses include $40 per win and $250 per various league leading statistics. I can't express how happy I am to finally be somewhere.[8]

But, as Irwin notes, at this level it is *all* about performance.

Even for the stars, it is not easy at this level because the average retirement age for *all* athletes in the United States is 33.[11] That number continues to diminish every year. Frankly, medical research has led to a shortening of professional sports careers. After decades of use, work and training of muscles and joints—from youth sports, through high school sports, through college, and then through an entire professional career—the body simply breaks down. Interestingly, researchers have found that professional sports careers are growing shorter and shorter as athletes retire younger and younger. For instance, the Wall Street Journal studied National Football League careers and found that the average career of an NFL football player across all positions has fallen from just under five years by nearly half—to a little above two and a half years.[12,13] Quarterbacks' careers have dropped the most, from six to three years. So, imagine that: even if you stayed all four years of college plus redshirted an additional year, the average quarterback will be out of the game by the time he is just twenty six years old.

On the women's side of football, inequality still presides. The 1st female NFL Coach, and Gold Medalist Jen Welter received just $1 for her opportunity to play professional ball with the Dallas Diamonds in 2004.

"It was a dollar a game, but that's technically what made us pro," Welter told AZCentral.com.[14]

And the retiring age does not just drastically drop for a contact sport like football here in the US.

In 2010, the average length of an NBA career was less than five years.[15] In tennis, the average age of retirement for men is 27 years old and women is 25 years old.[16] A Major League quality baseball player can expect an average career of 5.6 years.[17,18]

During that time, however, the athlete is focused on making money. He or she has to be, because these are the prime earning years for any athlete. Those millions of dollars have to last the next twenty years, fifty years, seventy years. Those dollars have to last the rest of the athlete's life. So during that period, the athlete must stay focused on the sport. This, of course, reinforces the athletic identity even more so. Similarly, as most people—when asked about themselves—lead off with their profession: "I'm a lawyer," or "I'm an accountant." So does the professional athlete: "I'm a pro ball player." This further reinforces the athletic identity above other roles they may play or other interests that might otherwise take that position for them.

While retirement comes for both genders, female athletes bear a much heavier burdon on creating a living with their next chapter. (This topic could be a whole book in itself. Please know this is just one story of female athletes having a much different retirement than most male professional athletes.)

World champion and gold medalist Abby Wambach, who won the Icon Award at the ESPY's with Peyton Manning and Kobe Bryant will face a much different retirement and second chapter.

She recounts with her Barnard College Commencement Speech,

As the three stood on the stage, "I had a momentary feeling of having arrived—like we women had finally made it," Wambach said. "Then the applause ended and it was time for the three of us to exit stage left. And as I watched those men walk off the stage, it dawned on me that the three of us were stepping into very different futures.

Each of us, Kobe, Peyton and I—we made the same sacrifices, we shed the same amount of blood sweat and tears, we'd left it all on the field for decades with the same ferocity, talent and commitment. But our retirements wouldn't be the same at all. Because Kobe and Peyton walked away from their careers with something I didn't have: enormous bank accounts. Because of that, they had something else I didn't have: freedom. Their hustling days were over, and mine were just beginning."

Abby, even with her worldwide fame and history breaking soccer career, has the a similar story to most— the need to HUSTLE post athletic retirement . . . [19]

OLYMPIC SPORTS

Always An Olympian, Never Former Never Past

—US OLYMPIC COMMITTEE

Olympians can often have it very different. For some, they fell in love with sports that permit them to play the game to pay their bills. When the International Olympic Committee opened up participation to professionals in 1992, the United States put together the NBA "Dream Team" to represent the nation in Barcelona. That team featured today's legends like Michael Jordan, Scottie Pippen, John Stockton, Magic Johnson, Larry Bird, Patrick Ewing, Chris Mullin, Charles Barkley and Clyde Drexler. The only amateur athlete named to the team was Christian Laettner, who was coming off his second NCAA championship in a row. With the growth of volleyball, players have opportunities to play in professional leagues around the world. Even events we see as backyard games are giving athletes opportunities to get paid to play, like badminton which is popular enough to merit professional leagues in southeast Asia and India.[20]

For many Olympians, however, they likely have a very high athletic identity because based on circumstances, they embody playing for the love of the game and the desire to play at the highest level of the sport. An athlete *must* play for love and desire to give up opportunities at stable careers in order to continue to play against elite competition on the largest stage. And the Olympic athlete's career may not be as long as some believe. It seems like every Olympic quadrennial we hear stories about competitors like Anne Abernathy—known as "Grandma Luge"—who competed at her fourth Olympics in Nagano at 44 years old[21] and gymnast Oksana Chusovitina who famously represented Uzbekistan at 41 years old in Rio in 2016.[22] And there has been an increase in the average age of Olympians across all sports since the 1980 games.[23] However, it has only increased three years, from just over 22 years of age in 1980 to just over 25 years of age in 2012.[24] The fact is, even Olympic careers are fleeting and Olympians retire from their sport career.

Much has been written about the sacrifices that America's Olympians make in order to pursue their dreams of athletic achievement at the highest level. Some Olympians—by virtue of their achievements or even their personal stories—become so ingrained in the public's image that they naturally fit with marketing campaigns for major corporations. Usain Bolt, for instance, competes in track as a sprinter—not exactly the largest spectator sport in the United States. At the professional level, track is like golf and tennis, in which top players earn prize money based on where they place in major events. But the prize money is often a pittance in itself. In 2012, for instance, CNN Money reported that only half of American track and field athletes ranked in the top ten in the nation earn more than $15,000 per year from their sport.[25] It is only the most famous athletes who then pull in the bucks that people traditionally think of when they hear the words "professional athlete." For instance, Usain Bolt reportedly earned over $34 million in 2017 according to Forbes, which includes a $10 million endorsement deal from Puma.[26] Michael Phelps is worth $55 million.[27] But should the Fastest Man In The World and the most decorated Olympian of all time expect anything less?

But take a guess at how much Scott Parsons makes from his sport and endorsements? Or Adam Nelson? Or Megan Kalmoe? Better question: do you even know who those people are? And that is the issue for these athletes. Parsons was a three-time Olympian in kayak, not exactly a spectator sport. He scrapes for every nickel to be able to compete. Nelson was a two-time silver medalist at the Olympic Games in shot put. Going to near-ridiculous heights to support his wife and children, he managed to obtain a $12,000 sponsorship from MedivoxRx despite competing in an event miles from the limelight.[28] And Kalmoe is an Olympic medalist and veteran in women's rowing all the way back to the 2008 Games.[29] She shares a $1,000 per month apartment with roommates and works a part-time job at a local YMCA, living just above the poverty line to support her sports habit.[30] But she may be even better off than her teammates like Grace Latz, who carries it with a grain of salt despite the fact, she says, "I slept in my car during training camp."[31] Even the sports that may only be high-profile every four years at the Olympics like swimming and track and field offer sponsorship and endorsement deals for medalists and champions that aren't available to athletes like Parsons, Nelson and Kalmoe. And they are far from the only ones. espnW broke it down prior to the 2016 Games:

> But isn't rowing a snooze? Doesn't it draw a TV audience somewhere between horseshoes and Ultimate Frisbee? Maybe. But the funding shortcomings aren't about popularity. They're ubiquitous. Speedskater Emily Scott applied for food stamps. At one point, heavyweight power lifter Sarah Robles was planning to live in a tent in her neighbor's backyard and pay $50 to use the shower. Gymnast Gabby Douglas' mother filed for bankruptcy. . . . Outside the top 10? Barely enough to buy a pair of Brooks Ghost 6 running shoes.[32]

But none of them would take it back. As Parsons says, these are "the kind of sport[s] that you do because you love it."[33]

Because of the sacrifices that the Olympian has to make simply to qualify for the Games—especially in the sports that people have never heard of—*it is not such a stretch to say that these athletes likely possess the highest level of athletic identity and foreclosure.* In college, they had dorms, training table, access to state-of-the-art training rooms and coaching staff. But once they leave those confines, it all falls on their shoulders. And many athletes give up careers and personal lives in order to pursue opportunities at this level. Because it is no longer just about competing to keep a scholarship but to win at the highest level, and every second of every day is devoted to that purpose, it goes without saying that the athlete at this level likely identifies *solely* as an athlete. (Of course with the caveat of family descriptors like: son, daughter, brother, sister, husband, wife etc)

And then, one day, even the professional athletes will do what all professionals in all professions do—even Olympians- they too will retire.

7

Retirement, Transition, and the Edge of the Cliff

Be comfortable in being uncomfortable.

—SUE ENQUIST,
11 time NCAA Softball Championship,
Hall of Fame UCLA Softball Coach[1]

Okay. So, I know you have already read a chapter on why I decided to write this book. And while I stick by everything that is in Chapter 1, the *real* "why" of this book is that I suffered the first death that Jackie Robinson talked about. I retired from volleyball, which led me off the Cliff after years of climbing my volleyball Mountain.

In my own story— I didn't really know I was deeply struggling in the transition until several years after. I had not processed my loss of sport— the loss of an athletic competitive outlet, teammates training structure and competition . . . . I basically dove full into what most graduates of 2008-2009 financial crash did at that time— find a job (any job) and then I worked toward building a career.

This book is not about me or my story, but I want to put a portion of my story in here so that you understand as the reader, more about what happened in my own athletic journey. And maybe why I am taking a shot Always An Athlete movement for others. I was never the best, but I know deep down I did give my best.

So here are three paragraphs around my personal transition and the moments that led to my eventual retirement.

From the time I was in middle school, I played club volleyball with some of the top teams in Southern California. I even played above my age bracket. I was recruited at the *high school* level to join Tesoro High School's then-brand-new volleyball team. Tesoro, having at that time just opened as a new school, was looking to establish its athletic bona fides early. And so the coach called me, we talked, and he recruited me to play there with promises of structuring the team around me and another incoming freshman. What 5' 9", 14-year-old Orange County girl would not have been tempted? Through high school, I continued to play on my club team as well. But then, my senior year, I was dealt a set-back: I tore my ACL in my left knee. Not good, but *especially* not good since I was going through the college recruitment process at the same time. I spent every day coming back from that injury, and somehow managed to land a walk-on roster spot at Baylor University with the promise that I'd get one of those scholarships. But my freshman year, I had another set-back: I injured my left knee again and had to have a second ACL surgery on the same knee. My freshman year was shot.

I continued recovering from my injury making up fun sideline songs with my other teammates who too were out of commission to play on the court. I did work hard and came back for my sophomore season and got to play again in what diplomatically would be called "limited minutes." And then I found out that I was getting recruited over with another defensive specialist who would be transferring in and there would be no opportunity for scholarship. After discussions with my coaches and athletic trainers, one thing was clear—competitive high-level volleyball was no longer a part of my path. There were no opportunities for advancement on the team. After only two years on a Division I roster I made the hard choice to step back as an active athlete and lean further into the other opportunities that were available to me on campus to help aid in my personal development. At nineteen years old, the activity and sport that I had put so much time, energy and emotion into was suddenly taken from me. How many other athletes out there can empathize? How many of you heard "the snap" or "the pop" at practice one day? How many of you found that when you came back from rehab, you'd lost a step or your movement was more limited than it was before? Even if you did not retire due to injury, there are many different reasons that athletes leave or are forced out of their sports:

Although transitional loss in sport can result from a variety of circumstances, some of the most relevant unique transitions experienced by athletes are being cut from a team, dealing with injury, and retiring from active participation.[2]

Other researchers identify "slumping"—disappointing athletic performance over a long period—as a source of loss.[3] And one of the most common reasons a player retires is "de-selection"—a transition characterized by circumstances in which an athlete does not qualify to play at the next level.[4] In the sports world, though, we just call it getting cut.

What comes next during the post-retirement period has been called many things. Many researchers call it the "transition." Prim Siripipat, former tennis star at Duke University and current ESPN host, calls it the "pivot,"[5] which I like because the word just feels sporty. I find those to be appropriate descriptions for what the athlete must do after retirement; an athlete must transition, an athlete must pivot. But what the athlete *endures* after retirement—*why* the athlete must transition or pivot—I refer to as the Cliff. We climb up the Athletic Mountain for years. But when we reach the top of our Mountain—whether it is at the end of youth sports, high school sports, college sports, or the professional and Olympic ranks—there is no hike back down the way we came. There is no ski-lift down or guide to take us. We reach the leading edge of the peak at some point, and we will go over that edge. The question is whether we prepare ourselves and take the plunge voluntarily, or whether we find ourselves suddenly falling over the edge and careening down the Cliff itself.

Importantly, I want to say that retirement and transition should not be confused with what I call the Cliff itself. **There is nothing inherently negative about retirement, even from competitive sports.** However, retirement is the event in the athlete's career that triggers his or her transition away from a predominant or overwhelming athletic role in life to non-athletic roles. For people who developed non-athlete roles in addition to their athlete role during the midst of their sports careers, the transition remains jarring *but not impossible to navigate*. It is even more difficult for those who discovered too late that their sport had overwhelmed all other parts of their lives. Despite the attention given to the financial disasters of athletes after they retire, there is a whole spectrum of non-financial consequences that elite athletes must deal with. Robert Laura of Forbes Magazine put it best in his 2012 piece, *How Star Athletes Deal With Retirement*:

There's a psychological side to retirement that often goes unaddressed in the traditional retirement planning process and not even the most skilled and decorated athletes of our time can avoid it. It requires equal if not more time and attention than more commonly addressed financial issues. It is a mental side that includes finding ways to replace your work-identity, managing your time and family relationships, and maintaining your mental and physical health.[6]

In an age when concussion-related research has the public digging into the post-retirement mental and physical health of athletes, it is optimistic that identity issues, mental wellbeing and physical well being of our athletes are becoming of greater interest to the research community. However, these are growing areas of research and there is still much to be uncovered.

Regardless of whether the athlete has additional roles they can promote or rely on, or not, every athlete to some extent suffers what Jackie Robinson called "the first death." In these instances, athletes to varying degrees have climbed the Mountain, only to one day find they are inevitably falling off the Cliff. And, unfortunately, the higher the Mountain the athlete climbs, the taller is the Cliff they fall from.

When I speak about the Cliff, it is important to understand that retirement and the transition are not the Cliff, *per se*. The Cliff, instead, is the consequence that the athlete must contend with once their career is over, and is characterized by losses and evolution in three different areas that I identify as Identity, Mental Health, and Physical Health. The consequences and evolution of each athlete in those three areas is collectively the Cliff. And it is my hope that this book and subsequent materials for athletes can help soften or shorten the fall.

Every athlete—regardless of how high their Athletic Mountain rose—experiences the Cliff in some form. For the high school varsity athletes who retire after graduation each spring, Dr. Chris Stankovich, clinical counselor and founder of Advanced Human Performance Systems asks parents to take note of unique stressors their retiring athletes may experience:

> First, sport retirement is often an abrupt, unwanted, stressful, and isolating experience for many kids. Even for student athletes who are realistic with their chances of playing college sports being small, the transition can still be difficult trying to re-prioritize goals, re-establish a new (non-athletic) identity, and develop new relationships outside of sports.

The support system of former teammates also vanishes, and often [high school] student athletes are left to experience all of these things alone and without much recognition from others, including family and friends. . . .

Even for kids who knew their sports careers would end after high school, many of them are still impacted by the loss. For some the stress comes from no longer competing at a high level, for others it's the team environment they miss, and still others are impacted by no longer wearing the identity of "athlete." . . . From my experience most athletes (including high school student athletes) do not actively seek help for the difficulties they experience with sport retirement and for some they aren't even aware of the impact of this transition and how it often spills over into other areas of their lives.[7]

The athletes with the most obvious difficulties with the Cliff are former college athletes and athletes at the professional and Olympic level. One of my mentors coached Division I softball for many years. After listening to the idea of this book early on in the process, she realized she had kept every email from former players over her 15 years of coaching. To help me with this book, she sent an email to all of them asking the question: "What was the hardest part of the transition?" She said the results were heartbreaking and stunning. Over 100 emails came pouring in within the first few hours after she sent the question. She realized I had tapped into the human spirit. Hearts were broken. Time, of course, had mended many. But there were still some who needed to talk about the difficulty.

For some of you reading, you might be wondering why it is so hard? While playing at those levels, the athlete's sports career is nearly all-consuming because during that period the athlete's entire life is performance-purposed: everything the athlete does must be intended to keep them performing at their peak level on the field or court. Or, at the very least, should not be a danger to it. Because it can happen so suddenly—especially for those who do not plan for it—retirement can feel like a sudden down-shift into reverse after years of cruising at 60 miles an hour in fifth gear. If you've ever heard brakes grind, that's the soundtrack for athletic retirement. The question, though, is how loud is the volume? Or, more appropriately in this book, how far is the fall off the Cliff?

We have the opportunity as a society to help soften the landing of athletes.

We as a society, can help and better prepare athletes for the inevitable transition, and I deeply believe our sports culture is ready for this type of conversation and sports programming.

THE CLIFF

8

The Cliff

Loss of Identity

It's tough when athletes make that transition.
I had to really humble myself and say, "You know what,
that's not my identity anymore."

—CHAMIQUE HOLDSCLAW,
Retired WNBA Player[1]

Many of the problems that the Cliff represents are rooted in one thing: the athlete's identity as an athlete. While I have discussed identity throughout the Mountain to give a sense of how it develops over time, it deserves some more consideration here.

I originally titled this chapter "Hung On The Wall." A couple of years ago, I worked as a nanny for the first time in my life. One of the boys that I watched was ten years old. He was not dramatic. He always put on a tough exterior. And he loved to play football. He and I connected pretty quickly because we shared sports journeys—mine already completed, his only beginning. After a couple of months, I knew that I'd made his inner circle when he asked me if he could show me something. Not knowing what he could possibly be up to, I figured he was either trying to prank me or had put something together to show off.

Turning the corner into his bedroom, I saw what he wanted to show me. On his bedroom wall, he had tacked up all of his football jerseys from teams he had played on. He told me about the rules of the game, strategy and plays. He regaled me with stories of wins, losses, and was very proud of how far his team had gone each season and big plays he made. Interestingly, the one thing he seemed to not care about: the participation trophies he had received. What was important to him was the jersey on his back which, to him, encompassed every season of growth and development.

I feel like my young friend's presentation that day is a microcosm for athletes across the world at every level. The jersey is not just something that we wear. It's not just clothes to distinguish us from our opponents. There is a deeper connection because the clothes *stand* for something. Our uniforms *represent* something deeper. New York Giants wide receiver Odell Beckham Jr. put it succinctly:

> You watch any of the gladiator or Spartan movies, on the field of battle is their helmet or whatever they are wearing. They won or lost in it. The jerseys are kind of like our armor. It is something to be remembered forever.[2]

Buffalo Bills safety Aaron Williams calls the jersey a reminder of "the journey to get in the N.F.L. and the journey to stay as long as possible."[3] And dang it if he isn't right for every athlete, if we replace "N.F.L." with "varsity squad," or "my favorite college team," or "Olympics."

The jersey is the ultimate manifestation of our identity as athletes. Something powerfully transformative occurs when an athlete puts his or her jersey on. We are warriors going off to battle. Our jerseys are *literally* stained with the blood, sweat and tears we have shed in victory and defeat. We pull it on, and we stand taller. We exude confidence. We know exactly who we are, what we are about, what we have to do and how we're going to do it. We honor those who came before us—the trailblazers and pioneers of the sport, the record holders, the legends and hall-of-famers. Our jersey makes us a part of that tradition and a part of that legacy. When we take off the jersey for the last time and hang it on the wall or put it in a drawer, it is like turning a piece of ourselves into a museum piece or hiding it away. Coaches and organizations recognize the importance of the jersey to the player. The jersey is deeply symbolic. Coaches frame the jersey on "Senior Night" to signify the ending of a chapter in their lives. And for the elite few, jersey numbers are retired in gyms and arenas throughout the country. When we take off the jersey, we lose our identity—some of us in whole, some of us in part.

Development of our individual identities has a long history of research by psychologists and developmental specialists. It has been one of the most discussed ideas throughout the world, throughout recorded civilization, and across multiple disciplines from philosophy to science and psychology in the modern age. Every person's identity can be complex or simple. It can be well defined and concretely articulated, or it can be ambiguous and open to further discovery. At the end of the day, though, our "identities" come down to each person asking themselves one simple yet thoughtful question: who am I?

There are several theories on identity formation and development. Some come from the philosophical school of thought, which is rooted in the reflections and rhetorical questions about our relationships with ourselves and our world posed by Enlightenment Age thinkers such as Immanuel Kant and René Descartes.[4] In the nineteenth century, pioneers in the new field of psychology such as William James, Charles Horton Cooley and G.H. Mead took the philosophical foundations of the previous age and began applying principles of empirical science to the study of identity formation.[5] Within the last century, a new approach was utilized that relied on self-labeling, dependent upon who our peers are: identity politics. But what *is* identity, at the end of the day? In 1986, a leading researcher named Peter Weinreich defined "identity" as "the totality of one's self-construal, in which how one construes oneself in the present expresses the continuity between how one construes oneself as one was in the past and how one construes oneself as one aspires to be in the future."[6] For the athlete, this question to "who am I" is almost always answered starting with "I am a fill-in-the-blank player." "I am a basketball player." "I am a professional football player." "I am an Olympic sprinter." "I am a varsity baseball player."

This answer is rooted in your entire history, your family, your friends, your church, *your teams, your coaches, your administrators, your teammates, your leagues, your colleges*, and everything that you were, are and aspire to be in the future. But more important than answering the question (which every person must answer on their own), is to understand how you get to be who you are, and whether what you *think* you are really is the sum total of your being. Are you really a fill-in-the-blank player and nothing else?

Every athlete reading this knows deep down there is so much more inside of us!

Individual identity is typically divided into the roles in which we see ourselves. It both compares and contrasts us with people around us based on relationships, experiences and circumstances. Some roles that people assume for themselves regarding relationships include identifying as a child, as a parent, as a sibling, as a grandparent. We identify ourselves as friends, enemies, acquaintances, and significant others. We identify with our culture and ethnicity. We identify ourselves based on experiences, such as being a Boy Scout, or being a scientist. Or, as I talk about in this book, being an athlete. People can adopt multiple roles, or they can engage in what researchers refer to as "role exclusion" or "role foreclosure," which is when people assume one or two identities and filter all others out.

Development of athletic identity in particular is a fairly recent topic of discussion among psychologists and social science researchers. The earliest research in the early 1990s defined athletic identity as the degree to which an individual identifies with the athlete role and looks to others for acknowledgement of that role.[7] Other researchers have defined it as "the degree of importance, strength and exclusivity attached to the athletic role that is maintained by the athlete and influenced by their environment."[8] At the end of the day, though, each of us who have played sports knows what it is because we have internalized it: it's the part of us that makes us say when people ask who we are, the first words out of our mouths are "I'm a ——— player."

But perhaps more important than the definition of athletic identity is how it forms. Like all roles and self-identifiers, it occurs over time and is influenced by our relationships with others, our experiences, and our circumstances. Recall way back at the beginning of the book Dr. Eric Martin's discussion of how the athletic identity traditionally comes into being:

> For an activity to become a passion, it must be significant in individuals' lives, be liked by them, and be something that they engage in frequently. More specifically, the activity that an individual may feel passionate about may not be merely an activity in which she or he participates. Rather, that activity actually becomes a central portion of that person's identity. . . . People who are highly passionate about activities such as football, writing, or teaching, do not merely play football, write or teach. Rather they are, or they have become, football players, writers and teachers.[9]

At the earliest stages of youth sports, when a child is first beginning to develop a broader understanding of his place in the world between parents, siblings, forming new friends in kindergarten and first grade, perhaps socializing more through religious institutions and youth groups, they engage in numerous activities that perhaps in the future they will develop a passion for. Without explaining *why* any person is passionate about sports (as such passion can come from parental influence, friend influence, or no other influence than the athlete simply enjoys playing sports or being active), what is clear is that as the child gets older, he begins to choose sports to the exclusion of other activities. The potential for an unhealthy balance between the athletic role and all others begins to set into place. If all the athlete knows is sports, or if all that is valued in those around her is sports or everybody around the athlete is servient to that role—such as in high school, if keeping up grades is valuable only to the extent it is necessary to remain eligible to play—the athlete develops a stronger athletic identity. Dr. Thomas Cieslak explains it succinctly in his doctoral work at the Ohio State University:

> Once an athlete begins a career in sport, he or she experiences a process of sport socialization. After participating on a beginner level (e.g., youth sport and interscholastic athletics), most athletes choose to specialize in a sport in which they are most skilled. As their sport career continues to develop, family, friends, coaches, teachers, and the media influence and support the goal of advancement in sport. This alludes to the fact that young athletes receive more attention and positive reinforcement than their non-athlete counterparts from their sport involvement and, subsequently, begin to form an athletic identity. . . .
>
> Early in life, those with high athletic identity begin to base their self-worth on athletic performance and tend to support their self-esteem through their strong athletic identity, which further develops if an athlete reaches elite levels (e.g., intercollegiate, Olympic, and professional [sports]).[10]

There is nothing inherently wrong in developing the athletic identity. However, with the prevalence of specialization in youth sports and high school sports, combined with the extreme focus necessary to succeed and continue playing at the highest levels in college, the pros and the Olympics, athletes over time are less and less exposed to other activities (including other sports). Michigan State University sport psychologist Scott Goldman puts it plain: "The amount of time, effort and energy an athlete puts into their sport exceeds almost *everything* else they've ever done in their life."[11] This essentially creates a feedback loop: the athlete measures his worth by athletic achievement, which drives him to focus on achieving greater success athletically, which requires him to forego other activities, which limits his world to athletics, and so he measures himself by achievement in the athletic world. It can too easily become a vicious cycle. Dr. Cieslak continues:

> Thus, athletes, as well as important people in their lives often focus on only one aspect of their personality [i.e. their role in the world as an athlete] and neglect the salience of other identities (e.g., family, friendship, religious, academic, romantic). This overemphasis on sport involvement may cause a lack of participation in other activities such as, but not limited to, school and social interactions.[12]

How many of us can relate to missing a school dance or important school function for a tournament? Or maybe being a part of student government was out of the question due to time constraints?

Development of all identity—including athletic identity—has been described by early psychoanalytic researcher Erik Erikson as the fifth stage of development of the human psyche.[13] It occurs first and most strongly during adolescence (ages 12 through 18) which, incidentally, is also the period when the most important people in an athlete's life—parents, friends, coaches—are more and more pushing for specialization. No wonder, then, when kids reach college and all they've ever known is homework, exercise and sports. Without other activities to provide positive reinforcement and by which to evaluate their own self-worth (or an alternative to the negative experiences that can be associated with youth sports and high school sports), it is no wonder that young athletes—at their most vulnerable stage—engage in identity foreclosure on a massive scale. As Dr. Cieslak writes:

> This lack of psychosocial development [of other identities] has been referred to as identity foreclosure. "Identity foreclosure is a construct used to describe people who have committed to an occupation or an ideology without first engaging in exploratory behavior. . . . [I]dentity foreclosure and athletic identity increased with the level of sport participation."[14]

Dr. Cieslak notes the imbalance in athletes who "have strong and exclusive athletic identities."[15] For these athletes, they may *only* identify as athletes, even to the exclusion of more obvious roles that they play in life, including the most fundamental roles such as son or daughter and brother or sister.

When Jackie Robinson spoke about an athlete's first death, he was talking about the identity crisis that accompanies retirement from competitive sports. When the athlete plays her last game or runs his last race, they look at themselves in the mirror. The conscious thought they have is, "what now" or "what's next?" But that is rooted in an even deeper, unconscious thought they are thinking which is, "all this time I've been an athlete. But what am I now? What else do I have?" The development of that identity comes from *all* of the reinforcements over the years that athletes receive. For this reason, retired NHL All-Star Al Iafrate makes a case similar to Robinson's:

> It's hard to replace the passion you have for a sport. There aren't many jobs that you retire from where you get to prove that you are the very best of the best in front of thousands and thousands of people every night.[16]

As early as high school, researchers are noting the loss of identity that athletes feel upon retirement. In 1990, researchers referred to the problem of "broken hearts and bruised egos" as a seasonal occurrence.[17] Katie Helms at the University of Arkansas, Fayetteville, noted it as follows:

> Here, high school athletes with a high identification with the sport role are particularly vulnerable problems caused by sport loss due to an increased focus on sport during a critical period when exploration and expansion of other interests are critical to the development of a well-rounded identity.[18]

In her study, Helms studied "loss levels" and "life satisfaction" of former varsity high school athletes a year after they graduated; "toward the end of the freshman year of college."[19]

I think every athlete can relate to this sense of loss. And at the very least, the sense of loss that comes when you no longer have the community and family of your teammates that you worked to build and maintain. Miles Wentzien, a high school athlete from Iowa, shares his experience:

> My favorite part about being involved with high school sports is the relationships that are made. Playing high school sports forms very close relationships among teammates that may have never happened otherwise. These relationships are very unique. Throughout the season I spend nearly every day working with my teammates. I remember moments in practice when I felt that I couldn't continue, or that I wasn't

strong enough to finish the drill. Then I looked over and saw the same exhausted expression on my teammate's face, and at that moment a bond was formed.

We knew that we could make it through anything, as long as we came together as a team. That feeling is what I will miss most about high school sports.[20]

This loss of self creates feelings of emptiness and desperation in some athletes. When all you have ever identified as is an athlete, and you lose that, what do you have left? (Answer: SO MUCH MORE!) Even if your primary identity is as an athlete, how do the other roles we play in life ever fill the hole of the dominant piece of us?

The complete loss of athletic identity is at the root of the problem and is intertwined with the other aspects of the Cliff, mental health and physical health. All of this ties together in why it is so important to transition with all the right tools and support systems. While tough, I believe it can successfully be done!

The hope is to bring into focus all the other attributes, passions and curiosities that make you/YOU! When you see yourself evolving and transforming, it becomes exciting and is truly powerful. You are breathing to this next chapter in life!

9

The Cliff
Mental Health

I didn't get out of bed. I didn't answer my mates' phone calls.
I was eating terribly, drinking heavily. A tough time. And look,
I didn't know at that stage that it was a form of depression.

—BARRY HALL,
Australian Football League all-star[1]

Disclaimer: there are some difficult stories that are included in this chapter. Please know this before reading further.

With the loss of identity, the Cliff is also characterized by more discernible mental health issues that athletes face when retirement comes. The feelings of emptiness and loss that athletes often feel can manifest in common symptoms of depression, anxiety issues and other mental health issues related to retirement from competitive athletics. While there is debate about how much more or less athletes suffer from mental health issues than the rest of the nation, the unique characteristics and circumstances that got the athlete up the Mountain in the first place make for post-retirement issues unique to the elite-level athlete. The most common and destructive mental health issues that athletes encounter include depression, anxiety disorders, substance abuse and suicidal thoughts.

Interestingly, most elite athletes at the collegiate and professional level have delayed mental health issues arising out of their retirement from competitive athletics. (Hi! That is me, I had a *delay* in my mental and physical health decline.)

In 2013, researchers from Georgetown University Medical Center published a study in which they found that active athletes actually had higher incidence of depression than athletes who had already completed their last game or race.[2] Those researchers suppose several possible factors contribute to depression during the performance-purposed years, including "the pressure to deliver peak performance, coupled with workload and lack of rest, [which] can lead to overtraining, chronic fatigue and depression."[3] Other stressors during college years include lack of free time and stress from schoolwork.[4] The sudden reduction in those stressors can often lead to immediate levels of relief.

Many of my friends and I can personally attest to this. I remember feeling a giant sigh of relief almost immediately after I told my coaches that I would not be playing the next year. The immediate expectation is no more practice to fit into a busy schedule, I could finally eat a cupcake without feeling guilty and, most importantly, *no more pressure to perform*! More time to myself. More time for a social life. More time to devote to schoolwork. Who wouldn't feel the pressure being lifted off almost immediately? However, sports psychologists find that this is often a short-term feeling. Helix Magazine—a science and medicine periodical published by Northwestern University—stated as much in the same year as the Georgetown study:

> Sports psychologists say that even though many student-athletes initially feel relief after finishing their athletic career, some still suffer depression and other mental-health issues for several years after graduation.[5]

Read that again: SEVERAL YEARS AFTER GRADUATION!

Caroline Silby, former national figure skater and practicing sports psychologist, believes it unfortunate that we don't talk about mental health issues for athletes in America today. Worse yet, we continue to fail to prepare our athletes for it. As she says, "even when athletes are happy about moving on and starting the next phase of their life and [are] excited about that possibility they're also simultaneously experiencing the sense of loss."[6] Expounding on this, she says "a lot of athletes will tell you they're relieved. But when you start pulling back the layers, they start to also experience this sense of loss."[7] Even when the athlete retires and feels these feelings, it can still be soon that they crop up again. For many, these feelings arise right around the beginning of the next season. As NBA All-Star Kareem Abdul Jabbar puts it, "the first training camp that I missed, I was like, 'Jeez, what am I going to do now?'"[8] To suddenly realize that from now on, you'll be sitting in the stands instead or on the bench often brings the point home. More importantly, "the stands" incorporates not just participation in sporting events, but the idea that the athlete now must find a new occupation or passion in life that can help fill the emotional and psychological void left by no longer being a part of an athletic team or of sports endeavors.

I don't know if you have ever watched the game from the stands—but it is a whole different experience than being the athlete competing in the game.

For many other athletes, the effects are more immediate. Australian football (*i.e.* soccer) star Barry Hall makes it clear that he chose retirement. Despite giving himself time to plan for it and to become okay with his decision, he still struggled immediately during the months following his retirement: "Did I struggle after the sport finished? Absolutely. I had two or three months . . . that I really struggled."[9] Athletes who do not choose to retire on their own, though, likely suffer from the impact on their mental wellness immediately. WNBA basketball star Lauren Jackson was "pushed out" of the game due to injuries, despite not being ready to retire. After meeting with the doctors, they told her "you will never play again, it's over. That was it. And I just remember thinking, OK. So I got out of the room and, yeah, I broke down and it was hard."[10] Whether the athlete gets to make the decision to retire for him or herself, or whether the athlete can see it coming (such as in the case of the college athlete who knows going into her senior season that this is likely her *last* season ever), or whether the change comes suddenly due to injury or other life circumstances, the effects of retirement from sports on mental health can begin to take their shortly after retirement takes effect. But what are those effects?

In 2015, an Australian survey of 244 retired athletes revealed that depression, eating disorders, and general psychological distress are the most common mental health issues facing former sports stars.[11,12] However, perhaps more concerning, is that regardless of the rate at which retired athletes *suffer* from various mental health conditions is that they have a higher rate of non-reporting. In other words, athletes are not good at asking for help, often for reasons related to their athletic identity and stigma perpetuated in the sports communities as a whole. These are issues that are significant and need to be addressed by every participant in sports and athletics—from fan to coach to the athlete herself or himself.

DEPRESSION AND ANXIETY DISORDERS

The most common mental health issue that the retired athlete faces coming down the Cliff is depression. Recent research has shown that athletes experience the same psychological stages of grief after losing their competitive sporting careers that people go through while grieving the loss of a loved one.[13]

The Anxiety and Depression Association of America has found that depression is one of the most common mental illnesses in the nation, affecting nearly 20 percent of the adult population every year—including among athletes.[14]

The Mayo Clinic has identified several of symptoms, including: feelings of sadness, tearfulness, emptiness or hopelessness; angry outbursts, irritability or frustration, even over small things; loss of interest or pleasure in normal activities, including sex, hobbies, and even sports; disturbed sleep patterns such as insomnia, sleeping too much, having an abnormal sleep cycle; feelings of tiredness and lack of energy; extreme changes in appetite and weight loss or gain; anxiety, agitation and restlessness; slowed thinking, speaking or bodily movements; feelings of worthlessness or guilt; fixation on past failures or self-blame; trouble with decision-making and concentration; changes in memory; unexplained physical problems such as muscle pain and headaches; and frequent or recurrent thoughts of death or suicide.[15]

Depression is especially acute after the end of competition. In the context of the Olympics, for instance, Scott Goldman of the Performance Psychology Center at the University of Michigan says:

> Think about the rollercoaster ride prior to the Olympics, and just how fast and hectic that mad dash is. This ninety-mile-per-hour or hundred-mile-per-hour ride comes to a screeching halt the second the Olympics are over. . . . [The athletes] are just exhausted; it was such an onslaught to their system. And when it's' all said and done, they're just physiologically depleted, as well as psychologically.[16]

It should go without saying, though, that the "onslaught" Goldman speaks of is common to *every* elite athlete—not just Olympians.

An aggravating factor for many athletes is retirement due to career-ending injuries. Silby states that such an abrupt end to a career—and, in many cases, a dream—can make retirement-related depression even worse:

> The key to how an athlete feels about his or her departure from sports is how much perceived control they have over that decision. The difference [is] between choosing to stop playing versus being cut or becoming injured and then taking you out of the sport. So the way in which that determination occurs and how much control the athlete has over that decision-making process really does impact how they do next with the transition.[17]

Regardless of the reason that the individual athlete falls out of competition—whether by choice or not—the loss exists. And it is that loss that preempts the depression and anxiety that the retired athlete can fall into. Unfortunately, the most acute—and the most devastating—symptom of depression and anxiety is suicidal thoughts and behaviors. This, of course, is the darkest mental health phenomena in the retired athlete. And don't be fooled: suicide is not a phenomena in and of itself.

As the American Foundation for Suicide Prevention suggests, it is one of the leading mental health crises America faces and the tenth leading cause of death in the United States.[18] Additionally, a higher risk of suicide has been found to follow loss of the athletic identity. In 2011, Fox Sports reported an interview with Dr. Judy L. Van Raalte from Springfield College in Massachusetts, regarding the correlation between the loss of athlete identity, ensuing depression, and suicide. Citing a 2009 study titled *The Athlete Versus the Jock*,[19] she discusses the difference between the "athlete" identity and the "jock" identity. In this study, "athletes" are identified as athletes who have positive mental health outcomes deriving from their involvement in sports, while "jocks" are identified as athletes whose athletic identities promote riskier behavior. Speaking with Fox Sports, Dr. Van Raalte stated that the "[a]thlete identity was associated with a decreased risk of suicide attempts, whereas jock identity was associated with an increased risk of suicide attempts."[20]

Dr. Robert A. Stern at Boston University's Center for the Study of Traumatic Encephalopathy has stated that suicide is one of the most complex human behaviors, and so "it can't just be explained by a specific factor."[21] More unfortunately, its complexity can be rivaled by its prevalence among retired athletes the world over. It seems every year, we hear about another retired athlete taking his or her life. Junior Seau was probably the most famous. But we've also heard about National Hockey League vet Todd Ewen, who took his life in 2015. Dave Duerson and Kenny McKinley. One of the most shocking incidents was in 2012 because coaches were literally faced with a suicidal player in Kansas City.

In 2012, Kansas City Chiefs linebacker Javon Belcher killed his girlfriend in their home before jumping into a car and driving to the Chiefs practice facility. Once there, he called out Chiefs general manager Scott Pioli, then-head coach Romeo Crennel and linebackers coach Gary Biggs to the parking lot where he shot himself in the head in front of them.[22] Pioli later told investigators that with the gun to his head, Belcher had told them,

> You know that I've been having some major problems at home and with my girlfriend. I need help! I wasn't able to get enough help. I appreciate everything you all have done for me with trying to help . . . but it wasn't enough. I have hurt my girl already and I can't go back now.[23]

Statistics website Sports Reference lists Olympians known to have committed suicide. Not all are due to mental illness, but many entries simply say "committed suicide" with no further explanation, the implication clear that *something* was going on.[24] In 2012, Russian judo champion Elena Ivashchenko, at only 28 years old, jumped from the fifteenth floor of her apartment after months of depression following the 2012 Olympic Games in London. Russian judo authorities said that despite the fact that she was a four-time champion at the European championships, her depression started when she failed to medal at the games, being eliminated in the quarterfinals.[25]

The loss of identity is often accompanied by loss of focus, lack of adequate feedback and positive reinforcement, and a general sense of melancholy. As boxing legend Sugar Ray Leonard said, "Nothing could satisfy me outside the ring. There is nothing in life that can compare to becoming a world champion, having your hand raised in that moment of glory, with thousands, millions of people cheering you on."[26] But more than that is the emotional shock accompanying the feeling that your life has peaked by the time you are 25 or 30 years old.

Part of the loss is losing your routine and, with it, your motivation. As NFL quarterback Trent Green says "I knew exactly what I was doing in March, June and September because there was a schedule. When you take that away, you suddenly have a lot more time on your hands. I've been out of the game since 2008, and I still have a tough time with it. I find myself thinking, 'What's my motivation today?'"[27] Part of it is losing the camaraderie. Former linebacker George Koonce said that "[w]hen I left the game and I was waiting for that phone call that never came, that's when things started to get blurry. It's even harder because you feel like you've got nobody to talk to."[28] I can't even imagine the feeling for college athletes and professional athletes retiring today who feel they cannot talk to any of their colleagues about their feelings. Maybe things move at such a pace that you don't even know that you are feeling that sense of loss, so it is harder to articulate.

A recent study at the University of Pittsburgh School of Medicine revealed that people who use social media frequently have more than double the likelihood of depression as those who do not use social media. I know for me, I can get into a toxic scroll where I will zone out and not even know that hours have passed.

And in our world, social media is a *huge* tool for athletes to connect with their fans and to be able to express themselves. And each platform is monetized.

According to the study, "highly idealized representations of peers on social media elicit {} feelings of envy and the distorted belief that others lead happier, more successful lives."[29] When I was forced out of volleyball, Facebook was still fairly new, and nobody knew how to Insta or Tweet yet. (Yet alone TikTok) But for today's athletes, who likely follow their former teammates, friends and maybe even coaches online, to get constant reminders of life on the field and on the court? To be reminded that the game has moved on without them on a push-button basis? I can only imagine how much tougher that makes the transition today than it did only a decade ago when I transitioned off the Cliff.

But at the end of the day, the depression and anxiety the retired athlete suffers from returns to the idea that their best years are behind them. Roman Oben, another NFL veteran, would likely say the Cliff is especially hard "because they [athletes] spend the rest of their lives being shadows of who they were"[30] at their peak: the Hollywood stereotype of the high school quarterback who still wears his letter jacket twenty years after graduating. The collegiate baseball player who can't seem to have fun on his employer's softball team. (Or takes it too seriously)

Too often, the loss of that identity manifests itself in feelings of inadequacy or an emotional void that cannot be filled. Feelings of helplessness can then fill in and lead to awful, destructive behaviors. Our athletes deserve better access to resources and inclusive community building events in their later years and in the immediate years after their retirement.

SUBSTANCE ABUSE

In 2009, former NFL defensive tackle Sam Rayburn was arrested for engaging in fraudulent behavior in order to illegally obtain Percocet and Lortab, both addictive painkillers.[31] In 2016, former NFL quarterback Ryan Leaf was released from prison after landing there due to an addiction to oxycodone.[32] Baseball legends Mickey Mantle and Babe Ruth drank and smoked their way into the Hall of Fame.[33] But substance abuse is not limited to superstars and Olympians. Without regard to social class, ethnicity or geography, the Drug Enforcement Agency and Center for Disease Control have noticed a "growing concentration" of drug—and especially opioid abuse—"in an unlikely subset of users: young athletes" of high school age.[34]

Unfortunately, substance abuse—sometimes more aptly called self-medication—is ubiquitous in the sports community. It can take one or both of the following forms: addiction and dependency. The National Institute of Health and the National Institute on Drug Abuse define addiction as compulsive drug use despite harmful consequences.[35] Addiction is commonly characterized by the inability to stop using a substance, failure to meet work, social or family obligations and, depending on the drug, tolerance and withdrawal. Substance dependence, on the other hand, occurs when the body physically adapts to a particular drug and requires more of it to achieve a certain effect (obtaining drug tolerance) and eliciting drug-specific physical or mental symptoms when the use of the substance is abruptly ceased (going through withdrawal). Addiction and dependency can occur simultaneously and both are signs of long-term drug use and, ultimately, abuse.

There is a long and strong history of the relationship between athletic life and drug abuse at all levels, across all sports, and for all numbers of reasons including self-treatment of untreated mental illness and dealing with stress and anxiety such as pressure to perform, injuries, physical pain and retirement.[36] Oftentimes, drug and substance abuse occurs during the career of the elite athlete, and can begin any number of ways. For some athletes, it is performance-enhancing drugs meant to push them to the next level. For others, it may be pain management drugs meant to keep them from sliding. For many athletes like Leaf, it begins with a simple injury requiring painkillers of some kind. In his case, he had his first taste of Vicodin when he was a 19-year-old quarterback coming back from surgery for a dislocated shoulder.[37] However, after only a four-year stint in the NFL, his addiction to painkillers continued despite the fact that the physical injuries of this once highly-touted player ceased occurring. As he puts it, Leaf "was an addict long before [he] ever took a drug. Perfectionism, competition, fame early on from the small town I was in . . . I didn't know how to deal with real life issues the right way as a humble human being."[38] Unfortunately, Leaf's story is all too familiar to the retired athlete.

Athletes too easily can become dependent on pain management drugs when returning from an injury. But even the most common drugs are used for their most common purpose throughout athletics: to take the edge off. For the retired athlete, the pain being managed may be not only the nagging injury, but the fresh wound of depression related to loss of their sport. Some turn to alcohol and other drugs as a coping mechanism and a means of escaping feelings of loss of identity, depression and anxiety common after retirement. Some studies even suggest that active athletes are at a higher risk of depression and addiction than the general public due to hardcore training regimens.

Some researchers believe that the intense physical activity engaged in by athletes during their prime years generates a chemical reaction in the body that primes them for addiction later in life. Endorphins and other chemicals released into the body and bloodstream of the elite level athlete can have the same addictive impact on the body as such highly-addictive opioids such as heroin.[39] Sometimes called the "runner's high" or "exercise dependence," the sudden stopping of training and movement that the body gets put through creates a void of chemicals on which the body has become dependent for balance.[40] In order for retired athletes to replace those chemicals without engaging in the physical activity to which they have become accustomed, they turn toward artificial means of getting those high-producing chemicals into their systems.

Frances Quirk, of the journal Performance Enhancement and Health, cites several studies that suggest that high-intensity physical training can produce chemical reactions that are as addictive as heroin. As he puts it, "a lot of retired athletes report fairly significant mental health concerns and an increased level of substance dependence" from the general population. As he states, "there are other factors that contribute to that in terms of pressure, isolation and competition, but there is a biological story" to the substance abuse as well.[41] Substance abuse is one of the leading mental health crises among retired athletes, and will continue to be as athletes use it to mask their depression and other issues related to their retirement.

SOCIAL STIGMA AND NON-REPORTING

Unfortunately, one characteristic of mental health issues for high-level athletes is the level to which they succumb to stigma regarding various issues. In 2013, Dr. Eugene Hong, team physician for Drexel University and U.S. Lacrosse, reported in the Philadelphia Inquirer that in a survey of over 800 sports medicine physicians, over 80 percent discuss psychological issues with their athlete patients regarding issues stemming from injury.[42] However, studies have demonstrated that athletes are less likely than the general population to report having received professional help for psychological and mental health issues.[43]

The question, of course, is why is this? One word: stigmatization. For decades leading up to the new millennium, social stigma of what we recognize today as common mental health issues was rampant across our culture. People suffering from anxiety disorders were described as "weird." People with depression were simply told to "get over it" and that "happiness is a choice." People with eating disorders were labeled "vain" (in the case of people suffering from anorexia nervosa or bulimia) or "undisciplined" (in the case of people suffering from compulsive overeating). And alcoholism—among other substance abuse issues was at one time described by many as simply a lifestyle or cultural hallmark as opposed to a biochemical dependency issue. While strides have been made to dispel these myths, the stigmatization of "mental illness" continues, especially in the sporting realm.

Mental health issues ought to be described as overall health and wellness issues no less than suffering from a sprained ankle or an ACL tear. Some steps have been taken. Famously, in 2010, Metta World Peace (neé Ron Artest) opened the door to finally changing the perception when he thanked his psychiatrist after winning the NBA World Championship with the Los Angeles Lakers. Unfortunately, the reason for the stigma arises out of the very nature of sports themselves. While Metta opened that door in a positive way, too often the dark side of mental illness in athletes crops up every time we hear about the most tragic cases such as

Junior Seau's suicide and the throngs of concussion-induced trauma suffered by NFL players and, increasingly, athletes in other contact sports.[44] And in 2017, ESPN columnist Kate Fagan published her work *What Made Maddy Run*, about the battles that University of Pennsylvania track athlete Madison Halleran fought against depression and anxiety before tragically taking her life. Furthermore, most of the research focuses on active athletes, or those who have suffered from traumatic injury like CTE. There is little research on the less devastating, yet entirely more common cases of depression that affect our athletes—both active *and* retired on a daily basis.

Despite the fact that the social stigma of wellness issues related to mental health has lessened over time with better research, there still exist misperceptions and myths about mental health issues as they relate to elite athletes. Part of the stigma that athletes face comes from fans who may perceive their favorite players as "super" men and women. Worse, they *expect* their favorite players to be super men and women. And, in efforts to live up to those expectations, athletes choose to forego seeking help that would be perceived as tarnishing that reputation. Part of the stigma comes from more internal sources like teammates, colleagues and coaches, that mental health issues are a "weakness," which is anathema to the "mental toughness" mantra repeated by coaches, teammates and even parents from the time that elite level athletes are children.

In her book, Fagan opines on the way in which mental health concerns are hidden or shunned in the sports community—both by those suffering and those who coach the suffering. As Fagan tells it, she was connected with an off-campus counselor by one of her trainers while she played basketball at the University of Colorado at Boulder:

> I was embarrassed about having to see someone. I told no one I was doing this. felt weak. The saving grace was that I was spared the discomfort—unfortunately, that's how it would have felt to me then—of walking across campus and into the building that housed counseling services. Everything I did, except for attending classes, was within the silo of the athletic department: lift, practice, study, train, eat—even worship. This was my safe space, my comfort zone. And guess what? There was no counseling center, no psychologist's office, within the athletic department building. The clear message: needing a psychologist is abnormal.[45]

Fagan completes the thought that all elite athletes—whether in high school, AAU ball, college and perhaps, especially, the pros—would ask themselves under similar circumstances: "How could an athlete with a mental health issue not feel like an outsider when she was literally forced out of the athletic department and pointed toward a building far away from campus and the athletic bubble?"[46] The obvious answer, of course, is that the athlete could not overcome those feelings. To be "weird" or "weak" is the greatest attack that any athlete—active or retired—could ever feel the need to defend against.

Unfortunately, most athletes view depression, anxiety and other mental health issues as an inherent weakness instead of as any other type of injury. Many athletes believe that they have the ability to overcome mental health issues on their own, as they might have a sprained ankle. In 2013, Dr. Ira Glick at Stanford University School of Medicine, recognized this and said that athletes "believe nothing can go wrong, they don't need help, they can overcome. And just for that alone, they don't want to go to therapy either for psychotherapy or medication."[47] Unfortunately, depression is often espoused as the "silent killer" or a "quiet epidemic" in this nation. Athletes do not realize that it *is* treatable, but it is more akin to that torn ACL which requires professional help to fix, than it is a sprained ankle which can be done away with ice, aspirin and a day away from practice. These efforts to remain "strong"—even in retirement, to continue to be the "superman" or "superwoman" that the fans remember—can overcome the common sense approach. As Fagan says, we—as society and the sporting community—"have little sympathy for injuries we cannot see and we cannot touch."[48]

Interestingly, popular culture is beginning to speak out more and more about mental wellness concerns in the sports community. The publicity from the public deaths and suicides of fan-favorite star athletes has led to people becoming much more aware of the issues, which has been a catalyst to combatting the stigma in hopes of championing the treatment of such issues as health and wellness issues instead of as weakness or attacks on masculinity or efficacy. Even the fictional world is beginning to address these issues. Or at least the stigma, if not the issues themselves.

For instance, USA Network's series *Necessary Roughness* ran for three seasons and followed a psychotherapist working with active players on a fictional football team.[49] More recently, in the 2017 season of the HBO series *Ballers*, a star NFL wide receiver is portrayed as dealing not only with his own mental health issues including anxiety, but also dealing with the stigma that he believes others carry for such issues;

eventually being mollified by his father's revelation that he—as a retired player—suffers from mental health issues, and that his son should not be afraid of dealing with them. Despite the need for our athletes, fans and coaches to avoid fictionalized and highly dramatic accounts of sudden breakthroughs as normal (these are, after all, television shows and not real science), I like the portrayals because they defy the notion for the public at large that just because an athlete suffers from mental health issues, something must be fundamentally wrong. Treatment is much more complex than is typically portrayed, but getting our athletes to at least admit that they may be suffering is the first and most important step.

These fears are the problem and need to be addressed more socially throughout the sports industry. For the retired athlete, suffering from mental health issues including—but certainly not limited to—depression, anxiety, feelings of inadequacy and loss and substance abuse need to be reported, need to be discussed, and ultimately need to be shown that they are not unique to any particular athlete but common to most. Only in this way can our retired athletes stay on a healthy path and maintain a positive athletic mindset for the decades of their life after their last competition ends.

Creating safe places for athletes, current and retired, to address their mental health is key in creating this new world that celebrates and focuses on the entirety of the athlete.

MIND. BODY. SPIRIT.

10
The Cliff
Physical Health

Once retired, I initially watched a lot of TV, gaining four dress
sizes on my five foot frame. It was very disheartening
but it helped me realize I had to find my next passion in life.

—SHANNON MILLER,
Olympic Gymnast[1]

The third part of the Cliff is when athletes fail to change their physical habits and routines. What I am talking about is, of course, diet and exercise. This likely seems like the most obvious way in which athletes fall off the Cliff because it is the most tangible. And by tangible, what I mean is that retired athletes have a common experience of waking up one day to find that they have put on a few pounds and are a little softer around the midsection. However, the physical wellness aspect of the Cliff is deeply intertwined with both the identity and mental wellness aspects of the Cliff and can be more complex for the athlete coming down off the Athletic Mountain than most people realize.

THE OBVIOUS

When Michael Jordan retired from basketball in 1998, he jumped from 212 pounds to roughly 240 pounds. Hockey player Mario Lemieux reportedly gained 25 pounds during a two-year hiatus from the National

Hockey League. Charles Barkley, who had already been dubbed "The Round Mound of Rebound" at the peak of his NBA career, weighed in at over 337 pounds during a televised weigh-in in 2001, 70 pounds over his playing weight.[2] But the big guys aren't the only ones having issues. Even the trimmest athletes become known for their weight gain after retiring. American gymnast Shawn Johnson won gold at the Summer Olympic Games in Beijing in 2008. But soon after, she became a target for body shaming after gaining twenty pounds.[3] Twenty pounds may not be a lot to a six and a half foot basketball player like Michael Jordan, but as Johnson tells it, "being 4' 11" and putting on 20 pounds looks like a lot."[4] As she recalls, she went "from this strict, regimented schedule to going through puberty on TV [*Dancing With The Stars*] and gaining weight," which is when she became "a huge target for criticism."[5] After putting on 20 pounds she returned to the gym, but realized she was at a loss. Her entire career had been so regimented that she did not know how to exercise on her own. While not as petite as Johnson ever was, I knew my fair share of athletes who had similar issues after they retired. *I am one of them!*

Often the reason for this is intertwined with the loss of identity. And it can be not only a symptom of depression or other mental health issues, but it can also be a cause and influence on depression and other mental health issues. In other words, while the athlete's physical health issues after retirement may seem simple, there are often more complex issues lying beneath the surface that the general population does not deal with on a daily basis.

The most important thing to consider about the athlete's fall off the Cliff as it relates to their physical health is that it is *not* based on bad habits. I identify "bad" habits as eating without purpose: overeating and junk food, even when you know better or don't have a reason to eat like that. I identify a "bad" habit as not exercising enough or correctly. But they are "bad" because they are reflective of a lifestyle that was *always* unhealthy based on physical needs and purposes. In other words, eating thousands and thousands of calories is not a "bad" habit when those calories are needed to perform. It only becomes a "bad" habit when it is no longer necessary for the lifestyle the athlete lives at the present.

Athletes, and especially those coming out of the most elite levels, often retain the same habits from their competitive days. Instead, the athlete's fall off of the Cliff physically is based on the athlete failing to adapt to their new lifestyle. What may have been "healthy" given their objectives to score points and win games may not be healthy when the objective is to make sure that your body will support you for the next fifty years of their lives.

During their peak playing days, an Olympic swimmer like Michael Phelps might pack away 12,000 calories *because* he needed the fuel to perform in the pool. An offensive lineman might not have any qualms about eating pounds of pasta and steak every day *because* he needed the weight to do his job. A professional soccer player might not be used to lifting weights every day because she needed to focus on agility instead of strength in her position. A high school swimmer might not know the proper posture for jogging because his sport never involved running.

Upon retirement, the athlete's lifestyle changes immediately. Their physical needs evolve instantly from being performance-purposed to being wellness-purposed. However, their habits and their mindset may still be performance-purposed because a mindset takes longer to change than a lifestyle. Even worse, they may not change their diet and exercise habits because they've never known anything *other than* a performance-purposed diet and exercise plan, and they are filled with uncertainty and myths about what they need to do for their bodies once they are no longer eating and exercising in order to score points and win games.

EXERCISE AND PHYSICAL ACTIVITY

As athletes, we don't know what we don't know. While we are climbing the Athletic Mountain, there is no way for us to fully understand what life will be like once we fall off the Cliff. And in one of the most tangible and immediate ways that we feel that is in the immediate change to our daily physical regime.

Anyone else deeply relate to sitting behind a computer 8-10 hours of the day? (Many times it can be 14+ hours on bad days)

In 2014, Shawn Sorenson, a health and exercise researcher at the University of Southern California, posed the following question:

> Twenty years from now, who's more likely to be a regular, healthy exerciser? A) The all-American athlete, with the ripped physique, seemingly infinite endurance, superhuman strength and supremely tuned agility? Or B) The decidedly less-impressive specimen sitting in the bleachers?[6]

If you've read the other chapters in this book so far, you can probably guess what his response was. Sorenson and his colleagues discovered that all alumni—regardless whether they played sports in college or not—reported the same average of five hours of exercise per week, and the same type of exercise: mostly cardio.[7] Worse to discover, among all alumni—including former elite college athletes—only forty percent met healthy exercise guideline ranges. In Sorenson's words, "former jocks were just as likely to become couch potatoes" as the average Joes and non-athletes that once cheered them on from the stands.[8] But why is this?

For the elite athlete, even at the high school level, daily workouts are crafted by our coaches and trainers. Furthermore, our workouts are developed for one purpose: to make us better at our sport. In other words, athletes do not exercise. Athletes *train*! But what's the difference? Exercise is movement for the sake of movement. Or, alternatively, for the instant gratification of feeling that burn, and that "runner's high." And there is nothing wrong with exercise. Millions of Americans exercise every day. But exercising can be for fleeting and weak reasons that don't motivate long-term devotion to getting out of bed and moving every day. Weight loss is a common motivator. But if the person doesn't see results right away, or if he or she reaches a point when they stop seeing results, the motivation to continue goes away. The opposite side of the spectrum for many people is the ambiguous desire to "gain muscle," which carries the same risk of short-term adherence if results are not immediately produced. For the retired athlete—whether recently or decades ago—sometimes they feel that they need to engage in physical activity only because they are "supposed to." For a retired athlete, the feeling that they are just *exercising* is one hundred and eighty degrees opposite from the mindset that they have spent years developing. For former collegiate hurdler Frank Miller, Jr. his "biggest challenge is exercising with no clear goal:"[9]

> Being healthy in general isn't enough to motivate me. I need a ball to chase and a score of some kind. I get bored without a semi-immediate reward.[10]

Tim Conley, a former offensive lineman at the University of Oklahoma and the NFL, recognizes that "for most former athletes, the sole motivation to exercise is their sport. Once that is done, the motivation ends. It becomes, 'What am I training for?'"[11] What could be more de-motivating for the high-level athlete than going from the gym because it feeds the passion . . . to going to the gym because you feel *obligated*?

But Conley hits the nail on the head without really knowing it. Once an athlete's sport is done, he may not be training. He may just be exercising. But therein lies the problem. Athletes are used to training—not just exercising. Training requires something more, both outwardly and inwardly. Training requires structuring workouts in order to achieve a specific, articulable goal and athletic (or at least physical) achievement. Baseball players lift weights trying to get an extra ten feet off of their slugging. When the ball goes that far, they restructure their workout to get another ten feet. A soccer player does yoga to improve freedom of movement in her core to react more quickly to fast changes of the ball. A tennis player does Pilates to increase core strength. For every active athlete, their workouts are performance-purposed—they are designed to win games, matches and races. And when I say designed, I really mean in a "research and development," scientific way. This means that coaches and trainers are creating not just practices and training regimens, but in a bigger sense they are crafting entire routines for the athlete. The athlete does not need to think about what he or she is going to do on any given day, because the coach has already done that. The coach has already created the structure of the day for them. And this is the biggest hurdle as it relates to physical exercise that the athlete runs into after they retire. Their physical activity must evolve from being performance-purposed to wellness-purposed.

Dr. Shawn Sorenson is a health and exercise researcher at the University of Southern California in Los Angeles. Over the last several years, he has collected stories from now-retired collegiate athletes about the mental block athletes run into when they suddenly realize they have no more structure created for them. It starts in youth sports, as Jennifer Lushao, a former Rice University swimmer, explains to Dr. Sorenson: "There's a routine and a lifestyle that you've built around this sport when you've been involved with it since elementary school. It just kind of dominates your life physically, mentally and emotionally."[12] But more than *having* the routine is that the athlete rarely has to be concerned with *what* the routine is, or *how* the routine is decided because everybody else is handling that for you.

Parents handle practices and coordinate travel in youth sports. In high school, suddenly coaches, parents and boosters are handling the logistics. In addition to having your practices, you have a regular school schedule that you will need to follow. In college, former USC swimmer Amanda Smith explains that "[e]verything is totally planned out for you—class scheduling, practice hours, tutoring. I am the kind of person who thrived as an athlete because I did great with structure."[13] Same goes for the professionals and Olympians who know when they have to be at practice, when they have to be in the weight room, and when they need to be on the bus to the airport.

However, once the athlete retires and falls off that Cliff, they may not realize that they are also losing a lot of the support that got them up the Mountain in the first place by providing that structure. At first, this can seem like a burden being lifted or even a sense of liberation. Swimmer Lushao explains:

> You literally go overnight from being required to be somewhere doing strenuous, structured physical activity over 20 hours a week to having absolutely no obligations to do anything physical whatsoever. The freedom was really mind-blowing. Sleeping in instead of going to a workout at 6 a.m. for the first time I was 11 was such a novelty.[14]

But this "new normal" can create a false sense of security in the retired athlete, at least as to their long-term physical wellbeing. It can be too easy to believe that because you have been an athlete—"a specimen" of the human animal, perceived as being the epitome of physically healthy by the rest of society—that you will *always* be that healthy. Physical wellness diminishes over time—not overnight. This, of course, is an awful fallacy, especially considering that many athletes *aren't* objectively healthy during their peak playing days, but merely fit a physical profile that is necessary for them to do their jobs. And often, that profile includes packing in the calories.

DIET

The Fastest Man Alive, Usain Bolt, famously fueled his 2008 Olympic performance by consuming over 47,000 calories worth of McDonald's Chicken McNuggets during the Games, an average of 5,500 calories per day. J.J. Watt loads up on 9,000 calories worth of sweet potatoes, avocadoes and stuffed French toast in order to be one of the best defensive linemen in the NFL. And Michael Phelps famously sparked the "Michael Phelps Challenge" when his 12,000 calories-per-day diet went viral while he was training for the 2008 Beijing Olympics.[15] Even Olympic table tennis players have to pack it in, burning anywhere between 2500 and 3500 calories per day during training and competition.[16] Probably the most obvious way that the climb up the Mountain makes for a longer fall off the Cliff later is maintaining high-calorie performance-purposed dietary habits even after the athlete's physical lifestyle has already and immediately entered into the wellness-purposed phase.

The most obvious way that life changes for the athlete after retirement is the move from an active to sedentary lifestyle. Lisa Talamini, director of nutrition and program development at Jenny Craig, explains:

> What happens to the athlete is not that different than what happens to a lot of people. . . . Maybe a few years ago they were more active, burning more calories on a daily basis. Now they're sitting in front of their computers at work. . . . [For an athlete], it just happens over a faster period with a larger number of calories.[17]

What is more insidious is just how slowly the bulk can arise. As Jeff Kotterman of the National Association of Sports Nutrition explains, "[a]t first, the body can handle that huge energy surplus, because it's still expecting to exercise. But after a while, even for the most gifted athletes, that extra dessert or fatty food is no longer dealt with the same way."[18]

For people ending competition after youth sports and high school sports, this change often takes the form of spending time at a desk doing schoolwork. For athletes retiring after collegiate and professional or Olympic careers, this often takes the form of entering the workforce and spending time at a desk doing the work that millions of Americans engage in, from running their own businesses, to selling insurance, to data entry. That change in physical activity is often not accompanied by a change in diet activity which has added to the overall physical health crises in the United States. Some health risks are likely unsurprising given the sport that certain athletes played during their competitive days. The most obvious—and probably the most researched—group I am thinking of is, of course, football players.

In 2013, a survey of current and former NFL players revealed that over 95 percent of all football players were "overweight." Over 56 percent were "obese."[19] Unfortunately, this is a problem that few in the sports industry are willing to accept as a systemic problem. Writing for The Daily Beast in 2014, Evin Demirel explains:

> Powerful sports entities like the NFL and the Southeastern Conference aren't shying away from obesity as an issue. But they want to confront it

on their own terms, framing it as only something they are helping society tackle rather than a problem they have also played a role in perpetuating. The NFL, for instance, has a fitness campaign designed to address childhood obesity. And researchers, doctors and professors affiliated with SEC schools recently convened to 'identify ways to markedly reduce America's obese and overweight populations through prevention,' as the SEC Symposium press release specified. These efforts are good and wide-reaching, but they don't address obesity treatment and the 'deconditioning' many former players need.[20]

Clearly, there is a problem in the culture that is setting up our athletes to fall off the Cliff harder as it relates to their diet. I don't mean to point shade directly at institutions, rather it is important to point out that society as a whole can do more. SEC and NFL (and all entities) I would love to see you take the efforts you have already made and take them further. Maybe a community bike ride? (More on that later . . . wink wink)

Athletic football players, though, aren't the only ones that are struggling. For many athletes at many places up the Mountain when their competitive journey finally ended, they are waking up months and years later to find their belts tightening. Chris Doemland was a former standout high school and college swimmer who woke up less than ten years after his last competitive meet to discover that he was pre-diabetic. It had happened slowly, not noticing as one extra pound turned into five extra pounds, then twenty extra pounds, then even more.[21] Lori Harrigan-Mack, an Olympian and three-time gold medalist with the U.S. Softball team ballooned up to 301 pounds after retiring in 2004. Mike Murburg, a former Princeton University wrestler, was almost 400 pounds at 58 years old. And at only 32 years old, former SEC Defensive Player of the Year and former WNBA player Vanessa Hayden weighed in at 366 pounds a mere three years after ending her career with the Los Angeles Spark. All three shared their stories on the 2014 season of *Biggest Loser*.[22] And every athlete who suffers becomes just one more health statistic suffering from the diseases that unfortunately accompany obesity such as diabetes, high blood pressure, high cholesterol, arthritis, sleep apnea and other ailments that make for a shorter, more painful life.

But then there is the other extreme of the athletic diet that many people don't consider as creating a horrible experience of falling off the Cliff later. That other side is the "light-weight" side, where the diet of the elite athlete is still performance-purposed. However, unlike football which often depends on sheer mass and strength, or running or swimming which rely on massive bursts of speed to be fueled, other sports rely on a *slight* diet. Consider gymnastics. In order for athletes like Shawn Johnson, Simone Biles and Aly Raisman to launch themselves into the air, to flip and twist and land, every ounce of body weight makes it harder to get airborne, harder to rotate the body, and harder on the landing. The same goes for sports like figure skating, competitive cheerleading and synchronized swimming. But worse than that, the ability to be a champion—to fulfill that athletic purpose—can also be judged by body types and diets during the peak performance period.

Consider this: sports like football, basketball, baseball, volleyball, swimming, sprinting and any number of other sports determine who wins and who loses by objective criteria—who scores the most points, or who runs the fastest, or who jumps the furthest. In sports like gymnastics, figure skating, cheerleading and many others, however, winners and losers are chosen by judges whose motives can be fairly influenced by technical proficiency, but also unfairly by things such as an otherwise-champion caliber gymnast's body type or look. After speaking with Johnson about her retirement, sports writer Dvora Meyers noted the characterization of the rivalry between Johnson and her teammate, Nastia Liukin right down to their body types:

> It was a rivalry characterized in terms of darkness versus light, force versus grace, a 'little ball of power,' as The New York Times put it, versus 'the flexibility of a prima ballerina.' Jock versus artist.[23]

Olympic gold medalist Dominique Dawes confirmed Johnson's critique: "Internationally, there still remains a stigma to that type of body type."[24] Athletes in these sports can sometimes feel pressure to obtain and maintain a particular "look" that—fairly or not—can be the difference between the podium and going home empty handed. As Johnson put it, during her training for the 2008 Olympics, she was only consuming about 700 calories per day: "I went as far as literally not eating any carbs. I wouldn't allow myself to eat a single noodle of soup. It got to the point where my body was like, shutting down."[25] The point, of course, is that during the climb up the Mountain, diet—as much as physical activity—is structured and designed for a performance purpose. And just like liberation from highly-structured physical activity, liberation from highly-structured eating habits can lead to long falls off the Cliff upon retirement.

Unfortunately, the habits that get developed during the performance-purpose years can often develop into poor activity and diet habits, if not straight-up eating disorders, *during* those years which then follows them through retirement. In 2011, Becci Twombley, then-director of sports nutrition at UCLA, reported that she would receive 15 to 20 calls per year from former athletes needing nutritional advice because they were struggling with clinical eating disorders such as anorexia and bulimia.[26] Compare that to Penn State's former director of sports nutrition, Kristine Clark, who told Sports Illustrated in 2009 that she would get "e-mail from former players five or six years after they've left saying, 'I'm in trouble. Please help me. I am prediabetic or my cholesterol is very high.'"[27] When I went to visit Andrea Hudy, the renowned strength and conditioning coach at the University of Kansas (now back at UConn), she told me that she has a regular only-half-joke with the outgoing basketball players each year: "Call me when your pants are too tight!" And to her credit, she has followed through whenever she has gotten the inevitable call from her former players. It's not in her job description to care, but she—and others like Twombley and Clark—do their best to make their former players a priority. This can be difficult, however, when they are in the midst of a season with post-season and championship aspirations for their current athletes.

This aspect of the Cliff requires helping athletes retrain their minds and bodies to begin living on a healthy, daily wellness-purposed diet. For the "big guys," this often can mean cutting down on total calories, carbohydrates and red meat after they retire because they don't need that much caloric intake to fuel their bodies anymore. For other athletes, like gymnasts, it can mean finally easing up on the uber-restrictive diets that they have been used to that were designed to keep them petite and in "flying" condition. The performance-purposed diet—whether it was expansive or restrictive—must often give way to a much more middle-of-the-road diet that promotes life-long wellness routines *and* permits them to indulge in a manner consistent with their friends, colleagues and family.

THE ALL-AMERICAN SELF

But perhaps one of the biggest hurdles for the retired athlete as it relates to the physical health fall off the Cliff is getting out of their own way emotionally and mentally. Yes, like I said at the beginning of this chapter, the other two aspects of the Cliff—Athletic Identity and Mental Wellness—are both fully entwined with the fall related to physical wellness. Too often I have seen my friends and former teammates be paralyzed by fear and embarrassment that keeps them out of the gym. I am not ashamed to admit today that in the past I have been ashamed that I am no longer the athlete that I once was. I've been embarrassed in the past that I no longer look like the athlete I once was. Those feelings have at times made my fall off the Cliff as it relates to my physical wellness harder than it had to be.

Here is the scenario. Maybe the athlete has just started her first job after college, mere months (maybe even weeks) after winning a conference or national championship. Or maybe the athlete got up, looked in the mirror and realized just how much weight he's put on in the last fifteen years since playing in his last professional game. Either way, it's time to get back into the gym because that's what athletes do. But there's not really a trainer that they know. The people that used to look after them have long since moved on to the latest bunch of athletes looking to the next season. They'll email you links to a couple of websites that might help when they get back into the offices later in the week. They'll give you the names of some personal trainers.

So, the athletes end up going to their local gym. Maybe it's one of the big, fancy gyms with lots of amenities and black card-style fringe benefits. Maybe it's the YMCA closest to the office. They walk into what should be "their" domain. But nobody recognizes them. There is no banter in the locker room. They walk out and see machine after machine. They don't really have a plan—just a vague feeling that *something* needs to happen. As a warm-up, they might pick a treadmill or maybe head over to the free weights. For the next hour, nobody recognizes them. Nobody is coaching them. And instead of working out next to teammates and with some of the greatest elites in sports, they are stuck between the old man lifting fifteen pounders and the woman with the muffin top barely using the treadmill as she tries to get rid of her baby weight or just get her body beach-ready for the summer.

Some athletes feel a sense of shame or embarrassment at this point. They can't help but feel lost. No more of the structure that came with playing elite and competitive sports. No coaches or trainers to guide them. And to be lost in an environment which society suggests they should already have a mastery of. Some athletes feel a sense of shame or embarrassment because they feel like they *shouldn't* be here—this is not their place. They belong next to the best athletes in the land—not old men and chubby beach bunnies. And for other athletes, the fact that they are in this position to begin with may be embarrassing for them as they look in the mirror when they are in their 30s, 40s and older and compare themselves to their 21-year-old selves who may have been state champion basketball players, All-American running backs, and World Series champions. At the end of the day, these are mental and emotional hang-ups that too often can prevent the athlete from easing his or her fall off the physical wellness part of the Cliff. It is clear that our sports industries are failing to give our athletes the tools to help them after the graduate or after their last game or after their last medal. This part of the fall off the Cliff can be shortened and the impact softened, but it requires a greater care on the part of the biggest players in the sports industry. Not every retired athlete has the knowledge, ability or resources to forge their own path from living a performance-purposed lifestyle to living a wellness-purposed lifestyle. Some of them don't know what they don't know. What we do know, however, is that from high schools to colleges and into the professional ranks, it is programs and franchises that have the most to gain and from the athletes modifying their bodies, and so they demand much. But just as someone once said, that "to whom much is given, much is required," those being given the fit athlete owe to those same athletes help transitioning from the lifestyle perpetuated by programs and franchises to the lifestyle athletes need for the decades after they have long since left the locker room

ALWAYS AN ATHLETE:

The Next Chapter of Your Life

11
Always an Athlete

Your whole life is sold out to the sport, and then one day it's
taken away. Now you've got to figure out the next plan.

—WALTER BOND,
Retired NBA Player, Motivational Speaker[1]

We're here to serve our players,
to care for them, to love them.

—DABO SWINNEY,
Clemson University Football Coach[2]

Loss of identity. Depression. Anxiety. Substance abuse. Obesity. Diabetes. The Cliff and the athlete's transition from living a performance-purposed life to living a wellness-purposed life is fraught with potential landmines. For the reasons laid out above, it is important to help our athletes develop strategies and discover healthy mechanisms and options to guide them off the Cliff in a manner that does not give them such a rude awakening on its impact. Or in many cases give the athlete the helpful information, community and mentorship once they realize that they are struggling with the transition, however many years out from retiring from competition.

THE THREE PILLARS OF THE ALWAYS
AN ATHLETE MINDSET

At the end of the day, the Cliff hits each athlete to varying degrees. But it always arises out of the same problem: lack of competition, structure of positive routine and loss of a community we were once so deeply ingrained in our daily life. Some may even feel like they have lost their sense of control and understanding of what to do next with their efforts and new amount of time. For this reason, I want athletes to take that Cliff face and turn it against itself; to turn it instead into columns that will support the weight of their identity, mental wellness and physical wellness for decades after their competitive careers are over. The same way that Michelangelo took marble from the stone cliffs of Carrara to carve columns for temples and masterworks, the modern athlete can take the walls of the Cliff to build the Pillars on which she or he will build their own temple and masterwork of mind and body. In this way, the athlete can conquer the Cliff. Just as the three aspects of the Cliff are *loss* of athletic identity, mental wellness and physical wellness, the Three Pillars of the "Always an Athlete" are made of *healthily* holding onto the athlete identity and promoting mental and physical wellness long after competition ends.

You often will find athletes—friends, family, strangers—who use phrases to describe themselves such as "*ex*-athlete," or "*former* athlete," or "I *used to* be a ——— player." I have personally never understood these types of self-describing phases, because the reality is that being an athlete is so much more than something we *used* to be. If playing a sport was simply something we did—no different than shopping for clothes or playing video games—then using phrases like "ex-athlete" and "former player" would be no more self-deprecating than the person who talks about how they *used to* work in retail. But we know that's not true. The competitive drive lives on deep within us and your experience developing yourself along your journey matters. You moved your body yesterday. You move your body today. Although to differing degrees and levels of intensity, you are still moving- still keeping wellness as part of your journey.

We know it can hurt to use those phrases to describe ourselves (albeit funny in some instances, like washed up water girl or caddy. But worse than that, we lie to ourselves whenever we use words like that because it diminishes that part of our personal story. It is like turning our back on what lit us up, what brought us joy and fulfillment. Perhaps that's why I like an old Marine Corps proverb: "Once a Marine, Always a Marine." Because being a Marine is a lifestyle and a mindset beyond simply a job or occupation that a person does for a few years.

Fun Fact: Olympic "Once an Olympian, Always an Olympian."

I believe the same is true of every athlete. Being "Always an Athlete" means keeping the most important and fundamental pieces of our athletic selves that we developed when our lives were athletically oriented. It means evolving, incorporating and molding our athlete selves with all of the other roles that we will play throughout the rest of our lives. Being "Always an Athlete" means looking to the future while honoring our past. And in order to do this, I believe that athletes need to turn the Cliff on its head by adopting as the Three Pillars of athlete wellness their Identity, their Mental Wellness and their Physical Wellness. Furthermore, these Pillars must be adopted as solutions to the Cliff long before athletes fall off the Cliff, which will place much responsibility on parents, coaches, teammates, administrators and fans to take efforts during their playing days to prevent the fall later.

ATHLETIC IDENTITY PILLAR

Simply defined as "the degree to which an individual identifies with their athletic role,"[3] especially to the exclusion of other roles, athletes must begin building their Athletic Identity Pillar in a healthy way very early in their career. Recall from the Mountain discussing how youth sports has become big business as specialization has occurred with more and more regularity even in the earliest years of an athlete's career. With many athletes today, they are suffering from burnout at an earlier and earlier age because of the focus not only on sports in general, but on exactly one sport. The negative impact of this at an earlier and earlier age is that the athlete engages in role *foreclosure* earlier and earlier. In the period of their lives when athletes ought to be focused on play at its most simple, they are beginning to view their life through one lens: one particular sport. They may be receiving the greatest amount of positive reinforcement from parents based on their play in Pee Wee football and Little League baseball; even more than the positive reinforcement they may receive for doing well on spelling tests and math tests in school. Worse, they may be receiving unfair amounts of negative reinforcement for failure to perform at a young age, *even though* they are excelling in other areas *like* academics. This simply has to be rendered unacceptable because it forms the foundation of loss of identity in later life.

As kids grow up, it is okay to continue to reinforce the athletic identity and to have fun with it. However, it should be reinforced as *one* identity— not the adolescent athlete's sole identity. As kids grow from elementary school age to high school age, they are going through the period of their lives when they are seeking their place in life. Typical activities include exploring interpersonal relationships as they begin dating at that age. They may be open to various other activities as school work includes specialized curriculum during the day, while sports may be relegated to afternoons. They may also explore other extracurricular activities like music, art, other sports, writing, after-school jobs and internships, student government, and any number of other activities. The parent and coach of the high school athlete must be careful not to discourage those other opportunities. In fact, they should be careful when the high school athlete begins to show signs of voluntary role exclusion and encourage them to engage in other activities. At this age, reinforcing a broader series of roles and interests is important to laying a foundation for an athletic career after college and even after a potential professional career.

The point in time when the athletic identity probably takes its strongest hold is through playing intercollegiate athletics. At this level, there can be a direct return-on-investment for the athlete. Specifically, the scholarship and now the NIL (Name Image and Likeness) money that can be made. Likely for the first time, the player is getting compensated for performance on the field and on the court in a very direct way. In order to keep a scholarship (or receive a scholarship, in the case of walk-ons), the athlete must maintain a minimum level of performance. This, of course, carries with it an increasingly large time commitment on the part of the athlete, but the result of putting in that time means that they have less time for other activities and outlets which may help them develop identity roles beyond their athletic role. Even the most obvious role in college sports—"student"—can too easily become a casualty and sacrifice to the athletic role because the college athlete has to embrace the athletic role in order to support themselves as a student, and in order to support their athletic role they have to embrace the student role in order to stay academically eligible to play. This, of course, feeds on itself and in the process of navigating that role-excluding echo chamber, the athlete can too easily become so caught up in *maintaining* those codependent roles that they have no real opportunity to explore and develop other roles. In order to combat this, college coaches and college administrators *must* take a more active role in providing an education to their players while they are still within the structure of the college. Curriculum and activities focusing on preparing student-athletes for the next phase, whether that phase occurs after graduation or after a pro career. (We are working on that!) Universities are in a unique position to do this because they still have their athletes in a "student" phase. This is likely where the greatest impact can be made, and it is incumbent upon the universities to do this. (And why when building this plan to help athletes, we are starting our focused impact at the collegiate level).

Finally, at the professional level, franchises can make better efforts to educate and prepare their players for life after the big leagues as it relates to identity. Perhaps more than at any level, those who make the professional ranks are at the highest risk of identity-foreclosure and having an exclusive athletic identity after retirement. After all, most Americans when faced with the question "who are you" will begin by stating what kind of business they are in: "I'm a lawyer;" "I'm a doctor;" "I'm a librarian;" "I'm a teacher." To not only get paid, but to be dependent on the athletic role to provide for themselves and their families, at this level the athlete will be at the highest risk of role-foreclosure. Fans and owners, managers and coaches can take steps to prevent this by encouraging hobbies outside of sports, by taking interests in their players as people and not merely as objects of adulation until they are put out to pasture. To ask more of our players to be people—not *just* supermen and superwomen—is what is needed.

But what about for the athlete who is about to fall off the Cliff? Or who already has, whether it started ten days ago or ten years ago? This is a tad more difficult because they may have already developed the athletic identity to such a degree that it is difficult to find their way to more. Writing for *The Players' Tribune* (an excellent online media platform founded by Derek Jeter, it publishes all things for athletes, by athletes), former NHL player Sean Avery put it succinctly:

> A lot of guys wish they could get back to where they were but that's the first thing that has to stop. And once you realize that all the things that allowed you to play your sport at the highest level—all the discipline and commitment and perseverance and talent will serve you well after you retire—you're ready to start training for the new season. It's the one called 'the rest of your life.[4]

At its heart, the Always An Athlete movement is about taking the best parts of our athletic identity and figuring out not how to get that back or make it our end-all-be-all, but instead adapting our athletic identity as a single part of our overall identity. To use that inner athlete that lives inside of us that is always ready to compete and have fun. We have to take the things that make us athletes at our core—drive, ambition, competitive fire, love of team—and find ways to embrace them in other pursuits. To be Always An Athlete does not mean giving up our athletic identity. If that were the case, this book would be titled *Never An Athlete Ever Again*! It means that we accept other roles that we may play in life: going to school and becoming a student, opening a business, exploring other potential passions like music or art, picking up *another* sport to become great at, being a father, being a daughter. It means that we continue to find outlets for our athletic identity to come out. **To be Always An Athlete means that we continue to embrace our athletic identity and make it a piece of who we are—not the sum total moving forward.**

In a way, it is like going back to your first game as a kid when you had an *idea* of what a game might have looked like but had yet to experience one for yourself. You might have been scared at the time because it was a new environment, or because you felt some pressure to perform already, or because you didn't want to look like you had no idea whether it was okay to stand on the sidelines or if you needed to sit on the bench regardless of the action on the field. If you're an athlete reading this book, you obviously got past that first game and those jitters. I'm asking you to get past this first step, ignore the jitters, and jump into the uncertainty again with gusto!

MENTAL WELLNESS PILLAR

As a society, we *must* make a concerted effort to educate our athletes from a young age through professional ranks and into retirement that having mental health problems is as serious as, for example, an ACL tear.

In terms of mental health, most athletes "power through" and think that they can face their challenges "alone" on their own, instead of seeking help. At times, some athletes feel embarrassed to admit, acknowledge, and share with others that they are struggling with daily life challenges and pressures. Seeking help and admitting to having problems are not a sign of weakness. Famous sport celebrities such as Simone Biles, Michael Phelps, Kevin Love, and Naomi Osaka are paving the way and putting "mental health" in the spotlight—demystifying the stigma and normalizing that "it's okay to not be okay".[5]

According to *Psychology Today*, a mental health condition is a "diagnosis that involves identifying when people's emotional, cognitive (thoughts), or behavioral reactions interfere with their day-to-day lives and responsibilities [such as] depression, anxiety, post-traumatic stress, and suicidal ideations". When we feel healthy, confident, and capable, we feel resilient managing our emotions and mindset while overcoming life's challenges. When we are not feeling healthy and not feeling resilient to take on obstacles, our mindset and emotions interfere with our problem solving, managing stress, and daily life activities like "getting out of bed".[6,7,8]

Quickly, I want to open up to be vulnerable to you, because even writing this book, I too have had mental health issues. When I started this idea, I did not fully understand the challenges that athletes, let alone people face. It started with wanting community. Then the mental challenges started showing up, especially when taking up this idea of trying to write a book and start something entrepreneurial, like Always An Athlete.

You don't know what you don't know.

After trying to "birth" this book and campaign to help athletes, I too can say I have been through some serious fires. I felt, and at times still do feel, a deep intense imposter syndrome and even at times depression that this idea and book was not good enough. Or that it is too academic? Or will anyone care? Why try when I feel like I am getting momentum—the next day can feel so dark?

One example that I find myself having to overcome is comparison. When I have anxiety and depression it is usually around circumstances. I am competitive and want to have answers to life's questions. Am I on the right path career wise? Why do I not have a partner yet? Will I ever be able to have kids? I also look at my body and wish I was stronger and leaner. (Yet, this has been in my head since I was 14 running around in spandex). As I have matured I am easier on myself and have given grace to keep pressing forward. One foot in front of the other.

Even as the storm in my mind passes, I force my focus my energy on gratitude . . . .and the winds begin to shift and light starts to break through the dark clouds.

Demonstrating a strong mental health focus means developing an increasing *awareness*, sensitivity, and action to the presence of psychological, emotional, and behavioral difficulties. Having a sense of freedom, ownership, autonomy, and control over one's own life, conditions, situations, and decisions can affect one's mental health.

Feeling "stuck" is real. Just as when we were competing and what fundamental movement seemed easy. . . . The next day you can feel "off".

Then there is a moment when there are too many of those "off" days where it becomes smart to reach out to get professional help. As athletes and competitive people, we can be hard on ourselves.

According to *Psychology Today*, certain athletes who "tend to worry about making mistakes and about being judged by others, and to feel extremely stressed, frustrated, or angry if they do not fulfill their own high expectations (Hill and Curran, 2016)" are more at risk [. . .] Having no clear sense of who they are outside of sport puts athletes at risk of mental health issues such as burnout (Coakley, 1992)."[9]

In short, there is no way to know where you are on your journey today. This book is meant to be a place that helps provide context that you are not alone. One of the best things that I think that we are doing is working to create a community of athletes who are experiencing the same transition.

The Always an Athlete cohort and mentorship program is currently ensuring strict confidentiality and providing education, prevention, and intervention support. Find out more on how to get involved at www .AlwaysanAthlete.com.

This urgent need calls for creatively providing an open forum for our athletes on *how* to find help and encourage them to feel comfortable and not shy away from such help. Remember that you are not alone. Lean on your Always an Athlete and Ball2Bike community. Reach out to our team. Ask for help and message your former coworkers, team members, coaches, instructors, family, and friends. Additionally, having a friend, teammate, or someone like a mentor to turn to and listen to can make such a huge impact on one's own mental health. It is recommended to lean on your community for support and seek out professional help such as certified therapists to support you. You can find these resources on www.AlwaysanAthlete.com. Mental health means being willing to learn healthy coping skills to alleviate stress and creating a life full of meaning, fulfillment, happiness, and connection.

PHYSICAL WELLNESS PILLAR

The last systemic change that is needed is paying close attention to the Physical Wellness Pillar for life-long wellness in our athletes. This— again—comes down providing education and training not only during the performance-purposed years, but, additionally, should include follow-ups starting "day-one" after our athletes have left the competitive realm. Evin Demirel at the Daily Beast sums it up best:

> This problem can be alleviated. Because not every former player has the ability or resources to chart their own path to a more normal weight and a longer life, the NCAA and the major college programs [and professional franchises] they played for should help.
>
> For one or two semesters after a student-athlete finishes his [athletic] career, if he's still enrolled and taking classes, the athletic department should pay for a nutritionist affiliated with the school to supervise his weight loss and work with him to maintain the best weight. Chart their blood profile and body fat percentage; make recommendations and encourage them along their path.[10]

The same is reasonably possible in the professional ranks, too. After all, if the NFL, NBA and MLB offer classes in financial literacy, and their players' associations do the same, why can't similar resources be made available on a wider scale to impact behaviors that have far-greater impact than spending habits, and that have far deeper roots than a signing bonus?

This is why Always An Athlete has been created—to be implemented at the programmatic and systemic level integrated into athletes' careers. Again, to get involved and enroll in the cohort and mentorship programs, apply on www.AlwaysanAthlete.com.

TRANSITION FROM A COMPETITION
TO A WELLNESS ROUTINE

You, athletes, who are now transitioning and taking on a new routine, don't forget to keep a structure, make exercise a part of your daily schedule, and set personal physical fitness goals. Make sure to MOVE *everyday*. Your habits can change very quickly when you fall out of the competition mentality and it is hard to get back into a rhythm. You will most likely be behind a computer most of your days. It's important to think about this next stage as your *wellness chapter* in your athletic journey. It is important to develop and maintain healthy sleeping, nutrition, learning, studying, and exercise habits. For example, you can sign up for a gym membership, you can take Cross-Fit, Class Pass, circuit training classes, or even hire a personal trainer. If you don't have a membership and choose to work out on your own, we learned from post-pandemic several online tools that you can watch fitness videos online and do at-home workouts, simply with a mat, barbells, or without any weights at all.

Have you tried a different active hobby? Or a different sport like dragon boat racing, sailing, dancing, or martial arts? Pickleball? (It has been taking the nation by storm!).

The possibilities are *endless*!

Some former athletes, especially those who have suffered injuries have turned to rock climbing, golf, or biking as an alternative due to the low impact on their joints. Other athletes consider new physical hobbies such as dance classes or outdoor physical challenges such as camping, backpacking, multi-day trekking, and hiking in nature.

Others sign up for a "mud run", "color run", "spartan race", triathlon, Iron Man, Century bike rides, Critical Mass monthly bike rides, or even a 5K in a costume for a fun physical challenge and worthy goal to strive for. I believe that these large activities are so popular because they are centered around community and a shared experience.

The important note to remember here is that, no matter what you decide to do next, you are always striving to be your "best self". There is no competition, but only a support group to guide you along the way and it is really you who is striving to beat your personal record.

As an athlete, you also already know the meaning of having a team or support group (virtual or in person). Downloading apps like Nike, My Fitness Pal, Strava, Apple Health, Fit Bit, etc. oftentimes have virtual groups, challenges, etc. where you have people cheering you on, you can track your progress, and you all are sharing your milestone "wins" together.

You will notice that exercising affects your day and will give you more energy. We all know that getting 8 hours of sleep, drinking 2-3 liters of water per day, eating a well-balanced diet, and exercising 30-45 minutes every day make all the difference. Maintaining a physical routine is often-times harder said than done—it requires intention, incentives, rewards, self compassion, discipline, and consistency. As an athlete, you know what it means to be disciplined and how all the hard work maintaining a work out schedule is worth it.

In short? Keep your physical routine and do your very best to maintain it!

More information and resources at AlwaysanAthlete.com

12

Why Should We Care?
We Need Widespread Change

The most successful people in the sport and corporate world
know that change is the energy—the driving force behind success
and without it, sporting organizations—and indeed athletes
and coaches will never realize their full potential[1]

—WAYNE GOLDSMITH ON BEHALF OF WG COACHING

There is a consensus among researchers and writers that for this evolution and reinvention to be most effective, in order to soften the fall
off the Cliff, there must be wholesale, systemic change by the biggest
stakeholders in sports today. Pee Wee Football and AAU youth teams
—that—are seeking shoe deals from the Nikes and Adidas's of the world
are stakeholders that can affect this change.

NCAA schools and conferences are stakeholders that can affect this
change. The National Football League, the National Basketball Association, Major League Baseball, the National Hockey League, Major
League Soccer and professional leagues across the nation and world are
stakeholders that can affect this change. The reason they are best suited
to effect this change is that they are the leaders in the sport industry.
The power to affect change lies with these large traditional institutions.
Ultimately, the greatest stakeholders are the fans—those to whom the
schools and professional franchises cater because, without the fans, those
programs would cease to exist.

Where that starts for athletes currently in the pipeline is re-orienting them while they are still performance-purposed. And the fact of the matter is that the people who have the most influence over the athlete while he or she is still performance-purposed is their *current* coach, their *current* athletic administration, their *current* general manager. But once they are out of the system, the people they will listen to most will be their *former* coaches, their *former* athletic administrators and their *former* general managers. This can be difficult, if for no other reason than no athlete wants to think about riding off into the sunset while they are at the height of their career. Super Bowl champion Aaron Taylor wrote in an open letter to the NCAA that "[m]ost athletes don't think about the fact that they'll be ex-athletes much longer than they'll be current athletes. Few among us ever take the time and effort to explore this reality and devise a 'Plan B.'"[2] Furthermore, no athlete *wants* to think about a life without sports. Steve Nash, NBA All-Star and senior producer at *The Player's Tribune* wrote that "[w]hen you're a teenager with outsized dreams and a growing obsession, and someone tells you this ain't gonna last forever, it's scary."[3] So maybe they ignore it, thinking the inevitable will go away.

But the fact is simple: retirement will catch up to every athlete, just as it does for every person who has a career at some point. Ultimately, the key to preparing athletes to build their Pillars from the Cliff instead of falling off is to get to them early. This responsibility does, at some point, fall on the older generations around them. And why not? Veterans at the professional ranks are doing the same as it relates to their rookies' finances. Adonal Foyle is a former NBA player and author of *Winning the Money Game: Lessons Learned From the Financial Fouls of Pro Athletes*. He tells a story about a flight for an out-of-town game. On the flight, he read an article about former NFL star Terrell Owens, who had just gone broke. According to Foyle,

> I was horrified. I went up front and grabbed three rookies, the youngest guys on the plane, and said, "You, you, and you: We're gonna meet and talk about finances. You need to have a financial strategy." They looked at me like I was crazy. They had no idea what I was talking about.[4]

The obvious question is: why can't we do the same thing for the non-financial dangers of retirement—falling off the Cliff—that we do for long-term financial security of our athletes? Why are we not getting more concerned earlier in their careers, *before* they finish their climb up the Mountain? And why are we not making efforts to heal our favorite man-made gods after they've fallen from Olympus?

WHY WE SHOULD CARE: STAKEHOLDER EDITION

If you are an athlete reading this book, active or retired, I assume that you already care. This book is for you. Since I began researching this book, my interactions and friendships with athletes representing numerous sports at every level—letter jacketed high school kids, former college athletes, professional athletes in the NFL and MLB, and numerous Olympic athletes—have generated exactly one response: "Wow! This is so great! I really wish people would talk about this!" But what about everyone else? What about our coaches, administrators, parents, family and fans? How many of you reading this are still not convinced you should care about the individual athlete after they retire? Perhaps not that we shouldn't *care*, but simply that we—the organization, the fans, the school, the whoever—have no reason to change or add to what *we* do to help our retired and retiring athletes from falling off the face of the Cliff? I believe that anyone reading this book who is or ever was an elite, competitive athlete will understand the reason that athlete should take steps to help him or herself. But why should those around the athlete? Why should the coach do anything other than coach the next generation once his players have graduated? Why should the general manager do anything other than generally manage his franchise for the next season once his guys have retired? Why should we be a part of the solution when we have games to win?

For the fans reading this book, I should hardly have to explain it. True, looking from the outside in, it can be difficult to put yourself into the position of a Final Four champion or a Super Bowl champion making millions of dollars. "Why can't they do it on their own?" Well, for the Final Four champion or the NFL millionaire, the answer to that question is "they can." But sports as a whole are more than just champions. And fans understand this even if they don't recognize it. What Bulls fan *doesn't* want a Michael Jordan rookie card, even though he's been retired as a player since 2003? What Oklahoma State fan would give up the opportunity to grab dinner with Barry Sanders even though he's been retired since 1998? And what *American* wouldn't want an autographed jersey of the 1984 "Miracle on Ice" team, or Julie Foudy from the 99ers hanging on their wall at the office? No matter how fleeting a career, our athletes are heroes that *we* love, support and believe in. And, like the warriors of old, the retired players become part of the legend. And who doesn't want to touch legend and myth? Why go to church if you don't want a part of what makes sports great?

What sports fan *doesn't* love the great underdog stories about sports: Sylvester Stallone in *Rocky*, Robin Williams in *The Best of Times*, Keanu Reeves in *The Replacements*, Kevin Costner in *Bull Durham*, and basically every single fictional Cleveland Indians lineup in *Major League*? Even our true stories become box-office fodder: *Rudy* is about an undersized football player who only wants to be on the field for one play at Notre Dame. *Friday Night Lights* is about one true season of Texas high school football. *Hoosiers* is about one true season of Indiana high school basketball. *Glory Road* is about Texas Western (now UTEP)'s improbable run to the NCAA basketball championship starting five black players against Adolph Rupp's all-white Kentucky squad in 1966. The quintessential "guy movie" is *Brian's Song*, about the friendship that developed between Chicago Bears Brian Piccolo and Gale Sayers. And who has never cried at the end of dramatizations of the Olympic underdogs like the 1988 Jamaican bobsled team in *Cool Runnings*, or Eddie Edwards, the not-so-high-flying-but-oh-so-loveable British ski jumper in *Eddie the Eagle*? We, as fans, *already* love our heroes, retired though they may be. To pretend otherwise is simply disingenuous.

I was posed this question—why should we care—a couple of years ago at a prominent well known conference by a fellow attendee. Well, it was not so much a question posed as it was an awful cynicism when this attendee bluntly told me "people don't care about the players. They only care about the wins." I was astounded at how short-sighted this was. Yes, in my own optimistic, Pollyanna way, I believe the most obvious reason to make executive change is because you *do* (or should) care about your players as people, even long after they have retired. They did, after all, build the foundation on which today's dynasties and traditions are built. Respect for our elders, and everything that goes with it. But I believe another less-obvious, but perhaps more impactful reason is this: the future of your fan base. *At a certain point, you have to look at your bottom line. And there is nothing wrong with that. This is America, after all. So at the end of the day, questions each mover and shaker in the sports industry ultimately must answer are: how will this generate more fans and more loyal fans that buy tickets, t-shirts, and television subscriptions.*

Today's Millennials are tomorrow's fans. As such, my generation is the hope for sports organizations' futures. According to NASCAR CEO Brian France in 2015, the "ability to manage and figure out the millennial fan and how that continues to unfold this year and over the long term is the most important issue in sports business."[5] Unfortunately, the reality today is that even the savviest executives and administrators are losing Millennial fans for a variety of reasons that many seem content to ignore. Frankly, gone are the days when fandom occurred due to the simplicity of life. You grew up in northeast Ohio, so you bought Browns shirts and Indians ball caps. Or you grew up in Philadelphia, so you went to Eagles games. Or you grew up in Los Angeles, so you watched the Dodgers. Or you went to a particular university, and began to follow their football program in the fall and their basketball program in the winter. For Baby Boomers and Gen Xers, their teams stood in as proxy warriors and a shared heritage between fathers and sons, mothers and daughters, neighbors and friends. New Yorkers and Bostonians saw their Yankees and Red Sox battle for them against their hated rival. Bruin alums keep the retort handy "we'll see what happens in March" when talking to their Trojan neighbors in November. Those days are gone, as life has gotten more complex and more complicated for the next generation of sports fan.

First-wave Millennials, now in their thirties, are a generation shaped by the awful and great economic forces of the twenty-first century. In 2016, the financial service firm Morgan Stanley reported the following about Millennials and their spending habits:

> Millennials have grown up in the shadow of the Great Recession, are saddled with higher education debt and housing costs, and are forming households later. These factors dramatically affect how Millennials spend . . .
>
> Worse, although Millennials are the most educated generation in history with 61% attending college, they've encountered a more challenging job market. Millennial employment rates plummeted during the financial crisis and still haven't fully recovered. In addition, more Boomers have opted to stay in the workforce for longer, which may be squeezing Millennials on the career front.[6]

And in turn, Millennials are squeezing sports in America.

The Millennial Squeeze starts, where else, but at the ballpark. In

30 For 30: The House That Steinbrenner Built, fans complain about the price of tickets at new Yankee Stadium in New York City, and about not being able to afford to take their kids to a game the way their dads could walk up and grab a couple of tickets on a gameday afternoon.[7] This is a common refrain at tailgates across America, as fathers recall their dads being able to get a ticket at the last minute to take their kid to a game. Unfortunately, gameday planning now feels like it can require a degree unto itself. I happen to be a Millennial. I played sports and I love sports. I'd love to go to a live sporting event. But for me—and millions of others in my generation—it is simply not feasible. For my friends with kids, tickets alone for a family of four top $400 for average seats at a mid-season NFL game, not to mention gas, parking, food and maybe a t-shirt.[8] Recently I was looking up *playoff* baseball tickets in October, to be able to be in the grassy knoll area behind the stadium for a game was $1,200. *With no guaranteed view of the field.* Yikes!

Even colleges are feeling the Millennial Squeeze, proof from de-creased attendance at games. The National Association of Collegiate Directors of Athletics released a report in 2015 that reported that "67 percent of millennials claim to attend sporting events less often or never."[9] Millennials blame pricing, despite the fact that attendance "is critical in maintaining another lifeblood of athletic departments: donations. Ticket sales and donations account for 41 percent of total revenue at Football Bowl Subdivision schools in 2014, according to a 2015 NCAA report. Factor in a predicted decline in future television revenue, and the down-ward attendance trend is even more problematic."[10]

The economic hurt that Millennials feel has led to the cable-cutting and alternative-modes-of-entertainment trend that professional and col-legiate sports organizations are now faced with. Recent trends demon-strate that Millennials watch sports less and less compared to even a few years ago. In turn with decreased attendance, Millennials are also shut-ting off the television when games are on. In 2017, L.E.K. Consulting, a global sports consulting firm, published its findings that sports organiza-tions have a "Millennial Problem."[11] In that report, L.E.K. published the following findings:

> Unlike their Baby Boomer and Gen X predecessors, Millennials follow a much broader range of both traditional and alternative sports as adults, and despite having less time on their hands, have a far greater selection of viewing alternatives.

Most notably, Millennials have increasingly bypassed traditional pay TV subscribership—the main staple of sports engagement for years—in favor of untethered media, a trend that is expected to continue in the years ahead. Recent data from ESPN pains a particularly stark portrait: For the fiscal year ending Oct. 1, 2016, subscribership shrank to 90 million, a 10% drop in just three years . . .

As Millennials continue to back away from mainstream media, they are likely to become increasingly disengaged from sports in terms of viewership and fandom—that is, unless industry heads are able to respond to these changes in a proactive manner.[12]

The data backs this up.

In 2016, for instance, ratings for the NFL among 18 to 34-year-olds—first-wave Millennials—hit their lowest point since 2008.[13] College sports—despite their captive audience of current students and alumni—are not immune to the effects. Universities are faced with increasingly empty seats in stadiums[14,15] and college sports television deals are absolutely tangled, with multiple cable providers each offering a different sports package that may contain tens or hundreds of sports channels which may or may not come with their own blackout schedules.[16] It's enough to infuriate even the most devoted fan, especially when there is a *de facto* blackout depending on which cable service provider services the fan's area; the most notorious, of course, being the Dodgers blackout[17], though even college sports get blacked out due to cable television deals—even in areas where the *only* cable provider is a competitor of the official cable network.[18] Even the Olympics are in trouble, at least among American Millennials. Nielsen reports indicate that the average American viewership of the Olympic Games has steadily been trending upward, with the median age of American viewers rising from 46.9 for the Beijing Games in 2008 to 48.2 for the London Games in 2012.[19] In 2016, the Rio Games saw a 30 percent drop in Millennial television viewers.[20]

This, in turn, presents an existential threats to American sports. As L.E.K. writes:

[T]he falloff in TV subscribership could have even farther-reaching consequences. When asked to list key reasons why they became sports fans in the first place, respondents cited 'watching games on TV growing up' as their top reason (30%) . . . Given that TV has been the historical conduit for sports appreciation, the decline in legacy viewership points to a concurrent falloff in sports fandom going forward.[21]

But beyond loyalty, Millennials are driving social responsibility through their loyalty, which creates opportunities for stakeholders to adopt the Always an Athlete philosophy in their fan programming.

Millennials are simply more socially conscious, and use their wallets to exercise that responsibility. For instance, 28 percent of Millennials report having participated in a boycott.[22] In 2015, the Global Corporate Sustainability report published findings that—globally—66% of consumers will spend more on a brand if it is sustainable, but 73% of Millennials said the same thing. And 81 percent expect their favorite brands to publicly declare their corporate citizenship.[23] Researchers at UC-Berkeley have found that "millennials strongly favor businesses with transparency and a clear commitment to give back to society."[24] As a case study, this may be partially responsible for the the Major Leagues decline in popularity among Millennials.

The good news, though, is that with Millennials' hesitance to spend money, they have become much more diligent in what they spend their money on. For this reason, Millennials are the most brand-loyal generation ever *if* you can get them. Talk about a silver lining! Point being, however, that sports organizations—professional, collegiate, even in high schools where booster clubs sell cookies for baseball uniforms and swim goggles—have a generation of fans and participants that they are in danger of losing because they do not cater to them. The next chapter will delve into the best way to engage the next generation of sports fans at every level of competition.

WHY SHOULD WE CARE: WE NEED A GLIMMER OF HOPE

The single greatest solution to preventing athletes from falling off the Cliff is earlier emphasis on non-sport aspects of our athletes' lives. And again more of an emphasis on non-specialized sports. I don't think it's a secret what my opinions are on specialization in youth sports and high school sports. I'm pretty firmly in the Swinney-Meyer camp.

At the lower places on the Mountain—youth sports and high school sports—the strategy needs to be implemented early that kids should not be focusing so exclusively on sports that it becomes their entire lives that early. A well-rounded sports experience ought to prevail, letting kids pick and choose which sports they want to participate in. Kids should also be encouraged to try *non*-sports activities in order to avoid burnout as well as to develop non-sports identifiers.

To this day, I wish that I would have learned an instrument, or at a very minimum learned how to read music.

From an early age, parents and coaches need to be approaching their child's sporting career with the idea that if their child is both talented and enjoys playing the sport, that it is *an* option—not that if they are talented and enjoy playing the sport that it is the *only* option to getting them to the next level.

If the athlete moves up the Mountain to college sports and certainly professional sports, this early-identification strategy still ought to take hold. Dr. Scott Tinley, author of *Racing the Sunset* and professor of sport humanities at San Diego State University, has considered several athletes who took this to heart:

> MLB Hall of Famer, Cal Ripken Jr. talked about how he had designed his life after sports 10 years before his last at-bat. The speedskater Eric Heiden shared stories about sitting in little wooden classroom desks as he sought entry to medical school with five Olympic gold medals in his backpack. . . . Former Cy Young Award Winner, Rick Sutcliffe told me that he would rather return to coaching young pitchers than travel as 'America's Guest.' And 1976 NFL Defensive Player of the Year Jerry Sherk told me within the first five minutes of our long relationship that the sooner I realized that the best part of my life was over, the sooner I could move on to a pretty decent second half.[25]

Remember Caroline Silby, the Maryland sports psychologist? As she said, "unfortunately, we don't really talk about it very much or prepare athletes for" how retirement from elite competitive athletics could impact them.[26]

I have found *no* universities or professional franchises that *require* athletes to go through any kind of training or curriculum designed to help them explore options for the day on which they eventually retire from sports through the problems they may encounter when they go over the Cliff. *However I have heard of some governing bodies within Team USA, starting to have discussions, but more geared toward career transition than holistic lifelong athletic life. A glimmer of hope and change. . . .

University athletic departments have been more apt to the mental health conversation and are sending students to general career counseling and psychiatric services centers on campuses when they are on the roster. However most are not able to help the athlete in any meaningful way after his or her graduation or draft day.

For the longest time I heard of *no* professional franchise or league that has implemented this type of support, though some offer programs like the NFL's Rookie Transition Program which tend to focus on "the best resources and practices for a successful *playing* experience both on and off the field," with little regard to a successful *retirement* experience which owners, managers and coaches know has a high probability of occurring sooner rather than later.

Recently, as of July 2022 (announced in October 2021). I was thrilled to see the newest NWSL team right up the road from me in sunny Los Angeles, Angel City Football Club unveil its Player 22 Future Program.[27] The initiative aims to support retired NWSL players interested in careers in the sports industry by providing funding for educational and professional opportunities.

Before we get into the good stuff I want to let you in on a fly on the wall moment.

When the executives from Angel City and retired athletes took the field to unveil this program—I was in the stands. I came to the game solo to meet a group of people in LA Tech. A networking thing to try to build community and to make connections to help level up my career. As soon as the announcers took to the field, I started filming. I already knew of the program and was excited to one day connect with the team. Maybe there would be a way we could collaborate? Anyways, I hope you can imagine me up in the stands—filming this all going down from afar.

I am also very glad to be able to add this to the book because for the longest time there was no examples of a transition program in the market.

Ok, back to Angel City. Two athletes specifically took the field to share this new program to the world.

There was great coverage from this moment, and Just Women's Sports covered the moment:

Saskia Webber, a part-owner of Angel City FC, and Angela Hucles Mangano, the organization's vice president of player development and operations came out before the game with a lineup of retired athletes.

Together they are "combined for three Olympic gold medals and a World Cup title in 22 combined seasons of professional soccer. The last thing retired players like Webber and Hucles- Mangano want to see is the next generation of athletes struggle in retirement as they did."

"This isn't just something Angel City is doing for Angel City," Webber said. "We want the whole league to embrace it, and hopefully all sports will embrace it."

We put our hearts and souls into soccer," Webber said of herself and her USWNT teammates. "We started the WUSA, and when I retired, for me personally, there was nothing. I was already 10, 15 years behind the people I went to college with. It was a reality check."

Webber emphasized that while some retired athletes quickly ascend to roles as a coach, general manager, broadcaster or even owner, these individuals make up one percent or less of retired players.

"What about the other 99 percent who aren't going to roll out of this and get an agent and get a broadcasting job?" Webber asked. "We don't want to forget them. We're going to pay as much attention to the 22nd person on that field and give as much opportunity to you as we would the marquee player, and that's what's important. In a lot of sports, those are the people that get left behind."

"It provides the education and guidance to fill that gap between when you retire from soccer and when you're going into your next career," Hucles Mangano added.[28]

I am thrilled that there is now a glimmer . . . the hope is active and I am certain it will continue to build.

At the end of the day, broad strategies must be encouraged from the get-go. Universities would do well to adopt a curriculum that their graduating seniors and draft-eligible players go through their final year to help them start thinking about their own retirement—whether it will come after graduation or in ten years. It should start weaning them off of the idea that they will have trainers, dieticians and coaches telling them what to do every day of their lives. Even though they may still have a season to go through, they ought to be thinking about that day when they're watching the next season from the comfort of their couch. Professional franchises and leagues ought to do something similar at the *beginning* of the professional athlete's professional career. If we have identified financial illiteracy as a problem that needs to be addressed, certainly the Cliff is as big of a problem—if not bigger. Players ought to be encouraged to take up other sports (a daring proposition for any professional athlete, I know!) and other activities that they may have never considered before as additional outlets for their personality and competitive spirit. But it needs to start early and be encouraged often. And I have one that I believe straddles (bike pun) the divide in so many different ways.

The last chapter in this book, chapter 15 is my dream for the world to help athletes connect with one another and find their next chapter in life. I have always believed that if you point out problems, that you must also point to solutions . . . .but before we get into the bike, I want to also outline some practical tools. Some of these tools are already innately built into our personality—but all can be implemented today for the retiring competitive athlete.

13
Solutions
Prepare

By failing to prepare, you are preparing to fail.[1]
—BENJAMIN FRANKLIN

This particular quote was also one of the favorites of legendary Coach for UCLA, John Wooden's. It is time tested and true, not only for athletics but for life.

This is a difficult journey because, at the end of the day, there are few external influences to help with this transition. People will offer suggestions and you might find some tips and tricks. But there is no personal roadmap to follow other than to be open to trying new things and finding the courage to embrace the unknown. As you take on the Cliff after climbing your mountain, the way you prepare is like your parachute. You will definitely want to have it ready to go! It will help you glide down into your next athletic chapter. Maybe with the right experts on board this mission, we will be able to help shape resources and events for athletes in the future. But it will take some time.

A good thing to celebrate is people are becoming more aware of the problems that athletes face when transitioning into a new chapter.

Since I started writing this book in 2014, we have seen a massive shift in culture as a whole, and specifically within the sports landscape. We now have seen important conversations rise and empathy (especially around mental health) extended to athletes.

The foundation of all suggestions that you may encounter is preparation. I hope you lean into preparation early and often for your next chapter from a competitive athlete into a wellness-based athlete.

PREPARE: SET GOALS!

When did Noah build the ark? *Before* the rain.

Would you show up to a match without a plan? Do you think you'd keep your starting spot for the next game if you hadn't studied game film on your opponent? Retirement from competitive athletics is no different. It is an indisputable fact for *all* of us competitive athletes: our playing days will come to an end. However, nobody ever wants to think about it in the middle of a season. It is human nature to avoid difficult conversations and to shove thoughts like this deep down. But just like planning for a game, you need to create a game plan *before* that inevitable day comes along.

One of the things that I wish I did earlier in my own career and what I advocate the most as athletes transition to the next phase of their life is the ability to think ahead and prepare while still climbing (the mountain) to the peak of their athletic career.

When should you start planning and preparing for your transition? Before the end of your athletic career. And one way to make sure that the transition is as smooth as it can be is to *prepare for the inevitable. . . .* The moment when athletic competition stops and the *structure* of this climb to the peak of the journey dissipates.

All athletes know that training is preparation towards achieving a goal or multiple goals (personal and team). Alongside of your current goals (if currently competing), you should have a tandem goal and plan for your retirement *before* you actually retire.

The same preparation and thoughtfulness that you have put into competing in your sport, whether solo or on a team, you should be working towards the new goal of being to transition with excellence. Outlining your plan (and ultimately your work back plan to achieve this goal) is critical to the success of your journey in the next chapter of your life.

As we outlined the Mountain and Cliff around the three pillars, I too encourage you to think about your transition and preparation in the same three pillars. (Mental Health, Physical Health and Athlete Identity).

One of the underlying frameworks to this overall discussion is the lack of *structure* when an athlete retires. However, if we start to think about preparing or building a new *structure* in this next season we are far more likely to be successful in the transition.

How do we identify and control the controllables? Another way to ask this question is how can we prepare?

You can't control the economy. You can't control geopolitical changes. You can't control the weather. However, you can control how early you start thinking about and implementing the personal structure needed for you to be successful in your post athletic career.

Just as you anticipate when playing sport, you need to anticipate and plan for your transition.

This is where I failed and honestly where I still struggle.

PREPARE: WHO

Who can you reach out to to help bring clarity and understanding to your upcoming new world? You are embarking on a new journey and in many cases a completely new path. There are many other athletes who have had to start from square-one too. Hopefully after reading this far in the book you are motivated to start putting a plan in place to help make you successful in the new challenge ahead.

Start having conversations with as many people that have already gone through the transition as possible.

One of the first people that you will think to have a conversation with is your coach. No matter how much you love your coach, there is no cultural precedent that your coach is going to have great advice for you or be invested in your journey out of sport. Remember, your coach is *incentivized* to focus on the new set of athletes funneling into the program rather than out. Your coach is always looking for the new talent to help build the program rather than equip the existing players. Why? Because it is his or her job to win. That is the current culture in sport. Hopefully with the release of this book the overall sport culture can change. And caring about an athlete does become part of the coach's job description to care about athletes leaving the program, but today it is not certain that they would be willing to spend time, energy and even follow up with you with a check-in to see how you are doing with your transition.

So who besides your coach can you reach out to that is part of the structure that helps make you successful today? Start outlining who you will bring on this journey with you.

PREPARE: PHYSICAL HEALTH

One of the key people to meet as early as you can is with your athletic trainer.

Your athletic trainer is going to be a key resource for you as you step into this next chapter of physical health. They will be able to share with you, because they presumably know your personal strengths and weaknesses. They should be able to provide some key workouts that you can do to maintain your current body. They know if you have a bad knee, ankle, or shoulder because they have been treating you for that injury. They also know the science behind training for competition rather than training and working out for wellness. Ask them to help you create a customized workout plan for your post retirement physical wellness. Their job is to make sure that you are healthy while you are in the care of the program/university/franchise. If you have created enough of a rapport with them, I hope that they would be willing to do this and help you chart this next chapter as a part of their job.

If this is not part of their job, I hope that Universities/Programs/Franchises write this into the job description of the athletic trainers so that their knowledge can be used to help the athlete in the transition.

This structure of key workouts is going to help you when you step into your local YMCA or gym and need some guidance on "what to do".

NUTRITION

Alongside your plan for physical workouts, you should also start to prepare to change your diet. Do you have access to a nutritionist? See if you can connect with a team doctor or nutritionist to help you better understand your own body and its needs as you prepare to go through the transition.

Do you know if you have certain food allergies? What foods should you focus on and what are foods that no longer serve your competitive state? If you can find or have access to that resource, be sure to use their knowledge to create a customized plan for yourself. You will need to revisit and edit that plan as the years go on and as your body matures.

However, creating a plan early will be a great starting point that you can implement day one after you retire.

Your physical health and your ability to keep your routines and habits connected to wellness will be a huge key in keeping your path free from obstacles that can arise if you neglect this important portion of the transition. (Diabetes, Heart Disease, etc). Your overall health and wellness is the foundational key to your overall ability to successfully transition into your next chapter of your life. It is also important to implement these strategies into the next chapter as current habits as soon as you can.

As soon as you can, explore other means of athletic expression. Do you like being outdoors? Do you now find yourself being drawn to water sports? Maybe you now enjoy running as a release? You may be going from a team sports environment to exploring something solo for you to move your body. Or you may be going from a solo sport to other types of activities that are more communal. Mix it up. If you are lucky, you may have been competing in lifelong sports: tennis, golf, surfing are the first to mind.

For me when I was playing volleyball, I wish I would have put a focus on other types of cardio in the last year that I played. Specifically, I wish that I had created a 90% volleyball routine and 10% bike routine. And as volleyball training came to a close, I wish I would have shifted the amount of % of time and energy into a bike or cycling routine as I did my volleyball.

While physical health may not be the first thing you may think of (because the assumption is you are currently in great shape), if you neglect this aspect of your transition—the other two pillars are severely weakened. Many times your mental health is deeply impacted by your ability to keep and maintain your physical health. All the pillars are interconnected.

PREPARE: MENTAL HEALTH

Earlier I mentioned you will need to outline the "who" you will take with you into this next chapter. The "who" *critical* for this key pillar and in this transition plan.

If you can bring more than one person. Surround yourself with a community of people who care about you and your mental well being. Who are the people in your life that you tend to talk to about both the good and the bad. Make a list of the people you feel safest to at this time where you can share your journey authentically.

It can include your greater community of parents, siblings, friends that are outside of sport. Alert them that you are already thinking about your transition out of sport and start having these conversations that may arise naturally as this will be a large change in your daily life.

Use the buddy system. Who on your team is transitioning out of sport that you are friends with that can help keep you accountable to the plans that you are putting in place? Ask them if they would be willing to be your accountability partner. Identifying others around you in your immediate circle will help you keep to a schedule and help you identify when you are falling out of this newly created structure that you are trying to form for the next stage of your life.

One of the main things that I wish I did was stay closer to my teammates. They would have been great resources to not only keep me accountable to the physical aspect of staying "in shape" but they could have also helped me with the mental aspect of the transition.

When we do things together, and not alone, we are more likely to come out the other side a success. When we isolate, we are more likely to fail. Mentally, being connected to teammates will help you because you will be going through the same life stage, together, and not alone.

I failed at keeping in touch with my teammates. I moved back to California and my proximity to them changed. I sought others along my journey after "team" but I never found the same type of accountability that I had in my previous season of training, practicing and competing with others.

One way to also prepare yourself for this transition is to prepare to find someone to talk to ahead of this transition. Give yourself enough time to find someone that fits the bill. Is there a mental health professional connected to your team? Now that mental health has become a more mainstream topic, more sports teams have a mental health professional on staff or at least the resource available. Can you set up checkpoints with this professional at certain points within your journey after you retire?

Finding a mental health professional is like dating. It can take a while for someone to be really able to connect with. So be sure to set out on the quest to find a right fit as soon as you can. Ask your friends and former teammates for personal recommendations. What are they like about their therapist? Do you think that you could match up well with them?

Reaching out to others who have gone through the transition is key, maybe they can provide recommendations. Ask questions to everyone you know.

How you prepare to create structure ahead of time should happen as soon as you start to see the end of your career. The earlier you can do it before the realization of "the end", the better.

PREPARE: ATHLETE IDENTITY

Although sports career changes are based on physical abilities, one is never too old to learn something new. I love the C. S. Lewis quote: "You are never too old to set a new goal, or to dream a new dream."[2]

In the athlete's world, at 25 or 30 years an athlete can be considered "old". At such a young age—you have aimed HIGH and have achieved GREAT things! And yet, as you turn this corner you are never too old to start learning and growing in life's wisdom.

With technology, upskilling, Massive Open Online Courses (Moocs), and the "Future of Work", we have more resources and information than ever before at our fingertips. We are fortunate to be exposed to so many different ways of learning and being. Moving forward, I encourage you to never "stop improving", never stop growing, and push yourself to learn something new every day. Even one of the world geniuses, Albert Einstein said: "*Wisdom is not a product of schooling but of the lifelong attempt to acquire it.*"[3]

Keep developing your passion for excellence. Just as you continue to "press yourself on the court" to get better and more effective at a skill, life will challenge you to continue to be curious and hone other skills. If you develop a passion for learning and the process of getting better everyday, you will not only have the opportunity to be more mentally healthy, help reduce Alzheimer's or dementia and other health problems, but also continue to grow and excel as you create new identities within your personal story. You have so much more within you to unlock.

Be a lifelong athlete AND a lifelong learner.

Did you know there are several types of learning such as visual, kinesthetic, reading/writing, musical, logical, and interpersonal styles. Discover yours and make it a daily habit, staying curious in your mind, body and spirit. Keep learning everyday. Education and knowledge are power. How will you use this knowledge, power, and responsibility and apply it to telling your life story?[4]

What have you felt like you could not try or pursue because of time commitments to your sport?

Try it. What was something that provided joy to you as you have journey thus far? What sparks your interest? Invest your time into exploring your curiosities about the world around you. You will meet new people as you open yourself up to new experiences and environments.

One of my favorite stories I have learned of a high profile athlete transitioning into another passion is the Hall of Fame pitcher, the Mariners and Diamondbacks legend, Randy Johnson.

Johnson retired from the game of baseball in 2010 but has made a great transition into becoming a professional photographer. Photography was not something new that he discovered after sport, rather he studied photojournalism at USC from 1983-85, and the "about" section of his photography website notes "Baseball became my occupation for two decades but my love of photography never left. Following my 2010 retirement, I was able to focus my attention back to this passion"[5]

Today, he is most often seen at NFL games where he adds to his growing sports portfolio. Beyond sports he loves to travel around the world shooting photos of wildlife in exotic terrains like Africa and Asia.[6] Randy Johnson is living a new chapter of his life pursuing a new passion that lets him express himself artistically, and the world is getting to see him lean into being excellent in another discipline. How cool is that?

I hope that one quick example is an encouragement to you as you continue to look and lean into your other passions. There are many other athletes that like you, have had to make the transition from their sport into their next chapter. (Admittedly, For some it has been harder than others).

Be proactive, in your pursuits outside of sports as early as you can in your career. Continue to try new things when opportunities are presented. When you prepare and seek resources that are currently available to you- you will not be caught off guard—rather you regain control of your path and your next steps.

ENJOY the unknown and the exploration of self as you keep forward along your path.

Best thing I could ever suggest is to not be caught off guard that your competitive career has come to a close, but to see down the road that the sun is setting and to plan (at least an outline) of your next steps for when you wake up the next morning.

You can only prepare for what you know is coming. *You can only control the controllables.*

Roman philosopher Seneca once said, "Luck is what happens when preparation meets opportunity".[7] When you prepare, you will be found with an opportunity to flex your plan. You may not feel lucky in the moment, but you will be thankful that you did put into place a structure to help give you the best opportunity for success.

You can not wait until the last minute to prepare. Start thinking about your transition as early as possible. In the long run you will be so much happier that you did.

If you are unsure of what to do next or how to prepare, please continue to tap into resources on the AlwaysanAthlete.com.

14
Inner Athlete

I must not fear. Fear is the mind-killer. Fear is the little-death
that brings total obliteration. I will face my fear. I will permit
it to pass over me and through me. And when it has gone past
I will turn the inner eye to see its path. Where the fear
has gone there will be nothing. Only I will remain.

—FRANK HERBERT,
Dune, 1965[1]

Dune's litany against fear may come from a work of fiction published in 1965, but it happens to be shockingly solid psychological advice. Repeated many times in the book, the words can be encouragement to a variety of people across the globe. And in this case, I hope it inspires you, the athlete, to take on the fear of the unknown. Because you have what you need. You are ready right now. Your *inner athlete* is inside of you, ready for the next chapter of your athletic life.

You could not scale the athletic mountain as high as you did without your inner athlete. The voice inside of you that refused to not give up. The voice that continues to push you further than you thought you could go.

In many cases it is the inner athlete, not the athletic body that is the reason you were able to scale the Mountain as high as you did. You can not excel as an athlete to your highest form without your inner strength helping you push past the fear, pain and the resistance of the environments that you scaled. Just as we outlined in Solutions, your preparation and your inner athlete combine to help you parachute that you can pull to help you glide and float into the next chapter of life.

Even if you have already retired, you know deep down that it is your inner athlete that pushes you to excellence in this new chapter of your life. It has allowed you to enjoy the view from the top of the mountain.

When the fear of the unknown comes closer and closer into focus, let the fear of failure wash past you. Your vessel may have been shattered (any one of your body parts), but you have the spirit inside of you to keep excelling. You are still here. And you are ready.

Here are some skill sets that you already have in your tool belt. Use these tools as you chart your new path.

GROWTH MINDSET AND SELF EFFICACY

In a growth mindset, people believe that their most basic abilities can be developed through dedication and hard work— brains and talent are just the starting point. This view creates a love of learning and a resilience that is essential for great accomplishment.

—CAROL DWECK,
Author of Mindset[2]

In addition to preparation, it takes a certain type of "growth mindset" to see the transition as an opportunity vs. a challenge.

Growth mindset is the ability to reframe any failure, mistake, or challenge into an opportunity. In doing so, one's growth mindset creates an opportunity to learn, adapt, grow, and improve. This may be one of the most important points in your personal journey and growth. A growth mindset allows athletes to "embrace learning, [as well as] welcome challenges, mistakes, and feedback.[3] And I believe your inner athlete has already been teaching you a growth mindset as you have climbed your athletic mountain.

A growth mindset allows room for error, failure, and mistakes. Remember the amount of times you didn't make the play? You didn't score the point?

Growth mindset builds off of feedback as a source of direction. Growth mindset encourages effort to try again. Knowing that we are capable of improving and learning—capable of change.

How many times did you get direction from your coach to adjust or adapt your style of play?

Your Growth Mindset is *everything* as you continue to develop and shape your new world.

Did you know that the brain is like a muscle that grows stronger and smarter when it undergoes rigorous learning experiences?

> People's beliefs about their abilities have a profound effect on those abilities. Ability is not a fixed property; there is a huge variability in how you perform. People who have a sense of self-efficacy bounce back from failure; they approach things in terms of how to handle them rather than worrying about what can go wrong.
>
> —From *Encyclopedia of Human Behavior*, 1994.[4]

Growth mindset and self efficacy, or the belief in one's own capabilities, go hand-in-hand in the learning, testing, failing, and iterative process. We adopt a growth mindset in what we focus on and, through action and insight, we create a narrative and beliefs from our experience. Therefore, we act on what we believe. We create results and we create our future based on our beliefs

Which if you really think about it—it is full circle.

With the combination of preparation and growth mindset, we are now gaining the ability to have an adaptable perspective. Approaching life as a "lifelong" curious learner, willing to make mistakes, willing to take risks, and willing to keep improving will make all the difference in having a smooth transition from sports into the real world.

With any stage in life, one of the best ways to work on mindset is to ask questions, think bigger, question the status quo, and see the world with fresh eyes. It also means reinventing oneself as part of one's curious investigation of self discovery. By asking questions and observing, you are ensuring that your perspective is aligned with your growth mindset.

GRIT

Grit is passion and perseverance for long-term goal . . . .
Grit is living life as a marathon not a sprint.[5]

—ANGELA DUCKWORTH,
Author the book on
Grit: The Power of Passion and Perseverance

What athletes have going for them while battling the "cliff" is developing one's "growth mindset" and underlying "grit". According to researcher and Author Angela Duckworth, she defines Grit on her website: " One way to think about grit is to consider what grit isn't. Grit isn't talent. Grit isn't luck. Instead, grit is about having what some researchers call an" ultimate concern"—a goal you care about so much that it organizes and gives meaning to almost everything you do. And grit is holding steadfast to that goal. Even when you fall down. Even when you screw up. Even when progress toward that goal is halting or slow. Talent and luck matter to success. But talent and luck are no guarantee of grit. And in the very long run, I think grit may matter at least, as much, if not more".[6]

When we talk about having grit in sports, the way a competitor can dig down deep and showcase perseverance, it is often praised and brought up as a character trait by coaches in all sports disciplines. Athletes have that "muscle memory" of demonstrating a resilient competitor mindset. Grit takes putting in the time, energy, structure, space, and commitment just like into any sport.

Grit is the ability to stay the course, stick to your healthy habits and discipline and know that you are giving it your 100%, even in the midst of hardship.

When this next chapter gets difficult, remember you have GRIT within your story and within your inner athlete.

CURIOSITY

Curiosity—asking questions—isn't just a way
of understanding the world. It's a way of changing it.[7]

—BRAIN GRAZER,
Hollywood Producer

In order to learn and make a change, one has to have the curiosity to observe, learn something new, and get out of one's comfort zone. As athletes you have curiosity and the desire to find out more built into your DNA. This will be a season where you will humbly realize how much you do not know. With this new landscape, you will need to ask more questions.

Let curiosity spur on your feelings of excitement—to wonder, to be empathetic, to understand, to imagine possibilities, and to be in awe of all that can be explored in the life ahead.

Since you are now "putting yourself" out there in new roles, new environments—a new "playing field" will emerge. It's good to never lose sight of the curiosity to learn, dive in, and ask questions. It's like being a "child again", not "knowing everything", and not being a master. Curiosity is becoming a "beginner" again and listening to a "coach and team members" again.

Know and explore your interests.

If you were given a blank page and you could learn a new skill, what are you most interested in learning?

Ask questions to everyone about anything that you find remotely interesting. Realize that you are starting over and the world is full of opportunities and choices. You never know where inspiration might spark.

Remember this season of innovation and disruption in your life will be pivotal as you move forward. Your unique quest for greater understanding will help you make more decisions as they continue to arise. As you were curious about your sport as a beginner, you too will take curiosity as an important tool to help uncover what is next in your journey.

STAY OPEN AND REMAIN IN A STATE OF GRATITUDE

The transition is not a straight line; you have
to Zig and Zag . . . and that is perfectly ok.

—JULIE FOUDY,
US Soccer Champion[8]

Wear gratitude like a cloak,
and it will feed every corner of your life.

—RUMI[9]

Like this job? Good zig move.

Bad job? Change it up with a zag. Learn from it and grow.

Lots of zig and zagging should be expected in this next chapter. You don't have to have it all figured out. Just remember to stay grounded in your present moment.

Why? Because in the present moment, this moment is a gift and an opportunity. Therefore, one's openness and response to situations, challenges, and "opportunities"-in-disguise will determine, again, the increasingly important, "growth mindset". Do you remember a time in your athletic story where the environment that you encountered or the people around you made you grateful? Do you remember listening and leaning into that moment?

Being in a state of gratitude enhanced the good moments. But just as gratitude is important in the good times, staying grounded in gratitude in the rough times is even more powerful.

Gratitude facilitates emotional control. Athletes who experience gratitude are likely to experience more positive emotions. This lowers stress, promotes problem-solving, and greater self-regulation. During this self-discovery phase of the transition, other key components such as optimism, positivity, promotion vs. prevention focus, flow, mindfulness, and confidence also make up one's mindset. The best ways to incorporate the aforementioned is to focus on practicing a Growth Mindset, being curious, and staying open. (See they all build upon one another)

We recommend keeping a gratitude journal or before going to bed to meditate on 5 things that you are grateful for. Wherever you can incorporate gratitude into your routine, you are shifting your focus to what you do have, and this grounding alone can release you from the trap of comparison.

FLOW STATES AND STRENGTHS

Time slows down. Self vanishes.
Action and Awareness merge. Welcome to Flow.[10]

—STEVEN KOTLER,
Author, journalist, and entrepreneur.
Executive director of the Flow Research Collective

The concept of flow is very relevant to sports and is used interchangeably with the popular sports term "in the zone" according to a study by Young and Pain.[11] As an athlete—you understand "Flow". You would find yourself in the moment, competing, and playing completely locked in to the task at hand. Once your mind clicked into a certain gear, your body and sport were aligned and you were completely locked within the game.

The authors of the Young and Pain study describe flow as "a state in which an athlete performs to the best of his or her ability. It's a special, magical place where performance is exceptional and consistent, automatic and flowing where an athlete is able to ignore all the pressures and let his or her body deliver the performance that has been learned so well."[12]

One of the best ways to get back into a state of flow is to know your strengths and lean into them.

Strengths Assessment

Understanding one's own strengths, values, mission, and purpose can further complement and strengthen one's growth mindset. Using assessments such as StrengthsFinder[13], VIA Character[14] Values Survey[15], Principles You by Adam Grant[16] RIASEC,[17] Predictive Index,[18] DISC,[19] etc. may help one determine and guide who they are, what they are good at, what they want to focus on, and how to best help others. Using your strengths develops confidence. Confidence develops trust where others can depend on you to leverage your values and strengths for good, for purpose, and for impact.

How to Get Into the Flow[19]

Having clear goals about what you want to achieve as well as the process to achieve those goals.

Concentration and focus on the present moment.

Participating in an intrinsically rewarding activity.

Knowing that your skills align with the goals of the task.

Feeling control over the situation.

It will be challenging to respond to the above until you are aware of your values, your priorities, and what gives you a sense of meaning and fulfillment.[20]

Your strengths may shift over time. But start to identify what innately is built inside of you so that you can take those strengths into the next chapter of your life.

WHAT IS YOUR WHY

Knowing your WHY is not the only way to be successful
but it is the only way to maintain lasting success
and have a greater blend of innovation and flexibility.

—SIMON SINEK,
Start with WHY[21]

If you noticed. We start this book with chapter one, WHY this book. Even as I began putting pen to paper, I started with WHY.

Think back on a peak experience, a period when life was really poignant, whether you did it alone or with a coach. Specifically, can you think of a time that was not fully connected to sports? Did you excel in any other areas of life?

What made this a pinnacle experience?

What mattered most to you at this particular moment?

Where have you been? With whom did you go?

What were you doing exactly?

What principles come to mind as you reflect on this moment? Several times through this activity, start to uncover and ask where your innate strengths lie.

After being more aware of your strengths, you're prepared to examine how you spend your time and look for opportunities to build on your strengths.

Make a list of your primary tasks at work, taking into account both what you believe you should be doing and what you really do. After that, take note of which of these areas plays to your strengths and which ones plays to your weaknesses. All of this is gray; there are no black and white answers. You can accomplish this by rating things or just writing in a journal about what you see. You can also start to measure how engaged and energized you were while working on a certain task.

Consciously, decide what to do about situations that are causing you to consciously lean away from your strengths.

Curt Liesveld, renowned learning and development senior consultant for the Gallup organization, often explained to leaders, managers, and employees that "you cannot be anything you want to be, but you can be a whole lot more of who you already are."[22]

Here is a sample "Why statement":

To empower and educate people everywhere so that they can improve their lives and achieve their goals."[23]

Lean into understanding your why, and it will help you build your next chapter.

SOFT SKILLS AS A LEADER

Emotional-social intelligence is an array of interrelated
emotional and social competencies and skills that determine
how effectively individuals understand and express themselves,
understand others and relate with them, and cope
with daily demands, challenges and pressures.[24]

Most of the work in life involves "showing up" and "soft skills". Soft skills in life is the "how". How do you go about executing and getting work done? And with whom? How do you work with them?

Developing your soft skills will be key to your future relationships, way of work, and goals. Having the emotional intelligence, awareness, and empathy allows you to effectively manage conflict as well as identifying and understanding your "team and stakeholders'" personalities, competing interests, work styles, and communication styles. Understanding motivations and leadership styles is very similar to how you would effectively work on a sports team as well.

Listed below are some examples of valuable soft skills:

Time management
Leadership
Communication
Creativity
Working under pressure
Adaptability
Teamwork
Problem-solving
Interpersonal skills

If you played on a team, you learned and gained these same skills in group competitive sports. The same applies here.

"Emotional intelligence is the single most important influencing variable in personal achievement, career success, leadership, and life satisfaction" (Darwin Nelson & Gary Low, 2011).[25]

You learned how to "read the court". It's the same as "reading a room". It's reading the dynamic, emotions, empathy, motivations, and behavior amongst everyone. Being aware and understanding these relationship dynamics are a part of emotional intelligence. Developing soft skills and one's own emotional intelligence will determine how one grows, advances, improves, and builds relationships both professionally and personally. Effective leaders practice and demonstrate a high social intelligence. Emotional intelligence will carry you through your career. These skills will also help you throughout your life as a lifelong learner.

STORYTELLING

I think stories are what move the world.
Whether it's an inspirational story or an informational one,
nothing in this world moves without story.

—KOBE BRYANT[26]

In storytelling, one of the best questions to help develop a story is answering the question of "what's next?". You are on your own Hero's Journey (a common framework used in storytelling).

The Hero's Journey involves challenge, struggle, transformation and overcoming an obstacle.[27]

You are now answering and crafting your own transformational journey.

You as a high performer can channel your mindset into building your own next chapter.

Kobe channeled his "Mamba mindset" when becoming a master storyteller after his iconic basketball career, which resulted in him winning an Oscar for "Dear Basketball."[28]

As you transition, it is important to remember all the values, purpose, and skills gained as an athlete, but how do you tell your story about what you've learned?

How do you share your story about your struggles and your successes?

Throughout the ages, human beings have been sharing stories across generations. A story entails a journey, twists-and-turns, and a moral lesson. What would you like to tell the world? How might we reframe the stories that we are telling?

Storytelling involves becoming vulnerable and revealing what others may not know about you. You now have the possibility of being seen and heard. Telling your story takes having courage and taking a risk.

No one else can tell your story except you. And it takes that self-awareness that one discovers by practice, feedback from others, and mistakes—just like how we learn about ourselves when playing a sport.

Communicating your story also takes practice. Take a look at The Moth Storytelling nonprofit[29] where hundreds of people, speak their truth, become vulnerable, "bare their souls" on stage, and "pour their hearts out" telling their stories. We all have stories to tell. You can also practice telling your story at Toast Masters International club[30], take a virtual Storytelling class at any improv theater like Upright Citizens Brugade[31] or get inspiration attending TedX[32] events in your local city.

You, yourself, are the only person who can stand up and self-advocate for yourself. You have to be your own greatest cheerleader and believe in yourself in order to "sell yourself". Telling your story means being seen and confidently being authentic without worrying about what the audience thinks of you. In life, we are constantly selling and sharing stories. How might you authentically "sell yourself and your story" to get others to believe in you, your mission, and your vision?

What can you offer to others? What are you seeking?

Who do you want to help and how might you contribute?

How can you add value?

These questions are all very important as you begin to chart your path forward. The answers to these questions will help you write your LinkedIn profile and help you navigate the job search ahead. They will help guide the stories that you would like to reveal and share with others. By telling our stories, we engage and connect with the community and world around us.

SEEK AND OFFER MENTORSHIP

I believe all the best managers are actually mentors.[33]
—GARY VAYNERCHUCK,
LinkedIn post 2020, with over 30,000 interactions, 1,250 comments and 1300 shares.

It is safe to say that this post struck a cord with the general population.

Lastly, receiving and giving mentorship is quite fulfilling. Navigating careers alone can be lonely (hence the need for community). Whether one's just starting off, becoming a leader, preparing for a promotion, whatever it is, we're here to help and we encourage you along your journey.

Here are some fun facts about why mentorship is so important.

Mentorship is a powerful tool to attract, develop, and retain. 67% of organizations report an increase in productivity due to mentorship as a result of a highly cross-functional and motivated workplace.

When you have a mentor, you are:

Five times more likely to get promoted,
Five times more likely to get a raise,
And there's a 60% increase in female and minority representation.[34]

When seeking out a mentor be sure to think about the three C's: Clarity, Communication and Commitment. The more you can define upfront, the better your experience will be.

DON'T HAVE A MENTOR YET?

If you are an early-career professional who doesn't have a mentor yet, we recommend that you seek one out as soon as possible. When you have a mentor, you develop confidence and strategies to move forward in your career. If the workplace or enterprise you work in is offering a mentoring program, it's a great opportunity to take advantage of. It's possible that you'd find mentors within your organization (Human Resources, Leadership Development training programs, or Employee Resource Groups) as well as at any trade organization, club, chamber of commerce, industry association, or industry conference.

As we continue to develop our mentorship cohorts, feel inspired and motivated to find your mentor and appreciate the ones you have. You can also seek mentors as part of the Always an Athlete program www.AlwaysanAthlete.com.

BECOME A MENTOR TO A YOUNGER ATHLETE

You influence others, positively or negatively, whether you know it or not. We encourage you to mentor those who are going through the same thing that you have gone through or are currently navigating similar situations. Offer insight into your past experiences and, perhaps, teach others from your lessons and mistakes.

If you have already transitioned into the next chapter of your life and have found your momentum and groove, look back at the programs you were a part of and see if there is a need of mentorship for the next generation of athletes.

Fulfillment comes from seeing others grow, learn, transform, and, eventually, shine using their strengths and talents for good. You can make an impact on others' journeys and make a difference in other's lives. Your presence and who you are can brighten someone's day and make all the difference in the world for someone else. Check out AlwaysAnAthlete .com to get connected in helping give back to the next generation of athletes.

You are enough and you are worthy of giving and receiving mentorship and guidance.

COMMUNITY

Normally, I will hit you with one quote, but when it comes to Community, there are too many quotes that highlight the need for belonging and fellowship to help balance out the journey ahead. It's like a firework show at the end of 4th of July. Community is the finale!

"The power of community is far greater
than any physician, clinic or hospital"[35]

—DR. MARK HYMAN

Alone we can do so little. Together we can do so much.[36]

—HELEN KELLER

"If you want to go fast, go alone.
If you want to go far, go together."[37]

—AFRICAN PROVERB

Best thing that we can say is "Get Involved!" because "No Man Is an Island."

"No Man Is an Island." You may have heard of this phrase. This phrase was originally written in 1624 by the English poet and cleric, John Donne (1572-1631).[38] He wrote them as he was extremely sick and almost lost his life.

I love that this quote is *so* old. It showcases to me that we have *always needed community*. We have always needed others to live a full life. We as a global community even understand this more deeply after going through Covid, when isolation globally was at its peak.

As you transition into this next chapter of your life, lean on others. Turning to a community takes vulnerability, courage, and humility to ask for help, lean on others, and trust in others to reciprocate and provide you mutual support.

Each person has a gift to offer to others—the gift of self. Friendships and relationships take effort, sacrifice, cultivation, intentionality, presence, trust, and time. It is a two-way street of being present to others while also asking and sharing your requests of what you need from them.

You don't necessarily need to continue being a coach, reporter, or working in the general sports industry. However, stay connected to your friends, your former teammates, and your coaches. Be intentional about sending out invites or holiday cards. Even better, you can set up a bi-monthly meeting with your close "core group" that you, at one point, saw these friends and teammates 5-10+ hours a day. In the real world, you will find it difficult to make time and will watch these friendships change and deteriorate. Stay on the "offense" when it comes to keeping your relationships.

I believe that if I had been surrounded in community and did not go through such isolation, I would have never been so sad and depressed—leading me to try to ask questions around WHY there were no resources, and WHY did no one point me to the bike. All of that isolation led me to want to build something for all.

One of the main things that I hope Always An Athlete becomes is a community of like-minded athletes where athletes can lean on one another and find common ground in both past experiences, current struggles and futuristic hopes.

When we feel connected to others within a community, we are less able to hide and retreat. People see and care for us and want to see us come back or be healed. Community, and the people you actively curate into your life to me may be the most important elements to a successful next chapter post competitive career.

The next chapter of this book is my original spark of inspiration to bring and maintain community. The bike!! I hope that the ideas spark inspiration and action in you as well.

THE SPARK THAT IGNITED THE FIRE WITHIN—
A SINGLE BIKE RIDE

15
Ball2Bike

Those guys [cyclists] are real athletes.
I don't think they even have lungs.

—BO JACKSON,
NFL Pro Bowler, MLB All-Star[1]

I love to ride all day!

—BILL WALTON,
UCLA Basketball Legend,
author of *Bill Walton's Total Book of Bicycling*[2]

PUTTING DOWN THE BALL, PICKING UP THE BIKE

The most important thing about any solution for helping athletes off the Cliff is that it is best to start early. Yes, even as early as youth sports. The specialization that takes place at such an early age is setting the groundwork for an awful transition later in life, especially for those who end up at the most elite levels of competition. Throughout those years, there needs to be a de-emphasis on specialization to permit kids to develop alternate role identifications for themselves. This does not mean that parents should de-emphasize *sports*. Far from it. What I am advocating is a balance, and giving kids the freedom to explore. Even the *push* to explore when they may be choosing to specialize on their own too early.

Given the popularity of sports and athletic participation, especially in youth and high school programs, care should be taken by relevant coaches, teachers, and other developmental staff to ensure the proper follow-up experiences necessary to mitigate negative experiences associated with the termination of these activities.[3]

One of the most important positive coping skills for athletes transitioning after retirement from *competitive* sports is the transition *into recreational* sports.[4] An athlete's willingness to continue to be involved in a *different* "athlete" role acts as a fantastic "buffer," because it helps the athlete maintain their athlete role[5] in some form, while allowing ample opportunities to explore and identify other roles and components of their lives, which can be as general as education or work, to other interests they may not have explored before, such as music, reading, writing, debate, politics, social justice, faith and spirituality, and any number of other parts of the machine that is "them."[6] **And this is the heart of this book—that we should not seek to give up our athletic mindset and identity, but that we ought to explore it and be open to modifying it because regardless of the other roles we lean on, develop, or recognize, we will always be athletes.**

For most people who played sports, recreational athletics may be a suitable alternative. The former high school track athlete plays intramural basketball in college. The former college swimmer who went on to law school ends up playing on her firm's team in lawyer-league softball. For many athletes who have competed at the most elite levels—especially in ball sports—though, these recreational leagues may not be available to them because their bodies are simply too worn down, especially from leg injuries. Even playing in a flag football game or running to first in a no-stakes softball game can be limited if pain shoots through your leg from ages-old injuries. I know that is what stopped me from playing a fair amount of recreational sports after I retired from volleyball.

I moved to Denver after college for a job. Most people would be thrilled to be there because who wouldn't love going up to Winter Park in January? I was unable to ski. My knees were tuned up so badly that I could not pivot and lean on them the way even a recreational skier needs to be able to in order to get off the bunny slopes. Lucky for me I was able to snowboard. But upon moving back to southern California, I discovered that my options were even more severely limited. I tried to get back into beach volleyball, but my knees were too injured for that. I couldn't run more than a few yards before I would get those shooting pains in my legs. On top of being out of shape, I was mentally and emotionally trapped. I was no different than a lot of athletes.

But then, in 2013, I re-discovered the bicycle. I advocate that the retired athlete pick up *any* activity that gives them a sporting outlet. But for me, and I believe for a vast majority of the elite level athletes out there, the bicycle offers the greatest solution for the largest number of people.

For those with these nagging leg injuries (which includes me and many of my friends from *many* different sports), there are really only a few sporting options available that permit those who want to truly compete do so. Or even if you just want an activity that will not make you want to sit down after two minutes. I discount running. While a fantastic form of working out, and certainly competitive, I believe that running is not the very best option for two reasons for most retired athletes. First, those lower leg injuries I complain about. Second, how many of us had to run during conditioning and practices, and hated it even when we were competing at our prime? I'd imagine that for many retired athletes, running is simply out. Kudos to people who can run, enjoy it, and have found it to be a great outlet.

In my opinion, this really leaves two options. The first is swimming. Swimming is a wonderful activity, and I am doing a lot of it while I prepare to go under the knife for a third time for my knee (a torn meniscus and torn ACL in the same knee; the opposite leg that I injured when I was younger. I hurt my knee, if you can believe it, playing in a Baylor Alumni game). Swimming is a "full-body activity" with lots of "core engagement," noted John Martinez, MD and medical staffer with USA Triathlon.[7] It is also one of the best activities "if you have joint issues," according to Irv Rubenstein, PhD, an exercise physiologist and founder of S.T.E.P.S. in Nashville, Tennessee.[8] One of the obvious drawbacks, however, is that not every part of the country has regular access to a pool big enough to make such activity stimulating for the former elite athlete. Those pools that are often are located on college campuses and YMCAs and may be restricted to certain hours that may not work well with a work schedule. And it just takes a certain kind of person to enjoy swimming in the ocean or a lake—outside of winter months.

For this reason, I firmly believe that cycling is the best option for the retired athlete. While there may be a *bit* of bias, LiveStrong states it easily:

> Cycling is a low-impact exercise that you can perform indoors on a stationary bike or outside on a bicycle. The repetitive motion of cycling

works the quadriceps and hamstrings, which are the muscles that support the knee joints. However, cycling does not put direct strain on knees, making it an ideal exercise choice for individuals with knee problems.[9]

Health Magazine reports cycling as one of the best low-impact workouts for weight loss, which may be a goal of the retired athlete who has put on a bit of a tummy since beginning the transition: "Cycling—indoors or out—is non-weight bearing and low impact, so you can work up a sweat without stressing your joints."[10]

Beyond this, cycling has started to take hold among athletes—both current and retired. Football players have started cycling as a form of training that is easier on the body than high-impact activities like running.[11] Bo Jackson—the consummate "athlete"—has not only fit cycling into his schedule since suffering from a devastating upper-leg injury but loves it so much that he created "Bo Bikes Bama"—a charity ride in Auburn held every year to help the people of Alabama. And Bill Walton—who can stake his most claim to fame as a three-time Player of the Year during John Wooden's championship stretch at UCLA, two-time NBA champion, or the Grate-est Deadhead of all time[12]—is perhaps the best ambassador for the bicycle as a *cause celebre* among retired and injured athletes. He credits the bicycle with helping him get back into form after a long history of serious back and foot injuries and more than 40 surgeries to manage them:[13]

> I have three bone fusions—both ankles and my spine, which has a titanium rod in it from the '09 operation. The fusions limit my motion, but enable me to get back in the game of life. These days, my bike acts as my wheelchair, my gym and my church, all in one. Always my first question to the doctor is: Will I still be able to ride my bike?[14]

Cycling is simply well-suited to the former athlete who suffers from long-time injuries.

But it also offers a lot of flexibility. The athlete can take up any form of cycling, which can include traditional cycling on a road bike or mountain biking if they are more outdoorsy or looking for more adventure. You can spend thousands on a custom road bike or pick up a used bike for less than a hundred dollars at your local bike shop. You can ride for fun, for competition, or even for simple transportation to go to work or run errands in your neighborhood. You can ride by yourself, or on a team, or in a club, or all three. *And cycling is available even in bad weather!*

Indoor cycling has been with us since the beginning of the modern gym. Sometimes called the "exercycle," the technology has progressed amazingly through the years. Every YMCA and gym in America has indoor cycles right next to treadmills. In the early 2000's, the world went through a "spinning" craze, which was really just another name for going to an indoor cycling class. Peloton, SoulCycle, FlyWheel, CycleBar and other indoor cycling studios have taken the fitness world by storm. LinkedIn published commentary on the reasons these studios are so popular, and most conform to the needs of the retired athlete, including the fact that classes offer a bit of the structure that elite athletes were used to during peak performance years, that classes offer a community centered around exercise and athletic pursuit, and they can be convenient and each tailors itself to a unique client experience. They also offer the best updated technology, and anyone can do it,[15] And in some cases they can access these rides and training from home.

I am clearly biased. But beyond being *one* activity, I believe cycling is the *best* activity for the athlete approaching or coping with the Cliff because it is foundational for discovering other activities and resources for the retired athlete, and it is easy to build on.

CYCLING FOR PHYSICAL HEALTH

It likely goes without saying that cycling is a good physical activity. But let's look at what the experts have to say anyway. In terms of physical health and wellness, experts are pretty well convinced on its impact. Between the ages of 20 and 40—during which most athletes retire—bone density and muscle mass peak.[16] It is also during this age "when we're at our most competitive and when our body and response time is best," notes Bryce Taylor, physical therapist and creators of the Halo Trainer.[17] Between 40 and 60, "cycling is lower impact than running, so it's good for decreased joint impact," says Taylor.[18] Cycling is very much a lifetime sport, too. In this age group, "researchers following more than 20,000 people in their 40s, 50s and 60s for 10 years found that casual cyclists who biked to work were 15% less likely to be obese or have high cholesterol and were less likely to have high blood pressure or pre-diabetes."[19] Even as you age, "cycling becomes largely a leisure activity with less susceptibility to lower extremity overuse injury or even spinal pain for that matter," notes Taylor.[20]

For the retired elite athlete, cycling is a fantastic activity. Retired

UCLA and NBA legend Bill Walton swears by his bike. Even when he was at his competitive peak, he was an avid cyclist in Southern California. He tells a story during his senior year, the legendary Coach John Wooden got all over him for wearing hair that came down to his collar. Coach Wooden threatened Walton that he had an hour to clean it up or get kicked out of practice. So Walton jumped on his bike and flew to a barber in Westwood. Upon getting trimmed, he jumped back on the bike and zipped back to practice. According to Walton, he "rode right through the tunnel, dumped [his] bike at the side of the court and stood at the back of the line hoping beyond all hope that Coach hadn't noticed [he] was three minutes late."[21]

Beyond saving him from a thorough lashing from Coach Wooden, however, Walton credits his bike with saving his life in later life. Despite a Hall of Fame career in both college and the pros, Walton has been unable to run or play basketball since 1986.[22] Throughout his life, he has had over 35 operations including bone fusions in both ankles, fusions in his spine, back surgery and knee replacement. However, Walton is only 67, and has a lot of life to live. According to him, the key to his recovery was neither miracle nor grit. "My bike is my gym, and my church and my wheelchair," he says.[23] Bo Jackson espouses the same. The greatest athlete of all time had his career cut short after a hip injury cut off the blood flow to his hip socket. This led to avascular necrosis—death of the joint tissue in the socket—which required him to get a hip replacement.[24] As Jackson has said, "I was looking for innovative ways to stay in shape, to get the exercise in. An artificial hip isn't conducive to a lot of running, so I had to do it in other ways, and cycling was the best thing for me."[25]

And this is the crux of why cycling is the best option for the elite athlete. As I said above, I pretty much discount most other athletic pursuits and exercise programs for athletes. Not because they are not good, but simply because the retired athlete has unique needs. Many, if not all, have had some type of injury that makes running and jumping painful. Sometimes to an unbearable degree. But perhaps the most important and unique need that cycling offers the retired athlete has less to do with the most obvious struggle with nagging injury, and with the greater lasting struggle of finding motivation to stay active.

Recall that for the retired athlete, the motivation to make it into the gym is nowhere near as strong as when they were in a performance-purposed phase of life. Athletes (or really anyone) who exercises to lose weight, for instance, often give up when the weight doesn't fall off immediately or in some noticeable way. Michelle Segar, a psychology researcher at the University of Michigan, wonders "how beneficial it can be to exercise in such a negative way, where you're constantly thinking, 'I'm not good enough, and I don't like my body.' Who wants to keep that up?"[26] I'd suggest that nobody does, least of all the athlete. And that's because, as discussed earlier, where the non-athlete may merely exercise, the athlete has to *train*. And this is where the bicycle can become a godsend for the retired athlete.

In 2012, researchers conducted a study with implications on motivation and physical activity. They found that starting a marathon training program made participants in the study feel a "growing connection with the cause, improved fitness and athleticism, and mutual training support."[27] Obviously, replace "marathon" with "cycling event" or "bike race" and it gives the retired athlete something to *train* for. It becomes a culture of training in and of itself. Will Dean's 2017 book about building the Tough Mudder movement is aptly titled: *It Takes A Tribe*.[28] And it is well known that in Tough Mudder and Warrior Dash circles, these are events which people don't *do*. These are events that people *train* for![29,30,31] Despite the fact that there are no winners and losers, a training culture pervades among participants. For the retired athlete who shudders at the thought of dragging tired knees and creaking elbows up a mud-covered hill, cycling events like a Bo Bikes Bama or Ball2Bike events offer that same motivation to work.

Cycling is a good foundation for other physical activity because it can be combined with other activities. If you enjoy running and swimming, then taking up triathlons may be for you as those can build on top of cycling. Classes can be incorporated into your routine if you need other people around you when you are exercising. This is definitely me. Some of my friends and family are much better at working out on their own. I like a class. I like a coach. I like people around me. Cycling gives me that option to help motivate me in my physical pursuits these days.

CYCLING FOR MENTAL HEALTH

Cycling is most obviously good for physical health. However, some people may not realize how beneficial the bicycle can be for mental health of all persons—including athletes. Numerous studies have shown that regular physical activity helps prevent or relieve stress, anxiety and depression. Momentum Magazine identified several ways cycling and physical activity in general provide mental health benefits.

First, even a half-hour of daily exercise improves people's subjective mood and well-being. It provides not only an escape from social media which bombards us with achievements of others and can create negative self-perception attitudes, but the very act of taking part in such physical activity is the type of positive activity that impacts our self-perceptions. Long term studies of adults have determined that high levels of physical activity are associated with decreased risk of clinical depression later in life. Aerobic exercise reduces anxiety and stress. Cycling outdoors has been determined to be associated with greater feelings of revitalization, more energy, less tension, confusion, anger and depression.[32] What may be less known is the research specifically related to cycling and mental health issues that affect retired athletes.

For instance, a Japanese study in 2013 revealed the effect of cycling on people suffering from depression. In that study, conducted using a stationary bike, a mere fifteen minutes of cycling was discovered to reduce their levels of cortisol—a hormone that causes stress and anxiety linked to depression.[33] And outdoor cycling has additional benefits.

In another study, volunteers pedaled a stationary bicycle while watching videos of green, leafy cycling trails. The first video was unedited. The other two were each edited to appear red and gray, respectively. After viewing the original, unedited version, cyclists reported less negative moods and felt like their cycling took less work, despite the fact their heart rate and breathing remained the same regardless of the video.[34] As one cyclist writes, it "ticks so many of the boxes" necessary to help with her own depression. Cycling is exercise. It provides "head space" as well as physical space. It gets you out of the house and into the sun. It can be as communal or solitary as you desire. It offers deviation from regular daily patterns, like taking your bike to work instead of the bus. It forces you to focus and be aware of your surroundings. And it tires you, properly, which aids with stabilizing sleep patterns.[35]

CYCLING TO HOLD ONTO ATHLETIC IDENTITY

As I discussed earlier, so many different things impact our sense of self and have spent years creating our "athlete identity." If what you miss from your career is the competitive nature of sports, then it goes without saying that cycling can be a wonderful competitive outlet. You don't have to try to be the next Lance Armstrong or compete in the Tour de France. However, there are amateur competitive cycling events throughout the

United States every year, across a variety of cycling disciplines. If it is the workout—the physical aspect—that you miss, cycling certainly has that element, too. If you miss the team aspect, cycling is broken down into teams. And if you miss the overall feeling of being involved in a "sport" and being around your colleagues in that sport, cycling is for you. As professional cyclist Juan Manuel Garate says, "even when a rider on another team doesn't have a bottle and he's thirsty, you give him one—100% of the time."[36]

The most important part of *re*-defining the athlete is not to withdraw or abandon the athlete identity altogether, but to incorporate it with other roles that we play. Cycling can be super beneficial for this purpose. For the athlete who loves being active, who loves "the sweat," cycling provides that outlet. For the athlete who misses the team atmosphere, cycling clubs provide an easy replacement as such groups have a clear objective on their rides: to get their members across the same line. For the athlete who misses competition and beating other teams, cycling events include not only mere rides, but also racing.

The athlete seeking a competitive outlet can race on his own, or if she is looking for a team in a competitive setting, there are certainly amateur racing teams that can be joined. Through these activities, cycling can offer community which can lead to developing other identities and other roles, as new interests may be discovered. After all, the goal with the bike for athletes I speak of is not necessarily to be performance-purposed the way cyclists are at the Tour de France. But it doesn't mean that it still cannot help scratch the competitive itch.

Beyond that, it is also a lifetime skill. A basic used bicycle can be had for around $100 in many places and holds up well for transportation purposes. How many college students—student-athletes and non-athletes—use bicycles for their main transportation from class in college towns across America? It is a family activity that can be joined in by your children. I believe a more focused bike world would be a way for us to help combat climate change.

Simply put, the bike is wonderful. Also, in terms of global popularity—the bike is going nowhere!

CYCLING FOR THE MOVERS AND SHAKERS

So why should college administrators, league commissioners and general managers adopt the bicycle into their athlete transition strategies? Again, it goes back to the bottom line and developing the loyalty of the Millennial and Gen Z fan: including the annual or semi-annual cycling event into a school, franchise or league's fan appreciation or fan experience calendar is a cost-effective, unique and unexplored means of Millennial and Gen Z brand identification and marketing. Adding in cycling-oriented programming—bike rides and bike races, like Ball2Bike events that are specifically designed to introduce athletes to cycling—is the best method for reaching the next generation of fan.

Millennial, Zennial and Gen Z trends in marketing are not just disrupting, but entirely upending the old models of generating brand loyalty. In the past, several marketing models could be relied on to develop marketing and branding strategies to engage consumers to the point of loyal consumption, such as AIDA[37] and the Hierarchy of Buying model.[38] These were easily practiced with Baby Boomers and the Greatest Generation, who were not as geographically mobile and certainly nowhere near as technologically diverse as today's young people. However, there exist several differences between my generation's sports fans and our parents and grandparents. We value authenticity over content. We want engagement with brands—not just advertisements. We want to co-create products, and we use multiple technology devices compared to earlier generations.[39]

However, the two most important differences for sports organizations moving forward in an era of ever-growing entertainment competition is that compared to our predecessors, the most recent generations are much more brand loyal, and they *expect* brands—including sports brands—to give back to society. According to Forbes, 60 percent of Millennials "said that they are often or always loyal to brands that they currently purchase. The sooner you build a *relationship and deep connection* with millennials, the better."[40] And fully 75 percent of Millennials say it's "fairly or very important that a company gives back to society instead of just making a profit. They are sick and tired of corporate greed and are still recovering in the aftermath of the financial crisis. We love brands that support their local communities and would rather purchase from them than competitors."[41] So how can sports organizations—both collegiate and professional—obtain the same level of loyalty from their fans that they have in the past?

Bill Sutton has applied Maslow's Hierarchy of Needs to the program and franchise fan problem. He suggests multiple levels through which franchises and programs must ferry their fans in order to achieve "complete love" of a particular team.[42] The first level is the establishment of physical needs: does the initial enjoyment provide a positive benefit to the fan. In other words, can the fan afford an introduction to the most basic experience offered, based on ticket prices, seat locations at venues, what Sutton refers to as "total experience costs" beyond the ticket, such as food, beverage, parking, etc. Only if the franchise or program can get this fan into the first game can it begin Sherpa-ing the fan up their own mountain toward "complete love of team." The next level that Sutton discusses is "Trust" between the franchise and the fan. The franchise, and even a league, must ensure that the fan believes their investment of time and money continues to be sound by demonstrating a desire to build a winning team and enhancing fan experiences. According to Sutton, "[t]hese initial two levels of the hierarchy must be met and firmly established within the first two to three years of the relationship if the relationship is to evolve to the higher levels."[43]

The next three levels, however, are about the fan internalizing the motivations for the relationship between fan and team. And it is in these last three stages that I believe cycling can be an important part of the strategy that any franchise or program ought to implement to build fan integrity, fan loyalty, and ultimately, fan consumption. At the Love and Community level, events such as these support the fan's feelings of identification with the team, and should "attempt to create and instill these feelings in others." At the Esteem and Recognition level, Sutton asks the question that all sports organizations need to ask: if "all mutually beneficial relationships are based upon some type of reciprocity," then "where is the reciprocity from the team/organization toward the" fan? Organized cycling fan events can help provide that reciprocity—the added benefit—especially to the Millennial fan, and can be used to reinforce the organization-fan relationship by older and younger generations, too. The National Association of Collegiate Directors of Athletics have identified delivering "offline experiences" as the first principle to engage the Millennial fanbase. According to the study's author, Brian Gainor of GMR Marketing, unique and memorable experiences and access are key:

> Don't take for granted that most millennial fans have never talked with a coach or former player (online or offline), walked on the field, gone in the locker room, or had their face/tweet featured on the scoreboard. These types of experiences are what turn the ordinary into the extraordinary for fans. These are the moments that convince millennials to turn off

Netflix, pass up a viewing party with friends, and decide to take a full day out of their lives to enjoy your live game day experience.[44]

However, I believe that Gainor's strategy is too narrowly focused on not only the gameday activity, but also the social media activity. Marketers have developed a brand-new form of consumer engagement (in this case, fan engagement) that particularly addresses the choices that Millennials make when determining when and how to spend their time and money. It is called "experiential marketing."

Experiential marketing is devoted to the one desire that is truly unique to the sports fan in young adulthood today: opportunities that create solid, concrete memories and feelings rather than "stuff" or even the fleetingness of a Tweet shown up on a scoreboard.[45] After all, what's more memorable: that time that I got a free t-shirt, that time one of my photos popped up on the scoreboard, or that time that I spent the day with Bill Belichik and Tom Brady cycling for a good cause? But experiential marketing, as it is understood today, is more than just showing up for an autograph session or other traditional "fan appreciation" events. It has to be a share-worthy experience. Some brands have had great experiences with this. Perhaps the most well-known recent experience was Budweiser's Whatever, USA event to promote Bud Light. Whatever, USA involved the Budweiser company taking over several blocks of a city—Catalina Island in 2015—to host what amounted to a large party.[46] Budweiser provided live entertainment from well-known performers like Snoop Dogg and others, free food, free beer, and mini events all over town. But events like these are about more than the party itself, as Bud Light Vice President Alex Lambrecht explains:

> Of course we want to make sure that the 1,000 people who come here have an amazing time. But ultimately we want those consumers to broadcast to the world how amazing it was, because we want to reach more than the 1,0000 people that are here.[47]

The year prior, when Whatever, USA was held in Crested Butte, Colorado, Bud Light received over 200,000 people applied for 1,000 available openings. Those who attended created more than 37,000 individual pieces of content from the event featured on their various social media accounts. It was simply a shareable event, and Millennials certainly shared! Now, this is not to say that a franchise or college team ought to necessarily throw a big party and hand out free beer. But it certainly illustrates the sheer power of such events to not only bring people together for that community experience, but to also create that social proof for their friends which is driving decisions on where they spend their money—including entertainment and sports.

But why would the fan get more out of a cycling event featuring your current and retired players? Most fan events that I have been to and participated in, there is some kind of barrier between the athlete and the fan. Getting signatures? There's traditionally a physical barrier: a table between the athlete and the fan. Meeting players? The jersey or setting can be a psychological barrier for the fan, creating an "us" and "them" distinction between fan and player or fan and coach; the impression for the fan that while they are "on the team," they still aren't really *on the team.* But to put your athletes—current and former—onto a bike? Kim Cross of Outside Magazine puts it plain, speaking of the celebrity athletes that pick up the bike for Bo Bikes Bama:

> Riding shoulder-to-shoulder with them feels like the Gods of Sport have come down from Mount Olympus to walk among the mortals. Except, on a bike, they are mortals too. They don't train for this. Their butts get just as sore. They struggle up hills like the rest of us.[48]

According to Norty Cohen, founder and CEO of agency Moosylvania, Millennials "will adopt brands. If you can create a friendship with these consumers, you really take it to the next level. They will go to great lengths to support you."[49] Furthermore, Millennials look for more social proof regarding which teams—like brands—to which they wish to devote their time and money. According to Geoff Smith, SVP of Marketing at CrowdTwist, "[s]ocial proof is the psychological concept that humans naturally look toward those around them to help make decisions."[50] When the franchise or athletic director endorses events that remove those physical and psychological dividers between fan and franchise or fan and program, it opens up the doorway to a much more tangible and, ultimately, more powerful form of loyalty from that fan, but also clearly communicates *why* other people should be loyal to this team: because they really are us.

So of all experiential marketing targeting Millennials, why should we make *cycling* the event that breaks down that barrier? Bo Jackson puts it best. When he founded Bo Bikes Bama in 2012, it was in response to the destruction wrought by the tornadoes that hit Alabama one year earlier. To help his home state, Jackson sought a way to raise money for the Governor's Emergency Relief Fund. Jackson took up cycling 20 to 30 miles a day, weather and schedule permitting, as exercise after hip-replacement surgery forced him to retire from the NFL and Major League Baseball in 1992. According to him, he "would rather get root canals" than exercise in his home gym.[51] When asked by Sports Illustrated "why cycling" for a fundraiser, Bo had this to say:

> Everybody always does a golf outing, but you can only get so many people involved in that because not everybody plays. And I wanted everybody to be able to participate. And what does everybody know how to do? Ride a bicycle. It's fun and it's good exercise. A lot of times when people are riding a bike, they don't even realize that they're exercising. So doing that was a no-brainer to me.[52]

Yes, Bo Knows Biking. But he chose cycling because Everybody Knows Biking, Too! Another lesson we can take from Bo Bikes Bama on why administrators and executives ought to take up the bike and encourage their athletes—current and former—to do the same is because events like Ball2Bike and Bo Bikes Bama infuse a greater amount of local pride into the fan-franchise relationship. Jackson uses Bo Bikes Bama every year to raise money for the Governor's Emergency Relief Fund in order to provide extra money for emergency preparedness and relief in Alabama, which ties Bo to the state and to the fans. Other events across the nation do the same. Some are organized specifically for charitable fundraising efforts, and have become national brands like the Susan G. Komen Race for the Cure which raises money at every event specifically for breast cancer research—fundraising is its *raison d'etre*. Others, like the Color Run, Warrior Dash and Tough Mudder, allow and encourage local organizers and participants to use the brand as a vehicle for charitable fundraising.[53,54,55] These events can help tie in a sports organization closer to the community itself. Additionally, though, to have a goal of that kind—raising money for a good cause—also helps put the fan on the same actual *team* as their favorite players. The same way that pitchers sit in the bullpen while batters sit in the dugout, they all gather in the same place for a common goal. In the same way, cycling events with your fan-favorite players will let them put on the same "uniform" and "play" for a common, team goal.

Cycling is great and cycling is wonderful for the fan because it removes those barriers and, for perhaps the only time, makes them feel like the athlete and themselves are on the same team. We're all wearing the same spandex and helmets. We're all riding road bikes. I'm literally riding and sweating next to "insert my fangirl or fanboy crush player's name here." It breaks down the divide between fan and player, bringing them closer together. This, in turn, brings the fan and the *organization* closer together. It diminishes the "fan/player" dynamic and builds a team dynamic. The fan grabs a screenshot and shares it with friends. The fan grabs a screenshot next to Bo and sends it to his colleague at work who dons a Bear Bryant hat and a Crimson Tide shirt every Saturday in the fall. A dad grabs a photo with him and his son straddling bikes with dad's favorite player growing up, long since retired. That becomes a moment for the dad to pass on *his* love of the organization to his son in a very personal, intimate and contextualized way beyond simply having followed the team as a child or having gone to the school as an adult. That son—a Millennial—then shares the photo on his Instagram, Facebook, Twitter, or whatever the next wave of social media will be, and it gets likes and shares—some even from the school or organization itself—helping to permanently cement him into their fanbase. Will he bring his Facebook Friends and Twitter Followers along for the ride? Maybe.

That's the hope, the momentum grows and ———.

For the bottom line, cycling and the events it produces with current and former players are beneficial to building the future fanbase. With the decrease in the number of Millennials who are showing up as loyal customers, it behooves the sports industry at all levels to apply experiential marketing techniques that will also help Millennials pass on their love for their teams to their kids someday. So, to that attendee who told me in 2014 that "it will never change. People don't care about the players. They only care about the wins," I'd suggest that they have no idea what they are talking about when it comes to what *my* generation cares about.

BALL2BIKE

For more stories about athletes—both current and retired—picking up the bicycle as a means of maintaining the athlete identity, helping with mental health and physical health, please visit the Always an Athlete website at www.AlwaysanAthlete.com

16
Conclusion

"Clear eyes. Full hearts. Can't lose."

—KYLE CHANDLER,
as Coach Eric Taylor in *Friday Night Lights*[1]

I want to commend you, the Athlete. No matter how your competitive career ended or will end, you will remain a competitor for the rest of your life. No matter what sport you played, the fire that propelled you forward is still inside . . . deep in your soul—you will remain an athlete.

You sacrificed time on the court and in the gym. Now, that "new court" or "new gym" has been traded in for a physical or "home" office. Where, before, you competed against your opponent and you competed against yourself, you may be, currently, competing on a team in your current company or building your own business. Personally, you may be competing with the beautiful and challenging realities of life. The ups and downs, the points won and lost—all that you experienced in sport, help you take on the ups and downs of life. You are now competing in a different arena on a different team, yet still competing against yourself—to become your "best" self.

You avoided "fun" things in the off-season and followed a strict diet to maintain a competitive advantage when competing in season. Perhaps, now, you are sacrificing, instead, to maintain your body weight. You want to be able to look and feel your best, for wellness rather than for a competitive advantage. Now you have to prioritize taking care of your physical body alongside increased responsibility in your personal life. It can be a mix of job, studying, family, friends, networking, volunteering to a meaningful cause. All these activities are now pulling for time as you strive for balance in your personal and professional goals.

You had a "pump up" song in the locker room and followed superstitions. Now, you have a "pump up song" to apply to the "daily grind" ritual as you go to work. You lock into the zone for deep work instead of locking in on the next play. You boarded planes at five o'clock in the morning for a single game. Now, you are up early, grabbing coffee commuting to your destination to get ahead of the work day and be a leader to your new job and overall community.

Your eyes narrowed on the next play, the next snap, the next pitch, the next serve, the next kick. You battled through the heat, the cold, the wind, the rain, the mud. Perhaps, your eyes are now narrowing in on spreadsheets, tech, and data on a laptop 8+ hours a day while juggling friends, family, finances, other commitments, traveling, and passion side projects. At a moment's notice, you are ready to pivot from one project to the next for another "fire drill" from your skip level boss. Always in ready position. Comfortable with change.

Coaches called you. Coaches visited you. Your teammates became your family. Your sports family pushed you further than you thought you could go. You, NOW, have the TIME to spend with friends, family, coworkers, the public, the community, neighbors, hobby/interest groups, and clients. There is a new possibility to network with new contacts, which in turn create new opportunities. Just as when you were young, you will come to realize that relationships are everything. And life truly is a team sport.

Even after months of rehab and injuries. These are traded in for new types of setbacks in work, family, business, and personal life. You are now more adaptable and understand the importance of a growth mindset in the face of adversity. "Point by point" has now become "Day by Day"

Your sport was not something you did. Your sport, your number, your highlight reel was a part of your story, but deep down in your DNA you will always be a competitor. It was a part of who you were. Perhaps, now, whatever passion you focus on or desire you go after—you are putting the hours behind the scenes when no one is watching. Now your work or product is on display on a Zoom meeting vs on the field.

So, we've come a long way through this book. This book has shed light on tools and resources to best shape your athletic identity, mental health, and physical health and rehabilitation. It has provided ways to reinvent oneself while staying authentic and true to your roots as well as accepting and embracing this new transformation, this new chapter. *This new opportunity.*

If you are a current athlete, then maybe this book is a fond look back at the Mountain so far and a roadmap on how to avoid falling off the Cliff someday. If you are already a retired athlete, then maybe this book is a look back at your own journey up the Mountain, and perhaps makes you wish you'd had a roadmap on your way down the Cliff. Maybe you'll recommend this book to a young athlete you know. If you are a parent, family or friend of an athlete, then I hope this gives you some insight into what goes on in the athlete's mind and heart not only as they climb the Mountain, but how abrupt and difficult it can be when they eventually fall off that Cliff. I also hope that through such insight, you will be there to help mentor them on that long journey down.

If you are a coach or an administrator, I hope that if you believe that your program or franchise has no further moral obligation to your play-ers after they leave your ranks that I will have persuaded you otherwise. And if not, then I hope that I persuaded you that there may be a financial obligation to follow through on what you've read here. At minimum, you will understand that keeping your player a part of the ——— family is just good business and will keep the community full of athletes surrounding your team engaged and energized.

And if you are a fan, then I hope that this book gives you a little insight into the life and death—at least the first death—of every athlete in this country. And I hope *you* will be inspired to do something to ease the pangs of the Cliff that hit your athletic gods and supermen and super-women on a daily basis. If all goes well as we hope to build this movement, maybe you can plug into a #Ball2Bike ride or an #AlwaysAnAthlete event and meet some of your heros, make new like-minded friends and stay a part of the athletic community.

Regardless of who you are, I hope that all readers understand the athletic journey a little better, and that this book will inspire each of you to help our athletes in the future. And personally, I hope to see each of you pick up the bike when you put down the ball, as a daily training space for you to keep your heart and mind balanced. At minimum I would love to see you join your fellow teammates on a commemorative alumni ride, once a year. If you hang up your shoes, and place that framed jersey on the wall. My hope is that you find the next athletic chapter, something that keeps your body moving and invigorates your soul. I hope whatever keeps you training and motivated reminds you of how many more miles your body still has left to give. Here's to seeing you out on that long road!

In the end. . . .

You may no longer have the structure of a practice schedule or the muscle-toned body you had at your peak. But you embrace the mindset and the heart of athletes across the land. This is my story, yes. But it is also every athlete's story. All of us, at some point, end our journey up the mountain that we fought so hard to climb. We grapple every day with redefining ourselves, being open and curious for what is next and writing the next chapter of our lives. Deep down we always define ourselves as athletes. To you, I say "THANK YOU!" You are my inspiration. You who stepped out of their comfort zones to compete—*and will always compete in life*—you are Always an Athlete.

Thank you, Athletes

FAMILY ACKNOWLEDGMENTS

To my Mom and Dad: You both continue to support all my wild ideas and dreams, you are my biggest treasures. Thank you for the gift of 50 years of marriage as an example of commitment, in good times and bad. Also thank you for driving me all over to help me play competitive volleyball and for making sacrifices along the way. Also, thank you for getting me a bike when I was young, so when I found it again 20 years later I remembered the freedom and excitement I had in childhood. Your seeds of love, perseverance and faith, grew this tree of a message in me. Love you both forever.

Doug: Thank you for showcasing your love of the ocean to me as a young one. You rode the everlasting wave for decades. We will forever be the fruit flies with blue eyes in our family.

Elissa, Kyle and Kenlie: thank you for all you do to support me in all my endeavors. I love you very much.

Kalen: thank you for sketching the front cover of the book (and forthcoming journal)! Also thank you for teaching me about all the athletes in skateboarding culture. I love you and you are an amazing talent!

Extended family: Many of you are athletes and competed growing up: swimming, softball, basketball, football, soccer, baseball. Thank you for being my inspiration. You are always in my corner, and I in yours. I am forever grateful. Love you to the moon and back.

NOTES

Chapter 1. Why This Book

1. Jake New, *A Long Shot*. Inside Higher Ed., January 27, 2015 (available at: <https://www.insidehighered.com/news/2015/01/27/college-athletes-greatly-overestimate-their-chances-playing-professionally>)(last accessed: September 5, 2017).

2. Kathleen Elkins, *Americans retire 8 years later than workers in China – here's the retirement age around the world.* CNBC Online, August 15, 2017 (available at: <https://www.cnbc.com/2017/08/15/the-average-retirement-age-in-the-us-and-other-countries.html>)(last accessed: September 6, 2017).

3. Rob Arthur, *Shrinking Shelf Life of NFL Players, The.* The Wall Street Journal, February 29, 2016 (available at: <https://www.wsj.com/articles/the-shrinking-shelf-life-of-nfl-players-1456694959>)(last accessed: September 7, 2017).

4. Jeff Nelson, *Longest Professional Sports Careers, The.* The Roosevelts, July 22, 2013 (available at: <http://www.rsvlts.com/2013/07/22/longest-sports-careers/>)(last accessed: September 7, 2017).

5. Melinda Beck, *Delayed Development: 20-Somethings Blame the Brain.* The Wall Street Journal, August 23, 2012 (available at: <https://www.wsj.com/articles/SB10000872396390443713704577601532208760746>)(last accessed: September 1, 2017).

6. Melinda Beck, *Delayed Development: 7* Ferris Jabr, *Neuroscience of 20-Somethings, The.* Scientific American Online, August 29, 2012 (available at: <https://blogs.scientificamerican.com/brainwaves/the-neuroscience-of-twenty-somethings/>)(last accessed: September 1, 2017).

7. Beck, *Delayed Development.*

8. Chris Bondarenko, *Why many high-performing sports teams are losing money at the gate.* Vision Critical, February 25, 2015 (available at: <https://www.visioncritical.com/gate-revenue/>)(last accessed: September 7, 2017).

Chapter 2. Introduction

1. Robert Laura, *How Star Athletes Deal With Retirement*. Forbes Online, May 22, 2012 (available at: <https://www.forbes.com/sites/robertlaura/2012/05/22/how-star-athletes-deal-with-retirement/#25e3cf622a4e>) (last accessed: August 29, 2017).

Chapter 3. Youth Sports

1. Jim Afremow, PhD, *The Champion's Comeback: How Great Athletes Recover, Reflect, and Reignite*. Rodale Books at 16 (2016).

2. Bruce Kelley, Carl Carchia, *Hey, data data — swing!*. ESPN Online, July 11, 2013 (available at: <http://www.espn.com/espn/story/_/id/9469252/hidden-demographics-youth-sports-espn-magazine>)(last accessed: September 1, 2017).

3. Sports Society, *What We Do*. The Aspen Institute (available at: <https://www.aspeninstitute.org/programs/sports-society/what-we-do/>)(last accessed: September 1, 2016).

4. Sports Society, *What We Do*.

5. Sports Society, *What We Do*.

6. Sports Society, *What We Do*.

7. Sports Society, *What We Do*.

8. Steven Covelman, John Cadiz Klemack, *Former Olympian Anita DeFrantz Continues to Serve as an Advocate for Athletes*. NBC Los Angeles Online, July 25, 2012 (available at: < http://www.nbclosangeles.com/news/local/Anita-DeFrantz-Olympics-Advocate-LA84-London-Rowing-Montreal-Moscow-Boycott-163618106.html>)(last accessed: September 1, 2017).

9. Alice Lee, *7 Charts that Show the State of Youth Sports in the US and Why it Matters*. The Aspen Institute, February 24, 2015 (available at: <https://www.aspeninstitute.org/blog-posts/7-charts-that-show-the-state-of-youth-sports-in-the-us-and-why-it-matters/>)(last accessed: September 1, 2017).

10. Christy Adams, et al., *The Importance of Outdoor Play and Its Impact on Brain Development in Children* at 13. University of Missouri-Kansas City (available at: <https://education.umkc.edu/download/berkley/The-Importance-of-Outdoor-Play-and-Its-Impact-on-Brain-Develpoment-in-Children.pdf>) (last accessed: September 1, 2017).

11. Adams, *Importance of Outdoor Play* at 13-14.

12. Donna L. Merkel, *Youth sport: positive and negative impact on young athletes*. Open Access Journal of Sports Medicine, vol. 4 at 152, June 15, 2013 (available at: <https://www.ncbi.nlm.nih.gov/pmc/articles/PMC3871410/pdf/oajsm-4-151.pdf>)(last accessed: September 3, 2017).

13. Project Play, *Facts: Sports Activity and Children*. The Aspen Institute

(available at: <http://aspenprojectplay.org/the-facts>)(last accessed: September 3, 2017).

14. Merkel, *Youth sport: Positive and negative impact* at 152.

15. Health Fitness Revolution, *Top 10 Health Benefits of Youth Sports*. Health Fitness Revolution, June 3, 2015 (available at: <http://www.health fitnessrevolution.com/top-10-health-benefits-youth-sports/>)(last accessed: September 12, 2017).

16. Abigail Hess, *If you want to be a CEO later, play sports now*. CNBC Online, January 11, 2017 (available at: <https://www.cnbc.com/2017/01/11 /want-to-be-a-ceo-later-play-sports-now.html>)(last accessed: February 1, 2017).

17. Michael Casey, *Want to succeed in business? Then play high school sports*. Fortune Magazine Online, June 19, 2014 (available at: <http://fortune .com/2014/06/19/high-school-sports-business-cornell-job-market/>) (last accessed: September 1, 2017).

18. Positive Coach Alliance website. https://positivecoach.org/.

19. Patti Neighmond, *Benefits Of Sports To A Child's Mind And Heart All Part Of The Game*. National Public Radio, July 1, 2015 (available at: <http:// www.npr.org/sections/health-shots/2015/07/01/418899249/benefits-of-sports -to-a-childs-mind-and-heart-all-part-of-the-game>)(last accessed: September 3, 2017).

20. Neighmond, *Benefits of Sports*.

21. Neighmond, *Benefits of Sports*.

22. Baker, Kendall, Kobe; (available at: https://www.axios.com/2019/07/17 /health-risks-specialization-youth-sports).

23. Project Play, *State of Play 2016* at 4.

24. Matz, Eddie *The kids are alright*: (available at: https://www.espn.com/espn/story/_/id/10496416/ are-youth-sports-ruining-kids-childhoods-espn-magazine)

25. Matz, *The kids are alright*.

26. Project Play, *State of Play 2016* at 7.

27. *2014 Summit Shareables*, espnW Online, 2014 (available at: <http:// www.espn.com/espnw/w-in-action/2014-summit/grid/11661226/2014-summit -shareables>)(last accessed: September 2, 2017).

28. Sean Gregory, *How Kids' Sports Became a $15 Billion Industry*. TIME Online, August 24, 2017 (available at: <http://time.com/4913687/how-kids -sports-became-15-billion-industry/>)(last accessed: September 2, 2017).

29. Michael S. Rosenwald, *Are parents ruining youth sports? Fewer kids play amid pressure*. The Washington Post Online, October 4, 2015 (available at: <https://www.washingtonpost.com/local/are-parents-ruining -youth-sports-fewer-kids-play-amid-pressure/2015/10/04/eb1460dc-686e

-11e5-9ef3-fde182507eac_story.html?utm_term=.e4d8caede24d>)(last accessed: September 2, 2017).

30. Herbert A. Simon and William G. Chase, *Skill in Chess*. American Scientist, vol. 61, no. 4 pp. 394-403, 402. July-August 1973 (available at: <https://digitalcollections.library.cmu.edu/awweb/awarchive?type=file&item =44582>)(last accessed: September 11, 2017).

31. John R. Hayes, *The Complete Problem Solver*. The Franklin Institute Press, Philadelphia, Pennsylvania 1981.

32. Malcolm Gladwell, *Outliers*. Little, Brown and Company, New York, New York 2008.

33. Gladwell, *Outliers* at 42.

34. V. Alan Spiker, *Growing Athletes: A Father's 15-Year Journey from T-Ball to Hard Ball*. at ch. 5.

35. Anders Ericsson and Robert Pool, *Malcolm Gladwell got us wrong: Our research was key to the 10,000-hour rule, but here's what got oversimplified*. Salon.com, April 10, 2016 (available at: <http://www.salon.com /2016/04/10/malcolm_gladwell_got_us_wrong_our_research_was_key_to _the_10000_hour_rule_but_heres_what_got_oversimplified/>)(last accessed: September 11, 2017).

36. Langston Wertz Jr., *Yo, this is why Kobe Bryant, the Black Mamba, wants to punt on AAU basketball*. The Charlotte Observer Online, May 2, 2017 (available at: <http://www.charlotteobserver.com/sports/article148210494 .html>)(last accessed: September 11, 2017).

37. Wertz Jr., *Yo*.

38. Myron Medcalf and Dana O'Neil, *Playground Basketball Is Dying*. ESPN Online, July 23, 2014 (available at: <http://www.espn.com/espn/feature /story/_/id/11216972/playground-basketball-dying>)(last accessed: September 11, 2017).

39. Matz, *kids are alright*.

40. Joseph Zucker, *286-Pound 8th Grade Prospect Jaheim Oatis Offered Scholarships by Alabama, More*. Bleacher Report, July 24, 2017 (available at: <http://bleacherreport.com/articles/2723544-286-pound-8th-grade-prospect -jaheim-oatis-offered-scholarships-by-alabama-more>)(last accessed: September 11, 2017).

41. Nathaniel Popper, *Committing to Play for a College, Then Starting 9th Grade*. New York Times Online, January 26, 2014 (available at: <https:// www.nytimes.com/2014/01/27/sports/committing-to-play-for-a-college-then -starting-9th-grade.html?mcubz=0>)(last accessed: September 1, 2017).

42.. Tim Casey, *When Will We Stop? The Absurdity of Youth Basketball Rankings*. Bleacher Report Online, January 20, 2015 (available at: <http:// bleacherreport.com/articles/2308941-when-will-we-stop-the-absurdity-of -youth-basketball-rankings>)(last accessed: September 11, 2017).

43. Langston Wertz Jr., *NBA and USA Basketball want your kid to play less, and here's why, The*. Charlotte Observer Online, October 18, 2016 (available at: <http://www.charlotteobserver.com/sports/high-school /article109084247.html>)(last accessed: September 11, 2017).

44. Matz, *kids are alright*.

45. Matz, *kids are alright*.

46. Matz, *kids are alright*.

47. Jacquelynne S. Eccles, PhD., *Development of Children Ages 6 to 14, The*. The Future of Children vol. 9, no. 2 pp. 30-44, 30 (Fall 1999).

48. Eccles, *Development of Children Ages 6 to 14* at 30.

49. Project Play, *Facts: Sports Activity and Children*.

50. Britton W. Brewer, Judy L. Van Raalte and Darwyn E. Linder, *Athletic Identity: Hercules' muscles or Achilles Heel?*, International Journal of Sport Psychology, 24(2) at p. 237 (1993).

51. Eric Martin, *Role of Athletic Identity and Passion in Predicting Burnout in Adolescent Female Athletes, The*. Miami (OH) University, Thesis-Dept. of Kinesiology and Health (2011)(available at: <https://etd.ohiolink .edu/!etd.send_file?accession=miami1312937508&disposition=inline>).

52. Atkinson, *How parents are ruining youth sports*.

53. *Nike Website, Nike Mission Statement Webpage*. Nike, Inc. (available at: <https://help-en-us.nike.com/app/answer/a_id/113>)(last accessed: September 30, 2017).

54. Aspen Institute, Don't Retire Kid ttps://www.aspenprojectplay.org /dont-retire-kid

55. Merkel, *Youth sport: positive and negative impact on young athletes*. Open Access Journal of Sports Medicine (2013).

Chapter 4. High School Sports

1. *Hoosiers* (1986 Metro-Goldwyn-Meyer).

2. Project Play, *Facts: Sports Activity and Children*.

3. NFHS, *High School Sports Participation Increases for 27th Consecutive Year*. National Federation of State High School Associations Website, September 12, 2016 (available at: <https://www.nfhs.org/articles/high-school-sports -participation-increases-for-27th-consecutive-year/>)(last accessed: September 12, 2017).

4. Project Play, *Facts: Sports Activity and Children*.

5. Lauren Feiner, *Pay-To-Play: Business Of College Athletic Recruitment, The*. Forbes Online, June 23, 2015 (available at: <https://www.forbes.com /sites/laurenfeiner/2015/06/23/pay-to-play-the-business-of-college-athletic -recruitment/#8e1ac73e9b57>)(last accessed: September 20, 2017).

6. Marc Williams, *Mesut Ozil quotes Arsenal club legend Tony Adams on Facebook and racks up the 'likes'*. The Independent Online, May 7, 2014

(available at: <http://www.independent.co.uk/sport/football/premier-league
/mesut-ozil-quotes-arsenal-club-legend-tony-adams-on-facebook-and-racks
-up-the-likes-9330794.html>)(last accessed: September 12, 2017).

7. Associate Press, *Coach known best for 1980 hockey gold*. ESPN Online,
August 19, 2003 (available at: <http://www.espn.com/classic/obit/s/2003/0811
/1594173.html>)(last accessed: September 12, 2017).

8. Katie E. Helms, *Campus Recreation Program Involvement, Athletic
Identity, Transitional Loss and Life Satisfaction in Former High School
Athletes*. University of Arkansas, Fayetteville Thesis and Dissertation (2010)
at 2 (available at: <http://scholarworks.uark.edu/cgi/viewcontent.cgi?article
=1059&context=etd>)(last accessed: September 15, 2017).

9. Jerry Rice, *Rice*. ed. Michael Silver. New York: St. Martin's Griffin.
pp. 20-23 (1996).

10. John W. Schoen, *Why does a college degree cost so much?* CNBC Online, June 2015 (available at: <https://www.cnbc.com/2015/06/16/why-college
-costs-are-so-high-and-rising.html>)(last accessed: September 12, 2017).

11. Lily Rothman, *Putting the Rising Cost of College in Perspective*. TIME
Online, August 31, 2016 (available at: <http://time.com/4472261/college-cost
-history/>)(last accessed: September 12, 2017).

12. Daniel Indiviglio, *Importance of College, The: A Self-Fulfilling Proph-
ecy*. The Atlantic Online, June 27, 2011 (available at: <https://www.theatlantic
.com/business/archive/2011/06/the-importance-of-college-a-self-fulfilling
-prophecy/241092/>)(last accessed: September 12, 2017).

13. David Leonhardt, *Is College Worth It? Clearly, New Data Say*.
The New York Times, May 27, 2014 (available at: <https://www.nytimes.com
/2014/05/27/upshot/is-college-worth-it-clearly-new-data-say.html?mcubz=1>)
(last accessed: September 12, 2017).

14. NCAA, *Estimated probability of competing in college athletics*, NCAA
Website, March 10, 2017 (available at: <http://www.ncaa.org/about/resources
/research/estimated-probability-competing-college-athletics>)(last accessed:
September 1, 2017).

15. NCAA, *Estimated probability of competing in college athletics*.

16. National Association of Intercollegiate Athletics Eligibility Center,
Registration Web Page (available at: <http://www.playnaia.org/page/register
.php>)(last accessed: September 15, 2017).

17. College Sports Scholarships, *Community College Athletic Scholarships – Junior College Sports Recruiting*. Webpage (available at: <http://
www.collegesportsscholarships.com/junior-juco-njcaa-recruiting.htm>)
(last accessed: September 15, 2017).

18. Ross Hawley, *Recruiting Column: Interview with NJCAA Executive
Director, Dr. Chris Parker*. USA Today: High School Sports Online, September 1, 2017 (available at: <http://usatodayhss.com/2017/recruiting-column

-interview-with-njcaa-executive-director-dr-chris-parker>)(last accessed: September 20, 2017).

19. Hawley, *Recruiting Column: Interview with NJCAA Executive Director*.

20. National Association of Intercollegiate Athletics, *NAIA Players in the Pros – NBA*, NAIA Website, September 10, 2005 (available at: <http://www.naia.org/ViewArticle.dbml?ATCLID=205294408>)(last accessed: September 15, 2017).

21. Alan Grosbach, *On to the Pros*, NAIA Website, June 10, 2015 (available at: <http://www.naia.org/ViewArticle.dbml?ATCLID=210143691>)(last accessed: September 15, 2017).

22. Aaron Sorenson, *Top DIII and NAIA Athletes Who Went Pro*, Next College Student Athlete Website (available at: <http://www.ncsasports.org/blog/2012/09/12/top-10-diii-naia-athletes-pro/>)(last accessed: September 15, 2017).

23. Anders Kelto, *How Likely Is It, Really, That Your Athletic Kid Will Turn Pro?* National Public Radio Online, September 4, 2015 (available at: <http://www.npr.org/sections/health-shots/2015/09/04/432795481/how-likely-is-it-really-that-your-athletic-kid-will-turn-pro>)(last accessed: September 1, 2017).

24. Kelto, *How Likely Is It, Really*.

25. Bob Cook, *NCAA Survey Sheds Light on Athletes' Youth Sports Experience*. Forbes Online, January 17, 2016 (available at: <https://www.forbes.com/sites/bobcook/2016/01/17/ncaa-survey-sheds-light-on-athletes-youth-sports-experience/#49b4ed82a122>)(last accessed: September 1, 2017).

26. NCAA, *Results from the 2015 GOALS Study of the Student-Athlete Experience*. NCAA Convention Powerpoint (January 2016)(available at: <http://www.ncaa.org/sites/default/files/GOALS_convention_slidebank_jan2016_public.pdf>)(last accessed: September 15, 2017).

27. Matz, *Kids are alright*.

28. Matz, *Kids are alright*.

29. Matz, *Kids are alright*.

30. University of Richmond Athletics, *2015 Men's Lacrosse Roster – Chase Bly*. Richmond Athletics Webpage (available at: <http://www.richmondspiders.com/roster.aspx?rp_id=40>)(last accessed: September 15, 2017).

31. Baylor Athletics, *Track and Field - Robert Griffin III*. Balor University Athletic Department Online (available at: <http://www.baylorbears.com/sports/c-track/mtt/griffin_robert00.html>)(last accessed: September 12, 2017).

32. Florida State Athletics, *Jameis Winston Player Profile*. Florida State Athletic Department Online (available at: <http://seminoles.com/sports/baseball/roster/jameis-winston/>)(last accessed: September 12, 2017).

33. Sally Jenkins, *Robert Griffin III: His military appreciation will play*

well in the NFL and would benefit the Redskins. The Washington Post Online, March 11, 2012 (available at: <https://www.washingtonpost.com/sports/redskins/robert-griffin-iii-poised-to-handle-the-pressure/2012/03/11/gIQAuOA45R_print.html>)(last accessed: September 12, 2017).

34. Jamie Newberg, *Jameis Winston picks Noles over Tide.* ESPN Online, August 3, 2011 (available at: <http://www.espn.com/college-sports/recruiting/football/story/_/id/6831127/jameis-winston-commits-florida-state>)(last accessed: September 12, 2017).

35. Karen Crouse, *Want to Play Football at Ohio State or Clemson? Try Playing Other Sports, Too.* New York Times, December 30, 2016 (available at: <https://www.nytimes.com/2016/12/30/sports/ncaafootball/ohio-state-clemson-multisport-athletes-fiesta-bowl.html?mcubz=1>)(last accessed: September 12, 2017).

36. Crouse, *Want to Play Football at Ohio State and Clemson.*

37. Crouse, *Want to Play Football at Ohio State and Clemson.*

38. Crouse, *Want to Play Football at Ohio State and Clemson.*

39. Rustin Dodd, *Withey's volleyball background was a building block.* The Kansas City Star, March 29, 2012 (available at: <http://www.kansascity.com/sports/college/ncaa/article302002/Withey%E2%80%99s-volleyball-background-was-a-building-block.html>)(last accessed: September 12, 2017).

40. Dodd. *Withiey's volleyball background.*

41. Jordan Ritter Conn, *Started From Yaounde, Now He's Here.* Grantland Online, June 27, 2014 (available at: <http://grantland.com/features/joel-embiid-nba-draft-philadelphia-76ers-kansas-jayhawks/>)(last accessed: September 12, 2017).

42. Sam Mellinger, *In Joel Embiid, the Kansas Jayhawks have a star-to-be.* Kansas City Star, October 23, 2013 (available at: <http://www.kansas.com/latest-news/article1126029.html>)(last accessed: September 12, 2017).

43. Gary Bedore, *KU Freshman Udoka Azubuike is the latest Jayhawk big man to salute soccer.* Kansas City Star, October 21, 2016 (available at: <http://www.kansascity.com/sports/college/big-12/university-of-kansas/article109789162.html>)(last accessed: September 12, 2017).

44. Jeffrey C. Adams, *Athletic Identity and Ego Identity Status as Predictors of Career Maturity Among High School Students.* University of Houston – Theses and Dissertations (2011) at 54 (available at: <https://uh-ir.tdl.org/uh-ir/bitstream/handle/10657/261/ADAMS-.pdf?sequence=2&isAllowed=y>)(last accessed: September 15, 2017).

45. Dr. Chris Stankovich, *Know! The Importance of a Balanced Athletic Identity Among Youth.* Know! Newsletter, Drug Free Action Alliance (available at: <https://preventionactionalliance.org/wp-content/uploads/2015/03/Know-The-Importance-of-a-Balanced-Athletic-Identity-Among-Youth.pdf>)(last accessed: September 15, 2017).

Chapter 5. College Sports

1. *Rudy* (TriStar Pictures 1993)(motion picture).

2. *Rudy* (TriStar Pictures 1993)(motion picture).

3. Michael Goodwin, *College Sports Industry, The; When the Cash Register Is The Scoreboard.* New York Times Online, June 8, 1986 (available at: <http://www.nytimes.com/1986/06/08/sports/the-college-sports-industry-when-the-cash-register-is-the-scoreboard.html?pagewanted=all&mcubz=0>) (last accessed: September 20, 2017).

4. Goodwin, *College Sports Industry.*

5. Goodwin, *College Sports Industry.*

6. Goodwin, *College Sports Industry.*

7. Dryer, Kim. Nick Saban Signs Record Contract SA WCBI.com (available at: <https://www.wcbi.com/nick-saban-signs-record-contract-extension/>) (last accessed: October 20, 2022).

8. Marc Tracy and Tim Rohan, *What Made College Football More Like the Pros? $7.3 Billion, for a Start.* New York Times Online, December 30, 2014 (available at: <https://www.nytimes.com/2014/12/31/sports/ncaafootball/what-made-college-ball-more-like-the-pros-73-billion-for-a-start.html?mcubz=0>) (last accessed: September 20, 2017).

9. Tim Parker, *How much Does the NCAA Make off March Madness?* Investopedia Online, March 13, 2017 (available at: <http://www.investopedia.com/articles/investing/031516/how-much-does-ncaa-make-march-madness.asp>)(last accessed: September 20, 2017).

10. Public Broadcasting Service, *Interview Andrew Zimbalist.* PBS Frontline Webpage, January 29, 2011 (available at: <http://www.pbs.org/wgbh/pages/frontline/money-and-march-madness/interviews/andrew-zimbalist.html>) (last accessed: September 20, 2017).

11. Mark Koba, *What a college athlete is worth on the open market.* CNBC Online, April 12, 2014 (available at: <https://www.cnbc.com/2014/04/12/whats-a-college-athlete-worth-in-pay-on-the-open-market.html>)(last accessed: September 20, 2017).

12. Butts, Mason. Next Gen Personal Finacne: Available at: (<https://www.ngpf.org/blog/question-of-the-day/question-of-the-day-how-much-revenue-do-college-sports-generate-for-athletic-departments-each-year/>) (Last accessed: October 25, 2022).

13. Jones, Rory, Sports Pro Media (<https://www.sportspromedia.com/news/ncaa-finances-2021-revenue-march-madness-college-sports/.) (last accessed: October 22, 2022).

14. Jones, Rory, Sports Pro Media (<https://www.sportspromedia.com/news/ncaa-finances-2021-revenue-march-madness-college-sports/.) (last accessed: October 22, 2022).

15. National Association of Intercollegiate Athletics, *Economic Impact*. NAIA Website. (available at: <http://www.naia.org/ViewArticle.dbml?DB _OEM_ID=27900&ATCLID=211802101>)(last accessed: August 7, 2019); National Junior Collegiate Athletic Association, *Economic Impact*. NJCAA Website. (available at: <ncjaa.org/about/host_championship/economic _impact>)(last accessed: August 7, 2019).

16. John Kean, *Telling the Campus Story Through Athletics: How to Position Athletics Communications In A Leadership Role*. NCAA Division II Brochure (available at: <https://www.ncaa.org/sites/default/files/D2_Toolkit _Communications_web_20160111.pdf>)(last accessed: September 20, 2017).

17. Shannon Crawford, *Kentucky Basketball: Millionaire Heaven*. Columbia Sports Journalism Anthology, June 9, 2014 (available at: <http:// columbiasportsjournalism.com/2014/06/09/banking-on-coach-cal/>)(last accessed: September 20, 2017).

18. Fred Mann, *Wichita State's Final Four run pays off in exposure for university*. Wichita Eagle Online, May 4, 2013 (available at: <http://www .kansas.com/news/article1114740.html>)(last accessed: September 20, 2017).

19. Ben Baskin, *Shatterproof at Alabama*. Columbia Sports Journalism Anthology, June 9, 2014 (available at: <http://columbiasportsjournalism.com /2014/06/09/shatterproof/>)(last accessed: September 20, 2017).

20. Baskin, *Shatterproof at Alabama*.

21. Dr. Doug J. Chung, *Dynamic Advertising Effect of Collegiate Athletics, The*. Harvard University Business School – Working Paper 13-067 at 2, January 25, 2013 (available at: <http://www.hbs.edu/faculty/Publication%20 Files/13-067_86a0b712-f29e-423f-b614-0165b770dd65.pdf>)(last accessed: September 20, 2017).

22. Chung, *Dynamic Advertising* at 2.

23. Chung, *Dynamic Advertising* at 2.

24. Chung, *Dynamic Advertising* at 2.

25. Mann, *Wichita State's Final Four run pays off*.

26. Nick Schultz and Abigail Schnable, *After Magical March, Culture Change Comes to Loyola*. Loyola Phoenix Online, Aug. 22, 2018 (available at: <http://loyolaphoenix.com/2018/08/after-magical-march-culture-change -comes-to-loyola/>)(last accessed: August 7, 2019).

27. Dawn Rhodes, *With NCAA success, Loyola now looks for gains off the court*. Chicago Tribune Online, Mar. 21, 2018 (available at: <https:// www.chicagotribune.com/sports/college/ct-met-loyola-basketball-university -publicity-20180321-story.html>)(last accessed: August 7, 2019).

28. Baskin, *Shatterproof at Alabama*.

29. Baskin, *Shatterproof at Alabama*.

30. Amy Perko and Jay Weiner, *College Sports 101 – Chapter 8*. Knight Commission on Intercollegiate Athletics at 23, October 2009 (available at:

<http://www.knightcommission.org/images/pdfs/cs101.pdf>)(last accessed: September 20, 2017).

31. Doug Lederman, *When Athletics May Influence Alumni Giving.* Inside Higher Ed Online, April 29, 2008 (available at: <https://www .insidehighered.com/news/2008/04/29/giving>)(last accessed: September 20, 2017).

32. Elise Young, *The Gridiron Payoff?* Inside Higher Ed Online, July 3, 2012 (available at: <https://www.insidehighered.com/news/2012/07/03/report -finds-alumni-giving-among-other-areas-correlated-football-success>)(last accessed: September 20, 2017).

33. Jonathan Meer and Harvey S. Rosen, *Impact of Athletic Performance on Alumni Giving: An Analysis of Micro Data.* National Bureau of Economic Research – NBER Working Paper Series (April 2008) (available at: <http:// www.nber.org/papers/w13937.pdf>)(last accessed: September 20, 2017).

34. Michael L. Anderson, *Benefits of College Athletic Success, The: An Application of the Propensity Score Design with Instrumental Variables.* National Bureau of Economic Research – NBER Working Paper Series (June 2012) (available at: <http://www.nber.org/papers/w18196.pdf>)(last accessed: September 20, 2017).

35. Kent Babb, *Baylor sports fans, in wake of another scandal, struggle with support and shame.* Washington Post Online, June 3, 2016 (available at: <https://www.washingtonpost.com/sports/baylor-sports-fans-in-wake-of -another-scandal-struggle-with-support-and-shamea-new-wave-of-sadness -leaves-football-supporters-questioning-everything/2016/06/03/67ec4d64 -2902-11e6-a3c4-0724e8e24f3f_story.html?utm_term=.3da0c3d3b556>) (last accessed: September 20, 2017).

36. Independence Community College. *ICC's opening day summer enrollment up 70 percent.* Independence Community College Website, June 5, 2018 (available at: <indycc.edu/news/1640770/iccs-opening-day-summer -enrollment-up-70-percent>)(last accessed: August 7, 2019).

37. Lindsay Ellis, *Baylor draws record-high applications despite scandal.* Houston Chronicle Online, March 20, 2017 (available at: <http://www .houstonchronicle.com/news/houston-texas/houston/article/Baylor-draws -record-high-applications-despite-11013274.php>)(last accessed: September 20, 2017).

38. Rebecca R. Ruiz, *Despite Scandal, Applications to Penn State Rise.* New York Times Online, November 30, 2011 (available at: <https://thechoice .blogs.nytimes.com/2011/11/30/penn-state-apps/>)(last accessed: September 20, 2017).

39. Sports Illustrated Staff: (Available at <tps://www.si.com/college/2022 /09/16/texas-report-thousands-spent-recruits-arch-manning-college-football>) (Last accessed October 20,2022)

40. Parker Gabriel, *Eichorst out as Husker athletic director; Nebraska begins search for new AD*. Lincoln Journal Star Online, September 21, 2017 (available at: <http://journalstar.com/sports/huskers/husker-sports/eichorst-out-as-ad/article_c811f0a1-52c1-5a82-8d76-209ddbbb52b9.html>)(last accessed: September 21, 2017).

41. Matt Galloway, *Banner day eludes 'unsatisfied' KU football in close loss to K-State*. Capital Journal Online, Oct. 28, 2017 (available at: <cjonline.com/sports/hawkzone/2017-10-28/banner-day-eludes-unsatisfied-ku-football-close-loss-k-state>)(last accessed: August 7, 2019).

42. Jimmie Kaylor, *The 5 Best College Football Coaches Who Have Been Fired*. Sports Casting Website, Mar. 13, 2017 (available at: <sprotscasting.com/sports/best-college-football-coaches-who-have-been-fired>)(last accessed: August 7, 2019).

43. Richard Johnson, *Why Les Miles was finally fired at LSU*. SB Nation Online, Sep. 25, 2016 (available at: <https://www.sbnation.com/college-football/2016/9/25/13036536/les-miles-fired-lsu-coach>)(last accessed: August 7, 2019).

44. Bill Vasko, *So You Want To Be a College Coach?* LinkedIn Website, June 20, 2014 (available at: <https://www.linkedin.com/pulse/20140620153938-33469656-so-you-want-to-be-a-college-coach>)(last accessed: August 7, 2019).

45. Jonathan Adams, *Jason Brown's Salary: How Much Money Did 'Last Chance U' Coach Make?* Heavy Online, July 24, 2019 (available at: <heavy.com/sports/2019/07/jason-brown-salary-last-chance-u-coach/>)(last accessed: August 7, 2019).

46. Pippa Raga, *We're Obsessed With Coach Martin's Family on 'Last Chance U'*. Distractify Online, Aug. 2019 (available at: <distractify.com/p/last-chance-u-coach-martin>)(last accessed: August 7, 2019).

47. Amy Daughters, *Why We Would Never Be a College Football Head Coach*. Bleacher Report Online, May 5, 2013 (available at: <http://bleacherreport.com/articles/1629795-why-we-would-never-be-a-college-football-head-coach>)(last accessed: September 20, 2017).

48. Dan Hope, *Clemson parts ways with volleyball coach Hugh Hernesman*. Independent Mail, USA Today Online, March 1, 2017 (available at: <http://www.independentmail.com/story/sports/2017/03/01/clemson-fires-volleyball-coach-hugh-hernesman/98575584/>)(last accessed: September 20, 2017).

49. *ISU Softball coach Shane Bouman let go*. WTHITV10.com, March 20, 2017 (available at: <http://www.wthitv.com/story/34957328/isu-softball-coach-shane-bouman-let-go>)(last accessed: September 20, 2017).

50. Rustin Dodd, *KU women's basketball coach Bonnie Henrickson fired after 11 seasons*. Kansas City Star Online, March 9, 2015 (available at: <http://

www.kansascity.com/sports/college/big-12/university-of-kansas/article13112879
.html>)(last accessed: September 20, 2017).

51. Nancy Spitler, *It's How You Win That Matters*. Clemson World,
Summer-Fall 2016 (available at: <https://clemson.world/dabo/>)(last accessed:
September 20, 2017).

52. Spitler, *It's How You Win That Matters*.

53. Spitler, *It's How You Win That Matters*.

54. NCAA Eligibility Center, *2016-2017 Guide for the College-Bound
Student Athlete*. At 31 (available at: <http://www.ncaapublications.com
/productdownloads/CBSA17.pdf>)(last accessed: September 20, 2017).

55. NCAA, *Scholarships Web Page*. NCAA Website (available at: <http://
www.ncaa.org/student-athletes/future/scholarships>)(last accessed: September
20, 2017).

56. Lynn O'Shaughnessy, *8 things you should know about sports
scholarships*. CBS News Online, September 20, 2012 (available at: <https://
www.cbsnews.com/news/8-things-you-should-know-about-sports-scholarships/>)
(last accessed: September 20, 2017).

57. National Center for Education Statistics, *Average undergraduate
tuition and fees and room and board rates charged for full-time students in
degree-granting postsecondary institutions, by and control of institution:
1963-64 through 2012-13*. Institute of Education Sciences, United States
Department of Education Website, Table 330.10 (available at: <https://
nces.ed.gov/programs/digest/d13/tables/dt13_330.10.asp>)(last accessed:
September 20, 2017).

58. Kristi Dosh, *Does Football Fund Other Sports At College Level?*
Forbes Online, May 5, 2011 (available at: <https://www.forbes.com/sites
/sportsmoney/2011/05/05/does-football-fund-other-sports-at-college-level
/#553c662171c2>)(last accessed: September 25, 2017).

59. NCAA, *NCAA Core Values*. NCAA Website (available at: <http://
www.ncaa.org/about/ncaa-core-values>)(last accessed: September 25, 2017).

60. Sean Gregory, *Should College Athletes Major in Sports?* TIME
Magazine Online, November 27, 2012 (available at: <http://keepingscore.
blogs.time.com/2012/11/27/should-jocks-just-major-in-sports/>)(last accessed:
September 25, 2017).

61. Megan Kalmoe, *NCAA: Revenue vs. Non-Revenue Sports*. Megan
Kalmoe Online Blog, January 24, 2011 (available at: <https://megankalmoe
.com/2011/01/24/rev-vs-nonrev/>)(last accessed: September 25, 2017).

62. Kalmoe, *NCAA: Revenue vs. Non-Revenue Sports*.

63. Peter Keating, *silent enemy of men's sports, The*. espnW Online, May
23, 2012 (available at: <http://www.espn.com/espnw/title-ix/article/7959799
/the-silent-enemy-men-sports>)(last accessed: September 25, 2017).

64. Jack McCallum, *Walk-Ons Are Now In the Running*. Sports Illustrated

Vault Online, September 5, 1984 (available at: <https://www.si.com/vaul t/1984/09/05/633947/walk-ons-are-now-in-the-running>)(last accessed: September 20, 2017).

65. McCallum, *Walk-Ons Are Now In the Running*.

66. Mark Titus, *Don't Put Me In, Coach*. Anchor Books, New York p.42 (2012).

67. *McCants et al. v. Nat'l Collegiate Athletic Ass'n*, Complaint at ¶ 91 (available at: <https://sports.cbsimg.net/images/blogs/Hausfeld-complaint.pdf>).

68. *McCants*, at ¶ 92.

69. NCAA, *Division I Results from the NCAA GOALS Study on the Student-Athlete Experience*, NCAA FARA Annual Meeting and Symposium Powerpoint, November 2011 (available at: <http://www.ncaa.org/sites/default /files/DI_GOALS_FARA_final_1.pdf>)(last accessed: September 20, 2017).

70. Jake New, *What Off-Season?* Inside Higher Ed Online, May 8, 2015 (available at: <https://www.insidehighered.com/news/2015/05/08/college -athletes-say-they-devote-too-much-time-sports-year-round>)(last accessed: September 20, 2017).

71. Jake New, *A Long Shot*. Inside Higher Education Online, January 27, 2015 (available at: <https://www.insidehighered.com/news/2015/01/27/college -athletes-greatly-overestimate-their-chances-playing-professionally>)(last accessed: September 15, 2017).

72. New, *A Long Shot*.

73. NCAA Press Release, *NCAA Launches Latest Public Service Announcements, Introduces New Student-Focused Website*, March 13, 2007 (available at: <http://fs.ncaa.org/Docs/PressArchive/2007/Announcements/NC AA%2BLaunches%2BLatest%2BPublic%2BService%2BAnnouncements%2B Introduces%2BNew%2BStudent-Focused%2BWebsite.html>)(last accessed: September 15, 2017).

74. New, *A Long Shot*.

75. Linda Flanagan, *When College Athletes Face Depression*. Atlantic Online, March 21, 2014 (available at: <https://www.theatlantic.com/education /archive/2014/03/when-college-athletes-face-depression/284484/>)(last accessed: September 20, 2017).

76. Jennifer J. Moreland, Kathryn A. Coxe and Jingzhen Yang, *Collegiate athletes' mental health services utilization: A systematic review of conceptualizations, operationalizations, facilitators, and barriers*. Journal of Sport and Health Science (2017) (available at: <https://ac.els-cdn.com /S2095254617300637/1-s2.0-S2095254617300637-main.pdf?_tid=20872038 -a01c-11e7-9ca6-00000aacb362&acdnat=1506143012_adb473809226 d0b89b9526c14a25b335>)(last accessed: September 20, 2017).

77. Daniel B. Kissinger, Richard Newman, Michael T. Miller and Daniel P. Nadler, *Athletic Identity of Community College Student Athletes: Issues for*

Counseling. Community College Journal of Research and Practice, 35: 7, 574-589 at 578 (2011)(available at: <https://www.researchgate.net/publication /233206863_Athletic_Identity_of_Community_College_Student_Athletes _Issues_for_Counseling>)(last accessed: September 20, 2017).

Chapter 6. Professional and Olympic Sports

1. King, Billie Jean, Brainy Quote (Available at: <https://www.brainyquote .com/quotes/billie_jean_king_121917>) (Last accessed October 22,2022)

2. Barbara Barker, *For WNBA players, the real money is overseas.* Newsday Online, November 19, 2016 (available at: <http://www.newsday.com /sports/columnists/barbara-barker/wnba-players-are-underpaid-shouldn-t-have -to-play-overseas-1.12639553>)(last accessed: September 25, 2017).

3. Barker, *For WNBA players.*

4. Spotrac, (Available at <https://www.spotrac.com/wnba/los-angeles-sparks /nneka-ogwumike-29888/>) (Last Accessed, October 22,2022)

5. Slate, WNBA Player's New Contract Is a Good Step- but It's Not Enough (available at https://slate.com/culture/2020/01/wnba-cba-contract -critique-progressive-inadequate.html)

6. Lee Feinswog, *Americans playing volleyball overseas are always aware of dangers.* Volleyball Magazine Online, January 20, 2017 (available at: <https:// volleyballmag.com/playing-overseas/>)(last accessed: September 25, 2017).

7. Peter Holley, *Why these pro players are willing to play basketball in Iraq for $20K a month.* Washington Post Online, March 17, 2015 (available at: <https://www.washingtonpost.com/news/early-lead/wp/2015/03/17/why-these -pro-players-are-willing-to-play-basketball-in-iraq-for-20k-a-month/?utm _term=.99264bb05e8b>)(last accessed: September 25, 2017).

8. Associated Press, *Volleyball Players Can Live Well, at a Distance, While Pursuing Olympic Dreams.* New York Times Online, March 22, 2014 (available at: <https://www.nytimes.com/2014/03/23/sports/volleyball-players- can-live-well-at-a-distance-while-pursuing-olympic-dreams.html?mcubz=1>) (last accessed: September 25, 2017).

9. Clint Irwin, *Life of a Non-Millionaire Professional Athlete, The.* Pacific Standard Online, August 6, 2013 (available at: <https://psmag.com/economics /my-economics-of-being-a-regular-professional-athlete-63770>)(last accessed: September 25, 2017).

10. Irwin, *Life of a Non-Millionaire.*

11. Tala Hadavi, *Professional Athletes Prepare for Life After Sports.* Voice of America News Online, March 20, 2011 (available at: <https://www.voanews .com/a/professional-athletes-prepare-for-life-after-sports-118377659/163130. html>)(last accessed: September 25, 2017).

12. SI Wire, *WSJ data analysis shows average length of NFL careers decreasing.* Sports Illustrated Online, March 1, 2016 (available at: <https://

www.si.com/nfl/2016/03/01/nfl-careers-shortened-two-years-data-analysis>)
(last accessed: September 1, 2017).

13. Rob Arthur, *Shrinking Shelf Life of NFL Players, The*. Wall Street Journal Online, February 29, 2016 (available at: <https://www.wsj.com /articles/the-shrinking-shelf-life-of-nfl-players-1456694959>)(last accessed: September 1, 2017).

14. Hammond, Sean, AZ Central, For Cardinals Jen Welter, Path to NFL has been unique (<https://www.azcentral.com/story/sports/nfl/cardinals /2015/07/28/arizona-cardinals-jen-welter-path-nfl-unique/30814029/>) (Last accessed, October 22,2022)

15. Aaron J. Lopez, *Life After NBA comes sooner than many players think*. Denver Nuggets Website, June 10, 2010 (available at: <http://www.nba.com /nuggets/features/junior_bridgeman_20100610.html/>)(last accessed: September 30, 2017).

16. Nick Wells and Eric Chemi, *Professional tennis is older than it's ever been*. CNBC Online, January 28, 2017 (available at: <https://www.cnbc.com /2017/01/28/professional-tennis-is-older-than-its-ever-been.html>)(last accessed: September 30, 2017).

17. Sam Roberts, *Just How Long Does the Average Baseball Career Last*. New York Times Online, July 15, 2007 (available at: <http://www.nytimes. com/2007/07/15/sports/baseball/15careers.html?mcubz=1>)(last accessed: September 20, 2017).

18. Seth Sandler, *NFL, MLB, NHL, MLS & NBA: Which Leagues and Players Make the Most Money?* Bleacher Report Online, March 18, 2012 (available at: <http://bleacherreport.com/articles/1109952-nfl-mlb-nhl-mls -nba-which-leagues-and-players-make-the-most-money>)(last accessed: September 30, 2017).

19. Purtill, Retired US soccer star Abby Wambach nails the gender pay gap's longterm damage (available at: https://qz.com/work/1285757/retired-us -soccer-star-abby-wambach-nails-the-gender-pay-gaps-longterm-damage/).

20. Mark Bailey, *Raj Ouseph: 10 things you didn't know about professional badminton*. Telegraph (U.K.) Online, August 11, 2016 (available at: <http:// www.telegraph.co.uk/health-fitness/body/raj-ouseph-10-things-you-didnt -know-about-professional-badminton/>)(last accessed: September 30, 2017).

21. Ross Newhan, *Known as Grandma Luge, Abernathy Slides for Pride*. Los Angeles Times Online, February 11, 1998 (available at: <http://articles .latimes.com/1998/feb/11/sports/sp-17896>)(last accessed: September 30, 2017).

22. Michael J. Joyner, *age of Olympians, The: Rio 2016 highlights younger, older athlete performances*. Sports Illustrated Online, August 11, 2016 (available at: <https://www.si.com/edge/2016/08/11/rio-2016-olympics-age-young -old-athletes>)(last accessed: September 30, 2017).

23. Joyner, *age of Olympians*.

24. Joyner, *age of Olympians*.

25. Charles Riley, *Olympians face financial hardship*. CNN Money Online, July 10, 2012 (available at: <http://money.cnn.com/2012/07/10/news/economy /olympic-athletes-financial/index.htm>)(last accessed: September 30, 2017).

26. *Forbes Website, Usain Bolt Profile Page*. Forbes Online (available at <https://www.forbes.com/profile/usain-bolt/>)(last accessed: September 30, 2017).

27. Mitch Strohm, *How Much is Michael Phelps Worth?* Fox Business Online, August 19, 2016 (available at: <http://www.foxbusiness.com/features /2016/08/19/how-much-is-michael-phelps-worth.html>)(last accessed: September 30, 2017).

28. Riley, *Olympians face financial hardship*.

29. Tim Struby, *Olympic medalist — and she lives just above the poverty line*. espnW, May 9, 2016 (available at: <http://www.espn.com/espnw/sports /article/15421001/us-rower-megan-kalmoe-money-struggles-olympians>)(last accessed: September 30, 2017).

30. Struby, *Olympic medalist. . . above the poverty line*.

31. Struby, *Olympic medalist . . . above the poverty line*.

32. Struby, *Olympic medalist . . . above the poverty line*.

33. Riley, *Olympians face financial hardship*.

CHAPTER 7. RETIREMENT

1. Enquist, Sue

2. Helms, at 16.

3. Lavallee et al. (1998).

4. Lavallee et al. (1998).

5. Prim Siripipat, *Moving on from sports: A college athlete's greatest challenge*. espnW Online, April 11, 2016 (available at: <http://www.espn .com/espnw/voices/article/15182997/moving-sports-college-athlete-greatest -challenge>)(last accessed: September 1, 2017).

6. Robert Laura, *How Star Athletes Deal With Retirement*. Forbes Online, May 22, 2012 (available at: <https://www.forbes.com/sites/robertlaura/2012 /05/22/how-star-athletes-deal-with-retirement/#7721e7b62a4e>)(last accessed: October 1, 2017).

7. Dr. Chris Stankovich, *How to cope with retiring high school athletes*. This Week Community News Online, May 20, 2016 (available at: <http://www .thisweeknews.com/content/stories/sports/2016/05/19/the-sports-doc.html>) (last accessed: September 15, 2017).

Chapter 8. The Cliff: Loss of Identity

1. RAG, *Athlete Identity Loss: Retirement*. Undefeated Sport Psychology Website, May 17, 2017 (available at: <http://undefeatedsportpsych.com /athlete-identity-loss-retirement/>)(last accessed: September 30, 2017).

2. Ben Shpigel, *Exchanging Jerseys: A Soccer Tradition Takes Off in the N.F.L.* New York Times Online, October 1, 2015 (available at: <https://www.nytimes.com/2015/10/18/sports/football/exchanging-jerseys-a-soccer-tradition-takes-off-in-the-nfl.html?smid=fb-nytimes&smtyp=cur&_r=1>) (last accessed: September 30, 2017).

3. Shpigel, *Exchanging Jerseys.*

4. James Côté and Charles Levine, *Identity Formation, youth, and Development: A Simplified Approach.* ———— at 10.

5. Côté and Levine, *A Simplified Approach* at 10.

6. Peter Weinreich, *operationalization of identity theory in racial and ethnic relations, The.* "Theories of Race and Ethnic Relations." Cambridge University Press, pp. 299-320 (1986).

7. B.W. Brewer, J.L. Van Raalte and D.E. Linder, *Athletic identity: Hercules' muscles or Achilles Heel?* International Journal of Sport Psychology, 24, 237-254 (1993).

8. Evelyn Monteal Oregon, *Examination of Athletic Identity and Identity Foreclosure among Male Collegiate Student-Athletes, An.* University of North Carolina at Chapel Hill, Department of Exercise and Sport Science – Theses (2010) (available at: <https://cdr.lib.unc.edu/indexablecontent/uuid:d9of35db-6927-4264-b7f5-0608fb499186>)(last accessed: September 30, 2017).

9. Martin, *Role of Athletic Identity and Passion in Predicting Burnout in Adolescent Female Athletes, The* (2011).

10. Dr. Thomas J. Cieslak, II, *Describing and Measuring the Athletic Identity Construct: Scale Development and Validation.* The Ohio State University – Thesis (2004) (available at: <https://etd.ohiolink.edu/!etd.send_file?accession=osu1091219903&disposition=inline>)(last accessed: September 30, 2017).

11. RAG, *Athlete Identity Loss: Retirement.*

12. Cieslak, *Describing and Measuring the Athletic Identity* at 2.

13. Saul McLeod, *Erik Erikson.* Simply Psychology Webpage, updated 2017 (available at: <https://www.simplypsychology.org/Erik-Erikson.html>) (last accessed: September 30, 2017).

14. Cieslak, *Describing and Measuring the Atheltic Identity* at 2.

15. Cieslak, *Describing and Measuring the Athletic Identity* at 2.

16. Robert Laura, *How Star Athletes Deal With Retirement.* Forbes Online, May 22, 2012 (available at: <https://www.forbes.com/sites/robertlaura/2012/05/22/how-star-athletes-deal-with-retirement/#29f139f2a4e7>) (last accessed: September 30, 2017).

17. Pearson and Petitpas at 7.

18. Helms, at 8.

19. Helms, at 11.

20. Miles Wentzien, *Voices of the Nation: What Will You Miss Most About HS Athletics.* National Federation of State High School Associations Webpage,

May 20, 2015 (available at: < https://www.nfhs.org/articles/voices-of-the
-nation-what-will-you-miss-most-about-hs-athletics/>)(last accessed: October
10, 2017).

Chapter 9. The Cliff: Mental Wellness

1. Luke Cooper, *Former Elite Athletes Reveal Mental Health Struggles
After Retirement*. Huffington Post Online, April 11, 2017 (available at: <http://
www.huffingtonpost.com.au/2017/04/11/former-elite-athletes-reveal-mental
-health-struggles-after-retir_a_22035114/>)(last accessed: October 1, 2017).

2. Sabrina Weigand, Jared Cohen and Daniel Merenstein, *Susceptibility
for Depression in Current and Retired Student Athletes*. Sports Health, vol. 5
no. 3, 263-266 (May 2013)(available at: <https://www.ncbi.nlm.nih.gov/pmc
/articles/PMC3658399/pdf/10.1177_1941738113480464.pdf>)(last accessed:
September 25, 2017).

3. Weigand et al., *Susceptibility for Depression* at 265.

4. Weigand et al., *Susceptibility for Depression* at 265.

5. Elena Schneider and Cara Cooper, *After Final Whistle, Former College
Athletes Face Relief, Depression*. Helix Magazine Online, June 18, 2013
(available at: <https://helix.northwestern.edu/article/after-final-whistle-former
-college-athletes-face-relief-depression>)(last accessed: September 25, 2017).

6. Schneider and Cooper, *After Final Whistle*.

7. Schneider and Cooper, *After Final Whistle*.

8. Jill Martin Wrenn, *end game, The: How sports stars battle through
retirement*. CNN Online, January 7, 2013 (available at: <http://www.cnn.com
/2013/01/05/living/aging-athletes-retirement/index.html>)(last accessed:
October 1, 2017).

9. Cooper, *Former Elite Athletes Reveal Mental Health Struggles*.

10. Cooper, *Former Elite Athletes Reveal Mental Health Struggles*.

11. Cooper, *Former Elite Athletes Reveal Mental Health Struggles*.

12. Amelia Gulliver, Kathleen M. Griffiths, Andrew Mackinnon, Philip J.
Batterham and Rosanna Stanimirovic, *mental health of Australian elite athletes*. Journal of Science and Medicine in Sport 18 (2015) 255-261 (available
at: <http://www.jsams.org/article/S1440-2440(14)00075-9/pdf>)(last accessed:
October 1, 2017).

13. Louise Ellis, *Clarke Carlisle has spelt it out: retiring from sport can be
a traumatic loss*. The Guardian (UK) Online, February 5, 2015 (available at:
<https://www.google.com/url?sa=t&rct=j&q=&esrc=s&source=web&cd
=13&cad=rja&uact=8&ved=0ahUKEwjbuMiez-nWAhUowFQKHTjnAgA4C
hAWCDAwAg&url=https%3A%2F%2Fwww.theguardian.com%2Fcommentis
free%2F2015%2Ffeb%2F05%2Fclarke-carlisle-retiring-sport-professional
-athletes-depression&usg=AOvVaw1jmP2SQgXSuguBcsjhe5GO>) (last
accessed: October 1, 2017).

14. Anxiety and Depression Association of America, *Anxiety and Depression Association of America Website, Facts and Statistics Webpage* (available at: <https://adaa.org/about-adaa/press-room/facts-statistics>)(last accessed: September 30, 2017).

15. Mayo Clinic Staff, *Mayo Clinic Website – Depression (major depressive disorder)*. Mayo Clinic (available at: <http://www.mayoclinic.org/diseases -conditions/depression/symptoms-causes/dxc-20321472>)(last accessed: September 30, 2017).

16. John Florio and Oisie Shapiro, *Dark Side of Going for Gold, The.* Atlantic Online, August 18, 2016 (available at: <https://www.theatlantic.com /health/archive/2016/08/post-olympic-depression/496244/>)(last accessed: September 30, 2017).

17. Schneider and Cooper, *After Final Whistle.*

18. American Foundation for Suicide Prevention, *Suicide Statistics Webpage, American Foundation for Suicide Prevention Website.* American Foundation for Suicide Prevention Website (available at: <https://afsp.org /about-suicide/suicide-statistics/>)(last accessed: October 1, 2017).

19. *Athlete Versus the Jock, The.* Journal of Sport & Exercise Psychology Vol. 31, Iss. 5 (October 2009) at 680 (available at: <http://connection.ebscohost .com/c/articles/44232623/athlete-versus-jock>).

20. Reid Forgrave, *Sports must wake up about depression.* Fox Sports Online, September 2, 2011 (available at: <http://www.foxsports.com/nhl/story /time-for-athletes-sports-to-wake-up-on-depression-issue-090211>)(last accessed: October 1, 2017).

21. Scott Tinley, *Why did Junior Seau kill himself? Exploring athletes and depression.* Sports Illustrated Online, July 2, 2012 (available at: <https://www .si.com/more-sports/2012/07/02/retired-athletes-depression>)(last accessed: September 30, 2017).

22. Lindsey H. Jones, *Belcher to Chiefs: I have hurt my girl; I can't go back.* USA Today Online, December 18, 2012 (available at: <https://www .usatoday.com/story/sports/nfl/chiefs/2012/12/18/jovan-belcher-kansas-city -chiefs-kasandra-perkins-murder-suicide/1777359/>)(last accessed: September 30, 2017).

23. Jones, *Belcher to Chiefs.*

24. Sports Reference LLC, *Sports Reference Website, Olympians Who Committed Suicide Page* (available at: <https://www.sports-reference.com /olympics/friv/lists.cgi?id=55>)(last accessed: September 30, 2017).

25. Foxsports, *Judo champ takes life over Olympics.* Fox Sports Online, June 18, 2013 (available at: <http://www.foxsports.com/olympics/story/russian -official-says-elena-ivashchenko-suicide-the-result-of-olympic-failure-061813>) (last accessed: September 30, 2017).

26. *Six Biggest Challenges Athletes Face When They Retire.* Olympic

Athletes' Hub Webpage, February 28, 2017 (available at: <https://hub.olympic.org/news/the-six-biggest-challenges-athletes-face-when-they-retire/>)(last accessed: September 30, 2017).

27. Jeffri Chadiha, *Life after NFL a challenge for many*. ESPN Online, May 31, 2012 (available at: <http://www.espn.com/nfl/story/_/id/7983790/life-nfl-struggle-many-former-players>)(last accessed: October 10, 2017).

28. Chadiha, *Life after NFL a challenge for many*.

29. Amit Chowdhry, *Research Links Heavy Facebook And Social Media Usage To Depression*. Forbes Online, April 30, 2016 (available at: <https://www.forbes.com/sites/amitchowdhry/2016/04/30/study-links-heavy-facebook-and-social-media-usage-to-depression/#1a418bec4b53>)(last accessed: October 10, 2017).

30. Chadiha, *Life after NFL a challenge for many*.

31. *Ex-NFL player Sam Rayburn charged in Oklahoma hometown of Chickasha*. The Daily Oklahoman Online, May 6, 2009 (available at: <http://newsok.com/article/3367165>)(last accessed: October 1, 2017).

32. Seema Yasmin, *Ryan Leaf out of jail and working to help others with addiction issues*. Dallas Morning News Online, August 2016 (available at: <https://www.dallasnews.com/sports/sports/2016/08/18/ryan-leaf-addiction>)(last accessed: October 1, 2017).

33. Paul Liotta, *With CC Sabathia checking into rehab here's a look at MLB players who have dealt with alcohol abuse*. New York Daily News Online, October 5, 2015 (available at: <http://www.nydailynews.com/sports/baseball/mlb-players-dealt-alcohol-abuse-article-1.2386185>)(last accessed: September 30, 2017).

34. L. Jon Wertheim and Ken Rodriguez, *How Painkillers Are Turning Young Athletes Into Heroin Addicts*. Sports Illustrated Online, June 18, 2015 (available at: <https://www.si.com/more-sports/2015/06/18/special-report-painkillers-young-athletes-heroin-addicts>)(last accessed: October 1, 2017).

35. National Institute on Drug Abuse, *Principles of Drug Addiction Treatment: A Research-Based Guide (Third Edition)*. National Institute of Health Website (available at: <https://www.drugabuse.gov/publications/principles-drug-addiction-treatment-research-based-guide-third-edition/frequently-asked-questions/there-difference-between-physical-dependence>)(last accessed: October 1, 2017).

36. Claudia L. Reardon and Shane Creado, *Drug abuse in athletes*. University of Wisconsin, Department of Psychiatry (2014) (available at: <https://www.dovepress.com/drug-abuse-in-athletes-peer-reviewed-fulltext-article-SAR>)(last accessed: September 30, 2017).

37. Yasmin, *Ryan Leaf out of jail*.

38. Yasmin, *Ryan Leaf out of jail*.

39. Justin McNamara, Marita P. McCabe, *Striving for success or*

addiction? Exercise dependence among elite Australian athletes. Journal of Sports Sciences vol. 30, iss. 8 (2012) 755-766.

40. Andrea Leuenberger, *Endorphins, Exercise, and Addictions: A Review of Exercise Dependence*. Impulse Journal for Undergraduate Publications in the Neurosciences (2006) (available at: <https://impulse.appstate.edu/sites /impulse.appstate.edu/files/2006_06_05_Leuenberger.pdf>) (last accessed: October 1, 2017).

41. *Retiring Olympic Athletes May be at Risk of Substance Abuse, Studies Suggest*. Partnership for Drug-Free Kids Webpage, August 1, 2012 (available at; <https://drugfree.org/learn/drug-and-alcohol-news/retiring-olympic-athletes -may-be-at-risk-of-substance-abuse-studies-suggest/>)(last accessed: September 30, 2017).

42. Dr. Eugene Hong, MD, *Depression in athletes: Is it being ignored?* Philadelphia Inquirer Online, October 16 , 2013 (available at: <http://www .philly.com/philly/blogs/sportsdoc/Depression-in-athletes-is-it-being-ignored .html>) (last accessed: October 1, 2017).

43. Bill Johnson III, *Beyond the Game: Athletes and Depression*. Huffington Post Online, September 23, 2015 (available at: <http://www.huffington post.com/bill-johnson-ii/beyond-winning-and-losing-athletes-and-depression _b_8174292.html>)(last accessed: September 30, 2017).

44. A. Pawloaski, *'Concussion' doctor says kids shouldn't play these sports until they're 18*. USA Today Online, September 5, 2017 (available at: <https:// www.today.com/health/concussion-doctor-warns-against-contact-sports-kids -t115938>)(last accessed: October 1, 2017).

45. Kate Fagan, *What Made Maddy Run*. Little, Brown and Co., New York (2017) at 80.

46. Fagan, *What Made Maddy Run* at 80.

47. Michelle Brandt, *Mental illness in sports: Why athletes don't always seek help*. Scope Online, October 30, 2012 (available at: <http://scopeblog .stanford.edu/2012/10/30/mental-illness-in-sports-why-athletes-dont-always -seek-help/>)(last accessed: October 1, 2017).

48. Fagan, *What Made Maddy Run* at 82.

49. Marc Siegel, *'Necessary Roughness' plays fast and loose with therapy*. Los Angeles Times Online, July 11, 2011 (available at: <http://articles.latimes .com/2011/jul/11/health/la-he-unreal-necessary-roughness-20110711>)(last accessed: October 1, 2017).

Chapter 10. The Cliff: Physical Health

1. Laura, *How Star Athletes Deal With Retirement* at 3.

2. *Retired athletes are fighting fat*. Washington Times Online, April 23, 2001 (available at: <http://www.washingtontimes.com/news/2001/apr/23 /20010423-022122-3981r/>)(last accessed: September 30, 2017).

3. Mike Larkin, *'My body was shutting down': Dancing With The Stars champ Shawn Johnson reveals she was only eating 700 calories a day as she prepared for 2008 Olympics.* Daily Mail U.K. Online, November 24, 2015 (available at: <http://www.dailymail.co.uk/tvshowbiz/article-3331474/Dancing -Stars-champ-Shawn-Johnson-reveals-body-shutting-eating-700-calories-day -prepared-2008-Olympics.html>)(last accessed: September 30, 2017).

4. Larkin, *'My body was shutting down'.*

5. Antoinette Bueno, *Shawn Johnson Opens Up About Dealing With Body Shamers: 'I've Hit Lows' With Eating Disorders.* Entertainment Tonight Online, November 19, 2015 (available at: <http://www.etonline.com/news /176411_shawn_johnson_opens_up_about_dealing_with_body_shamers>) (last accessed: September 30, 2017).

6. Shawn C. Sorenson, *Couch potato athletes: Why it's hard to stay active after competition ends.* Washington Post Online, July 25, 2014 (available at: <https://www.washingtonpost.com/opinions/couch-potato-athletes-why-its -hard-to-stay-active-after-competition-ends/2014/07/25/19fc0144-0b6d-11e4 -8c9a-923eccoc7d23_story.html?utm_term=.7e1cb3b507b7#comments>) (last accessed: October 10, 2017).

7. Sorenson, *Couch potato athletes.*

8. Sorenson, *Couch potato athletes.*

9. Sorenson, *Couch potato athletes.*

10. Sorenson, *Couch potato athletes.*

11. Sorenson, *Couch potato athletes.*

12. Sorenson, *Couch potato athletes.*

13. Sorenson, *Couch potato athletes.*

14. Sorenson, *Couch potato athletes.*

15. Sienna Hill, *10 Athletes With Insane Diets.* First We Feast Website, September 12, 2015 (available at: <https://firstwefeast.com/eat/2015/09/10 -athletes-with-insane-diets>)(last accessed: October 10, 2017).

16. Tia Ghose, *Here's What Olympians Eat for Each Sport.* Live Science Website, August 13, 2016 (available at: <https://www.livescience.com/55747 -what-olympians-eat.html>)(last accessed: October 10, 2017).

17. *Retired athletes are fighting fat.* Washington Times Online, April 23, 2001 (available at: <http://www.washingtontimes.com/news/2001/apr/23 /20010423-022122-3981r/>)(last accessed: October 10, 2017).

18. *Retired athletes are fighting fat.*

19. Rose Eveleth, *Obesity Could Be the True Killer for Football Players.* Smithsonian Magazine Online, January 31, 2013 (available at: <https://www .smithsonianmag.com/science-nature/obesity- could-be- the-true- killer-for - football-players-6188767/>)(last accessed: September 30, 2017).

20. Evin Demirel, *College Football Fattens Players Up and Then Abandons Them.* Daily Beast Online, October 4, 2014 (available at: <https://

www.thedailybeast.com/college-football-fattens-players-up-and-then-abandons
-them>)(last accessed: October 10, 2017).

21. Kate Penn, *York ex-athlete takes life back after health scare*. York Daily
Record, January 11, 2017 (available at: <http://www.ydr.com/story/life/2017
/01/11/york-ex-athlete-takes-life-back-after-health-scare/96147386/>)(last
accessed: October 10, 2017).

22. Jake Perlman, *'The Biggest Loser' premiere: Former athletes fight for a
return to their glory days*. Entertainment Tonight Online, September 11, 2014
(available at: <http://ew.com/article/2014/09/11/the-biggest-loser-premiere-2/>)
(last accessed: October 10, 2017).

23. Dvora Meyers, *"Athletic" Shawn Johnson Retires: How Gymnastics
Talks About Bodies In Code*. Deadspin Online, June 5, 2012 (available at:
<https://deadspin.com/5915913/athletic-shawn-johnson-retires-how-gymnastics
-talks-about-bodies-in-code>)(last accessed: October 10, 2017).

24 .Meyers, *"Athletic" Shawn Johnson Retires*.

25. Julie Mazziotta, *Shawn Johnson Opens Up About Eating Disorder: 'I
Would Eat 700 Calories A Day.'* People Magazine Online, November 23, 2015
(available at: <http://people.com/sports/shawn-johnson-talks-about-eating
-disorder-would-eat-700-calories-a-day/>)(last accessed: October 10, 2017).

26. Melissa Rohlin, *Leaving the sport, gaining an eating disorder*. Los
Angeles Times Online, July 28, 2011 (available at: <http://articles.latimes.
com/2011/jul/28/sports/la-sp-0729-eating-disorders-20110729>)(last accessed
October 10, 2017).

27. George Dohrmann, *I Want My Body Back*. Sports Illustrated Online,
June 8, 2009 (available at: <https://www.si.com/vault/2009/06/08/105822133
/i-want-my-body-back#>)(last accessed: October 10, 2017).

Chapter 11. Always an Athlete

1. Elrod, Jonas (Writer/Director). (2015). Fathers and Sons [Television
series episode]. In Elrod, Jonas (Executive Producer), *In Deep Shift with
Jonas Elrod*. Los Angeles, CA Oprah Winfrey Network.

2. Spitler, *It's How You Win That Matters*.

3. Todd M. Sabato, Tanis J. Walch and Dennis J. Caine, *elite young athlete,
The: strategies to ensure physical and emotional health*. Open Access Journal
of Sports Medicine, vol. 7 (2016) 99-113 (available at: <https://www.ncbi.nlm
.nih.gov/pmc/articles/PMC5012846/>)(last accessed: October 10, 2017).

4. Sean Avery, *Transition Season*. The Players Tribune Online, June 18,
2015 (available at: <https://www.theplayerstribune.com/sean-avery-why-i-
retired-life-after-hockey/>)(last accessed: October 10, 2017).

5. The Editors, Sportify It. Online October 22, 2022 (available at <https://
sportifyit.com/9-star-athletes-who-have-talked-about-mental-health/>) (Last
accessed: October 23,2022)

6. Cahak, Roger A: Meeting the Mental Health Needs of Athletes: Psychology Today (Available at <https://www.psychologytoday.com/us/blog/vitalogy/202109/meeting-the-mental-health-needs-athletes>) (Last accessed: October 23,2022)

7. Michele Kerulius, Mental Health , Young Athletes An Essential Guide, Psychology Today (Available at <https://www.psychologytoday.com/us/blog/sporting-moments/202205/mental-health-young-athletes-essential-guide>) (Last accessed: October 23,2022)

8. Taylor, Jim: Mental Health Should be a priority in sports: Psychology Today (Available at <https://www.psychologytoday.com/us/blog/the-power-prime/202101/mental-health-should-be-priority-in-sports-0>) (Last accessed: October 23,2022)

9. ESECC Business School, Putting Athletes Mental Health in the Spotlight, Psychology Today (Available at <https://www.psychologytoday.com/us/blog/be-in-the-know/202110/putting-athletes-mental-health-in-the-spotlight>) (last accessed: October 23,2022)

10. Demirel, College Football Fattens Players Up

Chapter 12. Why We Should Care

1. Goldmith, Wayne Sportify It Online October 22 2022 (aviailable at <https://wgcoaching.com/ten-reasons-why-change-is-so-hard-to-introduce-in-sport/> (last accessed: October 23, 2022)

2. Aaron Taylor, *Game face isn't the only face.* NCAA Webpage, September 3, 2014 (available at: <http://www.ncaa.org/about/resources/media-center/news/game-face-isnt-only-face>)(last accessed: October 1, 2017).

3. Steve Nash, *Life After Basketball.* The Players' Tribune Website, March 21, 2015 (available at: <https://www.theplayerstribune.com/steve-nash-retirement/>)(last accessed: October 10, 2017).

4. Maureen Callahan, *How pro athletes lose everything.* New York Post Online, June 14, 2015 (available at: <http://nypost.com/2015/06/14/how-pro-athletes-lose-everything-buying-cars-jewels-and-pet-tigers/>)(last accessed: October 10, 2017).

5. Brian Gainor, *Reaching and Engaging Millennial Fans.* National Association of Collegiate Directors of Athletics Report (February 2015) (available at: <http://grfx.cstv.com/photos/schools/nacda/sports/nacda/auto_pdf/2014-15/misc_non_event/ReportFeb15.pdf>)(last accessed: September 20, 2017).

6. Morgan Stanley, *Generations Change How Spending is Trending.* Morgan Stanley Smith Barney LLC., Website, August 26, 2016 (available at: < https://www.morganstanley.com/ideas/millennial-boomer-spending>)(last accessed: September 20, 2016).

7. "*30 For 30: House That Steinbrenner Built, The.*" (motion picture) (ESPN 2010).

8. Jimmy Burch, *Big-time sporting events put price squeeze on fans*. Fort Worth Star-Telegram, November 26, 2016 (available at: <http://www.star-telegram.com/sports/other-sports/article117276118.html>)(last accessed: September 20, 2017).

9. Brian Gainor, *Reaching and Engaging Millennial Fans*. NACDA Report, The, p. 1(February 2015)(available at: <http://grfx.cstv.com/photos/schools/nacda/sports/nacda/auto_pdf/2014-15/misc_non_event/ReportFeb15.pdf>)(last accessed: September 20, 2017).

10. Corcoran, *Now The Dang Millennials Are Killing College Football*.

11. Alex Evans and Gil Moran, *L.E.K. Sports Survey – Digital Entertainment Part One: Sports and the "Millennial Problem"*. L.E.K. Consulting, Executive Insights vol. xix, iss. 12 at ___ (March 2017) (available at: <http://www.lek.com/our-publications/lek-insights/sports-survey-digital-engagement-sports-and-millennials-part-1>)(last accessed: September 20, 2017).

12. Evans and Moran, *L.E.K. Sports Survey – Digital Entertainment Part One* at p. 1.

13. Leila Abboud, *Switch Off the Football*. Bloomberg Online, Bloomberg Gadfly, November 25, 2016 (available at: <https://www.bloomberg.com/gadfly/articles/2016-11-25/tv-sport-loses-its-allure-for-younger-viewers>)(last updated: September 20, 2017).

14. Kevin Stankiewicz, *Universities turn focus to young fans as football attendance declines*. Pittsburgh Post-Gazette Online, July 8, 2017 (available at: <http://www.post-gazette.com/sports/college/2017/07/09/NCAA-attendance-Pitt-football-tickets-millennials/stories/201707090131>)(last accessed: September 20, 2017).

15. Tully Corcoran, *Now The Dang Millennials Are Killing College Football Attendance; Here's Why*. USA Today Sports Online, July 10, 2017 (available at: <http://thebiglead.com/2017/07/10/now-the-dang-millennials-are-killing-college-football-attendance-heres-why/>)(last accessed: September 20, 2017).

16. Steven Godfrey, *cord-cutter's guide to (legally) watching college football, The*. SB Nation Online, September 8, 2016 (available at: <https://www.sbnation.com/college-football/2016/9/1/12684186/ncaa-football-without-tv-cord-cutting>)(last accessed: September 20, 2017).

17. Bill Shaikin, *It's ridiculous that Dodgers' historic run is not seen by majority of fans*. Los Angeles Times Online, September 2, 2017 (available at: <http://www.latimes.com/sports/mlb/la-sp-dodgers-tv-shaikin-20170902-story.html>)(last accessed: September 20, 2017).

18. Rustin Dodd, *Some fans left out of new Jayhawk Network deal*. Kansas City Star Online, September 4, 2013 (available at: <http://www.kansas.com/sports/college/big-12/university-of-kansas/article1122073.html>)(last accessed: September 20, 2017).

19. Todd Spangler, *NBC Turns to Digital Influencers to Draw TV-Averse Millennials to Olympics Coverage*. Variety Online, July 26, 2016 (available at: <http://variety.com/2016/digital/news/nbc-olympics-digital-influencers-1201823567/>)(last accessed: September 20, 2017).

20. Clio Chang, *How the Olympics Lost Millennials*. New Republic Online, August 17, 2016 (available at: <https://newrepublic.com/article/136096/olympics-lost-millennials>)(last accessed: September 20, 2017).

21. Evans and Moran, *L.E.K. Sports Survey – Digital Engagement Part One* at 2.

22. Brandon Carter, *Millennial Loyalty Statistics: The Ultimate Collection*. Access Development Website, September 12, 2017 (available at: <http://blog.accessdevelopment.com/millennials-loyalty-statistics>)(last accessed: September 25, 2017).

23. Sarah Landrum, *Millennials Driving Brands To Practice Socially Responsible Marketing*, Forbes Online, March 17, 2017 (available at: <https://www.forbes.com/sites/sarahlandrum/2017/03/17/millennials-driving-brands-to-practice-socially-responsible-marketing/#215b9a254990>)(last updated: September 25, 2017).

24. Kelsey Chong, *Millennials and the Rising Demand for Corporate Social Responsibility*. Haas School of Business, University of California Berkeley Website, January 20, 2017 (available at: <https://cmr.berkeley.edu/blog/2017/1/millennials-and-csr/>)(last accessed: September 20, 2017).

25. Tinley, *Why did Junior Seau kill himself*.

26. Schneider and Cooper, *After the Final Whistle*.

27. Emmy Hrube: ACFC Announces New Player Program; retirement of 22 (available at <https://justwomenssports.com/acfc-announces-new-player-program-retirement-of-no-22/>) (last accessed October 22, 2022)

28. Joshua Fischman: With New Program, Angel City Ensures Retired Players Not Left Behind (available at <https://justwomenssports.com/angel-city-angela-hucles-mangano-player-22-future-program/#:~:text=22%2C%20Hucles%20Mangano%20announced%20a,for%20educational%20and%20professional%20opportunities>) (Last access, October 22, 2022)

Chapter 13. Solutions

1. Benjamin Franklin, Available at (< https://www.goodreads.com/quotes/460142-if-you-fail-to-plan-you-are-planning-to-fail>) (last accessed, October 22, 2022)

2. CS Lewis, Available at <https://quoteinvestigator.com/2017/09/08/new-dream/> (last accessed, October 22, 2022)

3. Albert Einstein, (Available at <https://www.goodreads.com/quotes/314550

-wisdom-is-not-a-product-of-schooling-but-of-the>)(last accessed, October 22, 2022).

4. Malvick, Callielbert Einstein (Available at <https://www.rasmussen.edu /degrees/education/blog/types-of-learning-styles/>(last accessed, October 22, 2022.)

5. Johnson, Randy (Available at <https://rj51photos.com/about/>) (last accessed, October 22, 2022).

6. Dator, James (Available at <https://www.sbnation.com/2022/10/12 /23400828/randy-johnson-sideline-photographer-dead-bird-logo-nfl-mariners>) (last accessed, October 22, 2022)

7. Griffen, Jill/ Seneca (Available at https://www.forbes.com/sites/jillgriffin /2019/04/09/luck-is-what-happens-when-preparation-meets-opportunity /?sh=5253e1ae69c4 >) (last accessed, October 22, 2022).

Chapter 14. Solutions

1. Herbert, Frank. Dune (Available at <https://www.goodreads.com /quotes/2-i-must-not-fear-fear-is-the-mind-killer-fear-is>)(Last accessed, October 22, 2022)

2. Grand Valley State University (Available < https://www.gvsu.edu/ftlc /mindset-carol-dweck-183.htm>)(Last accessed, October 22, 2022).

3. Dweck, Carol, Mindset (Available at https://appliedsportpsych.org/blog /2021/04/revisiting-growth-mindset-as-a-core-capacity-of-sport-psychology/#:~ :text=The%20positive%20implications%20are%20many,%2C%20mistakes%2C %20and%20feedback.%E2%80%9D>) (Last accessed, October 22, 2022).

4. Kendry, Chera, Very Well Mind, Quotes from Albert Bandura on His Theories (Available < https://www.verywellmind.com/albert-bandura-quotes -2795687#:~:text=Ability%20is%20not%20a%20fixed,about%20what%20 can%20go%20wrong.%E2%80%9D>)(Last accessed, October 22, 2022).

5. Illene Berns-Zare, What is Grit and Why is it a Secret to Success? (Available < https://ibzcoaching.com/2018/01/what-grit-why-secret-success/>) (Last accessed, October 22, 2022)

6. Duckworth, Angela, AngelaDuckworth.com (Available < https:// angeladuckworth.com/qa/>)(Last accessed, October 22, 2022)

7. Grazer, Brian, Goodread(Available < https://www.goodreads.com/quotes /7799966-curiosity-asking-questions-isn-t-just-a-way-of-understanding-the -world-it-s>)(Last accessed, October 22, 2022)

8. Julie Foudy, ESPN (Available < https://www.espn.com/video/clip/_/id /23150351>)(Last accessed, October 22, 2022).

9. Rumi, Goodreads < https://www.goodreads.com/quotes/7368103-wear -gratitude-like-a-cloak-and-it-will-feed-every>)(Last accessed, October 22, 2022).

10. Kotler, Steven, Quote Fancy (Available < https://quotefancy.com

/quote/1722693/Steven-Kotler-Time-slows-down-Self-vanishes-Action-and
-Awareness-merge-Welcome-to-Flow>)(Last accessed, October 22, 2022).

11. Worthington, Valarie, Breaking Muscle, Being in the Zone: The Flow
State In Athletic Endeavors (Available <https://breakingmuscle.com/being
-in-the-zone-the-flow-state-in-athletic-endeavors/#:~:text=According%20
to%20a%20study%20by,of%20his%20or%20her%20ability.>)(Last accessed,
October 22, 2022) ·

12. Natelast, Mental Grit Consulting, Getting into Flow: How the Flow
State Helps Athletes Perform (Available < https://www.mentalgritconsulting
.com/flow-state/)(Last accessed, October 22, 2022)

13. Gallup Clifton Strenths Finder (Available < https://www.gallup.com
/cliftonstrengths/en/254033/strengthsfinder.aspx>)(Last accessed, October 22,
2022).

14. Via Character, Bring Your Strengths to Life (Available <https://www
.viacharacter.org/>)(Last accessed, October 22, 2022).

15. Personal Values Assessment (Available < https://personalvalu.es/>)
(Last accessed, October 22, 2022)

16. Principals You (Available < https://principlesyou.com/>)(Last accessed,
October 22, 2022)

17. Open Source Psychometrics Project (Available < http://openpsycho
metrics.org/tests/RIASEC/Last accessed, October 22, 2022).

18. Predictive Index (Available < https://www.predictiveindex.com/>)(Last
accessed, October 22, 2022).

19. DISC Personality Testing (Available < https://discpersonalitytesting
.com/free-disc-test/>)(Last accessed, October 22, 2022).

20. Natelast, Mental Grit Consulting, Getting into Flow: How the Flow
State Helps Athletes Perform (Available < https://www.mentalgritconsulting
.com/flow-state/>)(Last accessed, October 22, 2022).

21. Ramierez, Damien - Favorite Quotes/Passages from Start with Why
by Simon Sinek (Available < https://www.danramirezlibrarian.com/2016/02/26
/favorite-quotespassages-from-start-with-why-by-simon-sinek/>)(Last accessed,
October 22, 2022).

22. It's Your Yale: Focus on Your Strengths.(Available < https://your.yale
.edu/work-yale/learn-and-grow/focus-your-strengths-focus-success >)(Last
accessed, October 22, 2022).

23. Simon Sinek, SimonSinek.com (Available < https://simonsinek.com
/our-why/>)(Last accessed, October 22, 2022).

24. Griffen, Jill/ Seneca- No Idea.

25. Lonczack, Heather, Positive Psychology, Emotional Intelligence
Quotes & Do They Ring True? (Available <https://positivepsychology.com
/emotional-intelligence-quotes/>)(Last accessed, October 22, 2022).

26. Millen Josh, Kobe Bryant Search for Story (Available < https://www
.johnmillen.com/blog/kobe-bryants-search-for-story#:~:text=Asked%20in%20
an%20interview%20why,this%20world%20moves%20without%20story.>)
(Last accessed, October 22, 2022).

27. Wikipedia, The Hero's Story (Available < https://en.wikipedia.org/wiki
/Hero%27s_journey>)(Last accessed, October 22, 2022).

28. Millen Josh, Kobe Bryant Search for Story (Available <https://www
.johnmillen.com/blog/kobe-bryants-search-for-story#:~:text=Asked%20in%20
an%20interview%20why,this%20world%20moves%20without%20story.>)
(Last accessed, October 22, 2022).

29. The Moth (Available < https://themoth.org/>)(Last accessed, October
22, 2022).

30. Toastmasters (Available < https://www.toastmasters.org/>)(Last
accessed, October 22, 2022).

31. UCB Comedy (Available < https://ucbcomedy.com/trainingcenter/,>)
(Last accessed, October 22, 2022).

32. TedX Events(Available < https://www.ted.com/tedx/events >)(Last
accessed, October 22, 2022)

33. Vaynerchuck, Gary, LinkedIn (Available <https://www.linkedin.com
/posts/garyvaynerchuk_i-believe-all-the-best-managers-are-actually-activity
-6910555686783352833-FxoZ/?trk=public_profile_like_view>)(Last accessed,
October 22, 2022).

34. Dreami.io (Available < https://dreami.io/>)(Last accessed, October 22,
2022).

35. Mark Hymen (Available <https://twitter.com/drmarkhyman/status
/1183095020825567233?lang=en>) (Last accessed, October 22, 2022).

36. Brainy Quote (Available <https://www.brainyquote.com/quotes/helen
_keller_382259>) (Last accessed, October 22, 2022)

37. Pass It On (Available <https://www.passiton.com/inspirational-quotes
/7293-if-you-want-to-go-fast-go-alone-if-you-want>) (Last accessed, October
22, 2022).

38. Poem Hunter (Available <https://www.poemhunter.com/poem/no-man
-is-an-island/>) (Last accessed, October 22, 2022).

Chapter 15. Ball2Bike

1. Neal Rogers, *Bo knows the Tour de France: 'Those guys are real athletes'*. Cycling Tips Online, March 12, 2016 (available at: <https://cyclingtips
.com/2016/03/bo-knows-the-tour-de-france-those-guys-are-real-athletes/>)
(last accessed: September 1, 2017).

2. Jason Gay, *Bill Walton Is All About the Bike*. Wall Street Journal Online,
April 20, 2016 (available at: <https://www.wsj.com/articles/bill-walton-is-all
-about-the-bike-1461191925>)(last accessed: September 1, 2017).

3. Grove et al., (1997).

4. Grove et al., (1997).

5. Adler and Adler (1991) at 215.

6. Brown and Potrac (2009).

7. Linda Melone, CSCS, *Run. Bike. Swim. Which Suits You Best?* Energy Times, vol. 27, iss. no. 4 at 30 (July/August 2017).

8. Melone, *Run. Bike. Swim.* at 30.

9. Tanya Brown, *Low impact Exercises for Someone With Knee Problems.* LiveStrong Online, September 11, 2017 (available at: <http://www.livestrong.com/article/537951-low-impact-exercises-for-someone-with-knee-problems/>) (last accessed: September 15, 2017).

10. Selene Yeager, *Best Low-Impact Workouts for Weight Loss, The.* Health Magazine Online, June 28, 2017 (available at: <http://www.health.com/fitness/best-low-impact-workout-weight-loss#01-joint-friendly-low-impact-workout>)(last accessed: September 1, 2017).

11. Kevin Clark, *Rise of the NFL Cycling Nerd, The.* Wall Street Journal Online, December 29, 2015 (available at: <https://www.wsj.com/articles/the-rise-of-the-nfl-cycling-nerd-1451428267>)(last accessed: September 1, 2017).

12. *Bill Walton on the Grateful Dead.* Wall Street Journal Online, March 29, 2016 (available at: <https://www.wsj.com/articles/bill-walton-on-the-grateful-dead-1459263644>)(last accessed: September 1, 2017).

13. Patrick Redford, *Give Bill Walton His Damn Bike Back [Update].* Deadspin Online, November 14, 2016 (available at: <http://deadspin.com/give-bill-walton-his-damn-bike-back-1788970393>)(last accessed: September 1, 2017).

14. Roy M. Wallack, *People - Bill Walton*, Bicycling.com, August 24, 2010 (available at: <https://www.bicycling.com/culture/people/bill-walton>)(last accessed: September 1, 2017).

15. Stacie Shannon, *Rise in Popularity of Indoor Cycling Studios, The.* LinkedIn Online, February 11, 2016 (available at: <https://www.linkedin.com/pulse/rise-popularity-indoor-cycling-studios-stacie-shannon>)(last accessed: September 30, 2017).

16. Melone, *Run. Bike. Swim.* at 28.

17. Melone, *Run. Bike. Swim.* at 28.

18. Melone, *Run. Bike. Swim.* at 29.

19. Melone, *Run. Bike. Swim.* at 29.

20. Melone, *Run. Bike. Swim.* at 29.

21. John Henderson, *Bill Walton has long-running love affair with bicycles.* Denver Post Online, August 15, 2013 (available at: <http://www.denverpost.com/2013/08/15/bill-walton-has-long-running-love-affair-with-bicycles/>)(last accessed: September 30, 2017).

22. Henderson, *Bill Walton . . . affair with bicycles.*

23. Henderson, *Bill Walton . . . affair with bicycles*.

24. Rogers, *Bo knows the Tour de France*.

25. Rogers, *Bo knows the Tour de France*.

26. Erin Beresini, *Athletes Don't Exercise, They Train*. Outside Online Website, September 5, 2014 (available at: <https://www.outsideonline.com/1925541/athletes-dont-exercise-they-train>)(last accessed: October 10, 2017).

27. Karin A. Jeffery and Ted M. Butryn, *Motivations of Runners in a Cause-Based Marathon-Training Program, The*. Journal of Sport Behavior, vol. 35, iss. 3, p. 300 (September 2012)(available at: <http://connection.ebscohost.com/c/articles/78403557/motivations-runners-cause-based-marathon-training-program>).

28. Will Dean, *It Takes A Tribe: Building the Tough Mudder Movement*. Penguin Books, New York (2017).

29. Matthew Daniele, *1 Month Tough Mudder Training Plan*. Men's Fitness Online (available at: <http://www.mensfitness.com/training/mf-trainer/1-month-tough-mudder-training-plan>)(last accessed: October 10, 2017).

30. Francis Blagburn, *How to train for a Tough Mudder*. Daily Telegraph (UK), April 27, 2017 (available at: <http://www.telegraph.co.uk/health-fitness/body/train-tough-mudder/>)(last accessed: October 10, 2017).

31. Craig Ballantyne, *How to Prepare for a Tough Mudder*. LiveStrong Website, September 11, 2017 (available at: <https://www.livestrong.com/article/557913-how-to-prepare-for-a-tough-mudder/>)(last accessed: October 10, 2017).

32. Hilary Angus, *Pedaling Towards Happiness: 7 Mental Health Benefits of Riding Bikes*. Momentum Magazine Online, March 28, 2016 (available at: <https://momentummag.com/mental-health-benefits-of-cycling/>)(last accessed: September 30, 2017).

33. Megumi Ida, Itsurou Ida, Naoki Wada, Makoto Sohmiya, Masayuki Tazawa and Kenji Shirakura, *clinical study of the efficacy of a single session of individual exercise for depressive patients, assessed by the change in saliva free cortisol level*. BioPsychoSocial Medicine 2013, 7:18 (2013).

34. Wasmer Andrews, *Bicycling Can Sharpen Your Thinking*.

35. Sarah Strong, *How Cycling Helps in my battle with depression*. Total Women's Cycling Online, February 10, 2015 (available at: <https://totalwomenscycling.com/lifestyle/how-cycling-helps-in-my-battle-with-depression>)(last accessed: September 30, 2017).

36. Matthew Beaudin, *Why the sport of cycling is like no other*. Business Insider Online, May 3, 2017 (available at: <http://www.businessinsider.com/why-cycling-is-like-no-other-sport-2017-5>)(last accessed: September 1, 2017).

37. Jeff Fromm, *Secret to Bud Light's Millennial Marketing Success*. Forbes Online, October 7, 2014 (available at: <https://www.forbes.com/sites/jefffromm/2014/10/07/the-secret-to-bud-lights-millennial-marketing-success/#4a06be347054>)(last accessed: September 20, 2017).

38. Scott Stratten and Alison Kramer, *UnMarketing*. John Wiley & Sons, Inc., 2nd ed., Hoboken, New Jersey at pp. 3-6 (2017).

39. Dan Schawbel, *10 New Findings About The Millennial Consumer*. Forbes Online, January 20, 2015 (available at: <https://www.forbes.com/sites/danschawbel/2015/01/20/10-new-findings-about-the-millennial-consumer/#18dd960a6c8f>)(last accessed: September 20, 2017).

40. Schawbel, *10 New Findings About The Millennial Consumer*.

41. Schawbel, *10 New Findings About The Millennial Consumer*.

42. Bill Sutton, *How teams can use Maslow's hierarchy to build fan relationship*. Sports Business Journal Online, January 11, 2016 (available at: <http://www.sportsbusinessdaily.com/Journal/Issues/2016/01/11/Opinion/Sutton-Impact.aspx>)(last accessed: September 20, 2017).

43. Sutton, *How teams can use Maslow's hierarchy*.

44. Gainor, *Reaching and Engaging Millennial Fans* at 2.

45. Jeff Fromm, *How Brands Can Win With Millennials In The Experience Economy*. Forbes Online, July 27, 2017 (available at: <https://www.forbes.com/sites/jefffromm/2017/07/27/why-experience-innovation-matters-when-marketing-to-millennials/#349f940a7682>)(last accessed: September 20, 2017).

46. Kristina Monllos, *Inside Whatever, USA: Bud Light's Party Town as 'Content Factory'*. AdWeek Online, June 2, 2015 (available at: <http://www.adweek.com/brand-marketing/inside-whatever-usa-bud-lights-party-town-content-factory-165114/>)(last accessed: September 25, 2017).

47. Monllos, *Inside Whatever, USA*.

48. Kim Cross, *What Do Bo Jackson and Lance Armstrong Have in Common?* Outside Magazine Online, May 13, 2015 (available at: <https://www.outsideonline.com/1979356/what-do-bo-jackson-and-lance-armstrong-have-common>)(last accessed: September 25, 2017).

49. Melissa Hoffmann, *Attention Brands: This Is How You Get Millennials to Like You*. AdWeek Online, October 6, 2014 (available at: <http://www.adweek.com/brand-marketing/attention-brands-how-you-get-millennials-you-160575/>)(last accessed: September 20, 2017).

50. Geoff Smith, *Study: Millennials Are the Most Brand-Loyal Generation*. Inc. Online, September 30, 2015 (available at: <https://www.inc.com/geoff-smith/millennials-becoming-more-loyal-in-era-of-consumer-choice.html>)(last accessed: September 20, 2017).

51. Cary Estes, *Bo Knows Biking: Riding with Bo Jackson for Charity*. Sports Illustrated Online, April 17, 2014 (available at: <https://www.si.com/edge/2014/04/17/bo-bikes-bama-ride>)(last accessed: September 20, 2017).

52. Estes, *Bo Knows Biking*.

53. Tough Mudder, *Help Make A Difference – Run For A Cause*. Tough Mudder Website (available at: <https://toughmudder.com/fundraise-now>)(last accessed: September 20, 2017).

54. Warrior Dash, *St. Jude Warriors Give*. Warrior Dash Website (available at: <https://warriordash.com/get-involved/st-jude/>)(last accessed: September 20, 2017).

55. Color Run, The, *About*. The Color Run Website (available at: <http://thecolorrun.com/about/>)(last accessed: September 20, 2017).

Chapter 16. Conclusion

1. *Friday Night Lights* (NBC 2006-2011) (TV series).